The Private Voice

Other Books Written, Edited, or Compiled by Peter Gzowski

Peter Gzowski's Book About This Country in the Morning   (1974)
Spring Tonic   (1978)
The Sacrament   (1980)
The Game of Our Lives   (1981)
An Unbroken Line   (1982)
The Morningside Papers   (1985)
The New Morningside Papers   (1987)
A Sense of Tradition: A Century of Ridley College Memories,
1889–1989   (1988)

The Private Voice

A Journal of Reflections

PETER GZOWSKI

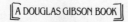

A DOUGLAS GIBSON BOOK

M&S

Canadian Cataloguing in Publication Data

Gzowski, Peter.
The private voice

ISBN 0-7710-3749-X

1. Gzowski, Peter.   2. Radio broadcasters – Canada –
Biography.   3. Morningside (Radio program).
4. Canada – Social life and customs.   I. Title.

PN1991.4.G96A37 1988   791.44′092′4   C88-094326-2

Printed and bound in Canada by T. H. Best

Design by T. M. Craan

A Douglas Gibson Book
McClelland and Stewart
The Canadian Publishers
481 University Avenue
Toronto M5G 2E9

To the memory of
Margaret McGregor Young Gzowski Brown, 1911–1949

CONTENTS

INTRODUCTION

TWO YEARS BEFORE I STARTED this book, at the end of my third season of hosting the CBC radio program *Morningside*, I published a collection of letters from listeners. In the spring of 1987, when, as you will see, this journal begins, I was putting the finishing touches on a second. Each of those books had added to my pleasure in the job (not to mention my income), but they had also left me feeling vaguely dissatisfied. Though they carried my picture on the cover, and though I had written introductions for them, and planned and orchestrated them, they were not *my* books, in the way those I had been writing before I returned to radio had been mine. I felt–you will read this in these pages too, or note it between the lines–almost guilty about them. Whatever had happened to me in the world of broadcasting, I still thought of myself as a writer, a writer who worked on the radio, perhaps, but a reporter first, a scribe. Not to mince words, I needed to write something of my own.

My plan at first was simply to keep a diary of the way the program worked. Though I thought the genre had been overused

–and, indeed, had employed some of its devices myself, in a book about hockey–I had enjoyed some of the early journals of professional athletes. I wondered if the same technique could be used to tell the story of a year in radio.

At the same time, I thought I might essay a bit of autobiography. For much of one season at *Morningside*, I had kept pinned to my office bulletin board – a handy receptacle for everything from the latest snapshot of my granddaughter to a map from an Icelandic telephone directory – which shows "Ottawa" where "Winnipeg" ought to be – a quotation from the British novelist Jean Rhys. "The only truly honest writing anyone can do," the quotation said, "is about himself."

The idea appealed to me. Like most journalists, I had spent much of my working life dropping in on the lives of people in the limelight and trying, with varying success, to capture them in print. Now, thanks to *Morningside* and some of my other (and less successful) adventures in broadcasting, I found myself at least on the edge of that limelight. I was neither comfortable with the attention my work had brought me, nor convinced it was my due. It was not what I had expected to achieve when I climbed on a train in 1954 to take a job with the Timmins *Daily Press*.

It bemused me, in fact–and still does–that someone who talks as haltingly and gropingly as I do (my producers say it is a sign of thinking out loud, and forgive me for it, but more realistic listeners simply say I stammer), and who runs his unfinished sentences on interminably, is working on the radio at all, not to mention with enough success to have made the cover of *Saturday Night*. Further, in common with everyone who's ever been written about, I had never been really satisfied with the pieces that other reporters had written. Even the most flattering of them, I thought – perhaps *especially* the most flattering, since I am, for instance, not nearly as nice in person as I try to appear on the air–had missed points that seemed to me central to my understanding of my craft, or in some other way had got things wrong. What would happen, I wondered, if I turned my reporter's eye on myself? With access to my own thoughts as I had not had access to, say, Wayne Gretzky's, I might come closer than before to that most elusive of the journalist's goals, truth.

So that spring, just after my fifth season as host of *Morningside* ended, I settled in to write.

I HAD WRESTLED with the diary form before.

Not counting the journal I began in the holiday season of, I think, 1947, when I would have been thirteen, and whose entire contents I can still recite ("January 1: Met Rhonda and all the gang"), I had tried it twice.

The first time was in the autumn of 1968. After the rug had been pulled from under a magazine I had been editing, I decided to take my wife and all of our five children to England. We booked passage on the Soviet liner *Aleksandr Pushkin*. To set an example for the kids, I resolved to keep a record. The example part worked out fairly well, though even Alison, my oldest daughter, stopped writing after about Madame Tussaud's. But my own efforts quickly declined into melancholy, with more gin spilled on them than I like to recall, and I gave up.

Years later, I was sorry I had. On our ocean voyage, Mickey, our youngest, then three, had somehow been listed on the passenger manifesto as remaining on board till Leningrad, some days after the rest of us were due to disembark at Tilbury on the Thames. We had been more than a little worried. With the Soviet penchant for following every rule to the letter – "iss not bossible" was the catch-phrase of our voyage – we imagined our little short-panted cherub, sucking his thumb in bewilderment as he wandered down the gangplank to Mother Russia.

We solved the problem in advance, thank heaven. But when our little cherub turned twenty-one a couple of years ago, I thought of our family crisis again. He was still living with his mother then, but spending most of his time downtown, studying to be a rock star. I threw him a birthday party at the Bamboo, on Queen Street, and there, in keeping with a family tradition that goes back to our distant Polish ancestry, I presented him with a signet ring. He had shown up with three guests who had hair like chimney sweeps and complexions that resembled those of the recently deceased (though they turned out to be pleasant to talk to), and, as I looked at Mickey showing them his replica of the crest my grandfather had given me, and entering, formally, the next stage of his life, I wished I had even my gin-sodden notes, however incomplete. They were all good kids, our five, as they are good young adults – bright, healthy, funny, irreverent. But I wasn't around for as much of their childhood as I wish now I had been, and a written record of some of the things we did and thought about together would have been nice to have.

Nearly twenty years later, when I was making some television films between seasons of *Morningside*, I tried again. On the day my plane left Toronto–at almost precisely the date this journal of another summer begins–I started to keep notes. As I travelled, I kept at it. I wrote on planes and in hotel rooms and sometimes, television being television, on the sites of the shoots themselves, while we waited for the light to improve or, once on location in southern Alberta, for a dam to be opened up-river so the rushing water would add drama to our shot. In late July, though, while I was playing some trivia in the Halifax Press Club, someone boosted my travel bag from my rented station wagon. Along with my favourite sweater, an airline ticket to Charlottetown, my Visa card, and half a mickey of Johnny Walker Scotch, I lost the several pads of lined foolscap I had filled with my felt-pen scrawl.

I got my notes back, as it happened. A friendly reporter at the Halifax *Mail-Star* wrote the theft up ("Star robbed in city" said a headline I was tempted to clip as proof of my celebrity), and the next day an even friendlier citizen reported finding it, dis-carded, in a men's washroom in Scotia Square. Though I thought the thief's literary judgement was unduly harsh, the incident took the wind out of my enthusiasm, and when *Morningside* resumed in the fall, I tucked my foolscap pads into a drawer, where, until I looked at them to help with some reflections I have included here, they remained.

Even with those notes, though, and as helpful as they have proved in the work that is now before you, I wished I had con-tinued. Writing about what was going on around me while it was happening–even in my rough-hewn traveller's scribblings–had forced me to think about it in a way I would not otherwise have done. It deepened the experience for me, and made me try to figure out not only some of the things that bothered me about it but many of the things I liked. I was beginning, I thought as I read my own notes over, to understand what I was doing.

THIS TIME, I resolved, I would not give up. Still, as I sat at the butternut table in my cottage on the May night in which this work began, I had little idea of the course I was setting out on.

The summer, I thought, would be a warm-up. I'd jot things

down as they transpired. If they triggered some memories, well, so much the better; I'd let them flow and see what happened. In the fall, when I returned to the program, I'd make the real beginning of my story.

Then, quite quickly, and in a way I could not have envisioned, the work took on a life of its own. My notes on my first lunch of the summer, with one of my oldest and most cherished friends, sent me tumbling through my memories. The very next day, the death of someone I had known long ago took me back to my first days in television. And so it went for much of the summer. Things happened; I wrote. I moved my word processor up to the cottage, and began transcribing my notes. They grew. Memory piled on memory. I wrote more. I continued to do other things, to travel a bit (though much less than I was accustomed to), and to dabble in some other projects, but the work I was now calling "my journal" had become an obsession. By midsummer, I was in the full flight of autobiography. The disks on my Macintosh, with its seductive ease of typing–even for an old four-fingered hacker from the Timmins *Daily Press*–were dangerously close to full. I cut. I reshaped. I revised. But by mid-August, when the *Morningside* unit came up from Toronto for our annual look ahead, I had a manuscript nearly as long as some of the books I've published. The autobiography seemed to cast light on the work I was doing–it was impossible, I now realized, to separate the way I did things from the way I had been prepared–but the season I had set out to describe had not yet begun.

Concerned now that the book had grown out of control, I turned to Doug Gibson, an editor and publisher whose work I had admired from afar, and who had established his own imprint at McClelland and Stewart. To my relief, Doug still had room for one more on his list for the fall of 1988. Under his cheerful and supportive guidance, I ploughed on, keeping notes in my scarcely legible longhand as the season unfolded, and, when I could make time on weekends or in the evenings, putting them into the machine, and often expanding my original musings as I did it. The obsession stayed with me, and became, if anything, even stronger.

Just after the calendar year turned, it became clear to both Gibson and me that I had done enough. The plot that had emerged unbidden from the events of the year–my flirtation with the possibility of leaving *Morningside* for another career alto-gether – had resolved itself. The book, though still based on the form that had inspired me, had taken a shape quite different from the one I had set out to do. But, in its raw form at least, it was there, stored in the electronics of my disks. In the process of assembling it, I had learned far more – not only about my job, but about myself and why I do what I do – than I could possibly have anticipated. I knew, at last, what the book was really about.

Now the real work began. I took some time off in the winter, holed up in the cottage again, and, while snowmobiles roared up the fairways where I had watched golfers, and crows squawked in the February cold, went over my notes some more. On into the spring I slugged away on weekends and around my other chores. When the *Morningside* season came to an end – the one I had not been sure I would finish – there was still work to do. Once more to the cottage and once more into the machine, until, finally, the journey you are about to begin with me was in the shape it seemed to want to hold.

Two notes, if I may, before we set out.

One is about the editorial process. I come, as you will discover as you follow me through some of my early adventures, from a tradition of hard and collaborative work, and though in my years as a writer I have fought with editors as vigorously as I have fought with writers in my years as an editor, those fights, at their best, have been based on a deep respect for the discipline and an abiding love of the craft. The struggles over this book have been as rewarding as any I can remember. Most of all, I am grate-ful to Doug Gibson, who, in his patience, understanding, and counsel, more than lived up to the reputation he has gained. He is, indeed, the heir to some of the figures I have mentioned in this book.

But I would also like to thank some other people who have read this work in one or other of its versions or helped me think my way through it. Gary Katz, my early-morning companion, was an invaluable adviser on matters of both fact and – I hope – fair-ness, as he has been for me at *Morningside*, though at whatever price to his own dignity he kept his pencil off the passages in which he appeared. Gill Howard, who also appears here, not only put up with more readings (and voiced more solicited opinions) than anyone ought to be obliged to, but also put up with fourteen months of intrusions on the time that would otherwise have belonged to her. Edna Barker, who had nurtured my often ungainly prose through five books before this one, kindly read this manuscript as well and, once again, helped me say better some things I wanted to say. Eleanor Sinclair added her impeccable copy editor's touch, and Shelley Ambrose, whom you will meet in these pages just as I met her, was invaluable. Finally, Peter Sibbald-Brown, who gave me, among many other useful suggestions, the title this book now bears, also gave me the pleasure of his laughter when, as sometimes he did, he read over my shoulder at the machine.

This very personal book is, of course, all mine. But it would not have been what it is without my friends.

The other note is simply about honesty. Yes, as I say, I have written every paragraph in these pages more than once, sometimes revising what I had originally set down–and then revising it again – months after I first recorded it. I have folded autobiography in among contemporary events, and welded pieces of memory together.

But I haven't cheated. In adopting the diary form, however I may have amended it, I have recognized that I have given up the privilege of hindsight, and though I have polished and reworded many of the things that were going through my head after I knew what decisions I would make based on them, I haven't tried to make myself look more prescient than I was. What you are about to read is what I did between the end of May 1987 and the middle of January 1988, what I thought about while I was doing it, and how I came to be there at the time.

PETER GZOWSKI, Lake Simcoe, July 1988

My once-smooth golf swing: LEFT, *at Betlyn, the family cottage,
in the 1940s;* RIGHT, *at the '87 Gzowski Invitational.*

Gill, trying to out-handicap her mother at the Queen's Plate.

CHAPTER ONE

End of the fifth Morningside season . . .
Two women in my life . . . A gossipy
lunch . . . The two lives of a young police
reporter . . . Edmund Wilson at the Park
Plaza . . . A morning Scotch with P.E.T. . . .
On trying to be Dick Cavett . . . "Bet you
don't remember who I am" . . . Looking
over June Callwood's shoulder

Saturday, May 30, 1987, Sutton, Ontario, late at night: Rain drenches the cottage as I write, pounding on the clerestory high above my head, running in torrents down the new pine siding. On the screened verandah overlooking the Hedge Road, the sky-lights leak prodigiously; puddles deep enough for tadpoles shine on the floor. But here in the main room, with its open cherry-wood kitchen and the scattering of still-unfamiliar furniture around the iron fireplace, I am as cozy as a bearcub. The cottage, which my cousin Jack rebuilt from scratch for us this spring, is riding out its maiden storm in style.

I peer into a tall pane of shatterproof glass. A sweep of these windows encloses the dining area at the back, looking south, across a cedar deck. By day, the view is of the first fairway of the Briars, my $200,000 lawn as my friend and neighbour and some-time partner Peter Sibbald-Brown calls it. This whole gentle, evergreen part of the world, with its rolling lawns and azure glimpses of Lake Simcoe, is the home turf of my adolescent sum-mers, full of family memories, and I have returned to it with nostalgia and affection. Nowhere are those memories more redolent than at the Briars itself, where I loped and gambolled as a boy, too arrogant and supple to know that golf was hard. From the deck, in daylight, I can see the bunker that caught the errant tee-shots of my grandfather, the Colonel, who took up the game in his sixties, and watched in frustration mixed with pride as my own drives grew ever longer with my gangly frame. When I stand on the lawn that is now mine, I hear him still, pipe clenched in his teeth, happily goddaming as he flailed the sand.

The smoothness of my golf swing has evaporated with the cockiness of my youth. I spray balls from the tee now (when I hit them at all) like a howitzer gone berserk, specializing in gigantic banana-shaped curves to the right – slices – and, if there were a pool as to which member of the club will be the first to test the temper of my glass this summer, I would bet on me. But the course provides a lovely prospect. In the morning, I will take my coffee to the cedar deck, to watch the seagulls and the swallows in the rising mist, and hope to restore my drooping ego by spotting, among the early hackers, a swing as unpredictable as mine.

Tonight, in the rolling storm, the shatterproof windows are opaque. Only my reflection stares back, set against the wash of rain and the velvet country dark.

I look tired.

I *am* tired.

Yesterday, at noon – well, noon in the Maritimes, where we are heard live – I finished my fifth season as host of *Morningside*. We ended with a flourish: forty minutes with Pierre Trudeau, the only interview he deigned to give to English radio on his disagreement with the Meech Lake Accord. I handled it reasonably well, I think, which is not always the case with major political interviews. The whole affair, in fact – the last-minute trip to Montreal, the scuffle with *The National* when we caught them running a bootleg line into our studio, the fuss afterward (someone came around from CBC Enterprises to suggest we package a cassette for the retail trade) – was exhilarating. But the excitement was a reminder of how much the season had taken out of me: nine solid months of rising before dawn, chugging my way up the gloomy streets, stepping into the airless office and plunging once again into the mound of mail and research.

I love it, of course. It really is the best job in the country. Ken Lefolii, who's been my friend for nearly thirty years – we were young together on the old *Maclean's*–told an inquiring magazine writer last year that the reason I seem to work so hard is that I'm talking for a living to all the people I would like to talk to if I just had time to kill. He's probably right. But I'm getting old. I'll be fifty-three this summer, the age Ralph Allen died, and every year the price of doing *Morningside* grows higher, the grind more gruelling. By spring, my tank is empty, and as each long season draws to a close, I wonder about stopping. This year, I wondered harder than ever. During the final stretch, when I was desperate for a rest, but when the statisticians were counting the audience, management decreed that I was irreplaceable. The ruling rankled. I still can't accept ratings – bean-counting, as I've learned to call them–as a measure of CBC radio's success. When the time came to negotiate for next year, I was grumpy. I held out for a lot more money, and, when they met my demands, I stuck the proffered contract in a drawer unsigned. I really was uncertain – or so I was convinced – and, for the last day or two, the thought crossed my mind that the Trudeau piece would make a lovely way to go out, like Ted Williams hitting a home run his last time at bat, tipping his hat to the crowd and disappearing into the dugout, never to be seen in his baseball suit again.

In the end, I have decided to do it one more time. While yesterday's program was still winging its way across the country on tape, I dug the contract from the drawer and signed it. In the crunch, I just couldn't face not being here next year. As Ralph used to say, you can always quit. Besides, as I sometimes forget, the last time I left here, in 1974, my life turned sour–there were eight years and a lot of misery between radio engagements. It's been a long way back.

THIS IS THE FIRST extended time I've had to myself for far too long. After each of the two previous *Morningside* seasons, I've jumped right into a schedule of shooting for television. The first time, in fact, I caught a plane on a Saturday morning, still hobbling from the pain of a hamstring I'd pulled in the annual *Morningside* wrap-up baseball game the day before (Old Farts vs. Upstarts, and you don't have to ask which I am), trying to stretch a solid line-drive into a single. This year is different. My television show has been, as the hockey players say so delicately of their ex-girlfriends, gassed. I have mixed feelings about the cancellation, as I have about all television, but not about the time it has left me to do other things, or none at all, this summer. I have some tidying up to do on a new collection of letters to *Morningside*, which will be published in the fall. Peter Sibbald-Brown and I are beginning work on a book we're doing about Ridley College, my old school. The second annual Gzowski Invitational golf tournament is scheduled at the Briars in a couple of weeks (too soon to tame my own errant game, I'm afraid), and I have a few pleasant functions to attend around the country. But other than that, I'm free until Labour Day, when *Morningside* returns to live programming (the summer air will be filled by sit-in hosts), and, as they say, it's a long, long time from May till then.

Sunday, May 31, 6 a.m., still at the cottage: And still a long way from being able to sleep in. I know, from summers past, that I will keep this rhythm for a while. No matter how late I stay up the night before, my body will stir with the dawn. Whether by genetics or by training–I supported myself one year at university by rising at midnight for an eight-hour newspaper shift before my classes began–I'm a lark, as they say, not an owl, better in the morning than at night. It's a helpful attribute at *Morningside*, to be sure (though not conducive to a fruitful social life). But wherever I am, I cherish the morning hours. They're mine: no phones, no visitors, no intrusions.

Up here, of course, there's no newspaper at the door either, and, away from the office or not, I am as addicted to a morning paper as I am to cigarettes or coffee. In a while, I'll go to get the Sunday *Toronto Sun*, and take it with my coffee to the deck. But right now, that feels like too much trouble. Funny, isn't it? There's an honour box right near the golf-course pro shop, and in the city I'd walk comfortably down to it. But here in the countryside, I'll climb into my car to do my errands, just like everyone else.

The weather's better than last night, and even here inside the cottage there's a bouquet of post-rain freshness in the air. With the golf course still empty, I'll sit and dawdle for a while.

Her name is Gillian, by the way, so the "G" is soft – Gillian Howard. As Tina Srebotnjak used to say, when Tina was an irreverent *Morningside* producer (and good friend) and I was falling in love, she is the third of my J's – Jenny, Jan, Gill. We've been together five years now, and I am still as impressed by her ability to sleep in as I am enchanted by her loveliness.

Circadian rhythms are not the only characteristic we don't share. By the calendar, she's much younger than I am – she turned thirty-five in April – but in other and more important ways she is at least as, or more, grown-up: realistic where I'm moody, outgoing where I'm introverted, blithe where I'm too solemn or full of my own importance. She cries easily, laughs more easily still, and sulks not at all. Even in the things we do share – a taste for cooking, a love of games and puzzles, a delight in the ridiculous – she is different from me. She cooks instinctively, for instance, where I labour over recipe books. She rode in equestrian events until her sensible fear of injury got the better of her, and will spend hours trying to break her own record on the Ms Pac-Man I bought her one Christmas.

But her joy is in the playing, where I'm out to win. I have introduced her to golf since we started coming up here, and, while she whacks the ball with her natural athlete's grace and gusto, she cares neither for putting nor about her score. Instead, she's interested in what birds she sees or in the trilliums in the out-of-bounds – where I, this season, go for other reasons. Her insouciance drives me to distraction, but, slowly, I may be learning from her, as I'm learning the names of birds and the tricks of raising house plants or, in our apartment in Toronto, tropical fish.

She longs, I know, for children of her own, and the only sadness in the difference in our ages is that she came into my life when new parenthood was behind me. But, reluctantly – for though we seldom speak of it, I know how deep the longing is – she accepts my unyielding refusal to start again, and takes what compensation she can from sharing my pleasure in the five I had with Jenny. She reminds me of birthdays, and comes with me to John's inaccessible guitar recitals or Mickey's occasional appearance in some Stygian hall of rock. My kids, in turn, approve of her and like her company. They seek her counsel when I'm not around (she knows more about Alison's romantic life than I do), and swap stories of my ineptitude. "And *last* night," she will say to them, while they fight to restrain their giggles, "he strained his duck sauce through a colander, and kept the bones and stewed vegetables while the gravy ran down the sink." I met her at the race-track, when I was working on the book I finished the first year I was back on the radio. She worked in the publicity office there, where her father, a distinguished litigation lawyer, is a trustee, her brother a trainer, and her mother, a quick-witted ex-Nova Scotian (who, as I said in the book, might have been president of a corporation if she'd been born at a different time), is a legendary handicapper. She was, and is, utterly unimpressed by whatever I've achieved. She's a devoted *Morningside* listener (or was when she worked race-track hours—she's in the movie business now), but if I left the radio tomorrow she'd take it in stride. She goes through life the way she plays bridge. If she misses a slam by finessing the wrong way—or, for that matter, by not having counted trump—she smiles her merry smile and waits for the next deal while I curse her inattention. In her life, there are more important things. Let her sleep.

ON FRIDAY, when I ceremoniously handed my signed contract to Gloria, she seemed relieved, and gave me a congratulatory kiss on the cheek. In her heart, though, she had probably been certain all along I would return. I sometimes think she knows me better than I know myself.

Gloria is Gloria Bishop, the executive producer of *Morningside*, a patrician redhead with the posture of a gymnast, on occasion the bluntness of a sergeant-major, and the saving ability to laugh at herself. I like her a lot, although when she was first proposed for the position she holds now I wasn't sure I would.

That was three years ago. Nicole Bélanger, the producer who had brought me back to radio, had reluctantly decided to move up into the bureacracy. I was concerned. Nicole had gone out on a limb to offer me the job; there were those in high office who felt I was yesterday's man. I still felt dependent on her, and feared the prospect of answering to someone else. Nicole had paved the way, though. All good producers are loath to cross the line between those who actually *make* radio and those who only think about it, and she, a canny handler of people, had bargained hard to ensure that the program she was leaving would stay on the course she had set for it. As one of her conditions, she had arranged for me to have a say in who might succeed her, a veto, as it were, over who would be my boss.

That summer, Donna Logan, who'd just become head of the AM network, called me at home to ask what I thought of Gloria. I said I had only a general impression, though I remembered her in the early 1970s as a producer in Montreal and had enjoyed her efficiency when she produced the '76 Olympics for radio, where I'd done some work.

"She thinks you think she's a tight-assed Westmount Wasp," Donna said.

"She does?"

"She says you said so."

"Well, I . . . uh, I might have."

"If she was," said Donna, who was a newspaper executive in Montreal before she joined the CBC, and knew Gloria socially, "she isn't now. I think you should talk to her."

I flew to Montreal. Gloria met me at the airport. "I hear you said I was a tight-assed Westmount Wasp," she said, smiling, and took me to Sherbrooke Street for an al fresco lunch and a bottle of wine. We've got on ever since.

She's had a tough year. Her mother is dying, slowly and painfully. In the middle of the last season, the relationship she'd been having off and on since her marriage broke up came to an end. Not long afterward, she was narrowly beaten out of a job at the United Nations, which would have given her international status (not to mention a glamorous life, an apartment in New York, and about $125,000 U.S. a year), and at which she'd have been superb. As well, she still misses Montreal. But none of that ever shows at *Morningside*, where she is fair and open and tough, rare qualities around the CBC. She is a powerful example of the kind of woman who a generation ago might have bloomed unnoticed in the domestic air–or, I suppose, like Gill's mother Nancy, have applied her gifts to other pursuits. She turned fifty last year, and some friends threw a party for her, six men in dinner jackets, Gloria the only woman. In reply to our speeches, she said, "When my mother turned this age, her life was to all intents over; mine, now, holds endless possibilities."

As I sit here in the midnight rain, so does my summer.

Monday, June 1: Anesty's restaurant, Toronto: Lunch with Fulford: gossip, gossip.

I have been friends with Robert Fulford even longer than with Ken Lefolii.

We met in the autumn of 1955. I had just come down to Toronto from Timmins, where I had discovered newspapering, to return to university, in the hope that I might *learn* something this time. To pay my way, I took the job that first convinced me I could get up in the mornings: police reporter on the night beat. My salary was paid by the Toronto *Telegram*, but, in a curious exception to those days of ferocious competition between the *Tely* and the *Star*, my assignment was to cover the overnight police news for them both. I would go into headquarters at one o'clock in the morning and stay until nine, and, the cop shop in those days being at 149 College Street, I would make my way afterward across the road to classes; in between, I would monitor the police radio, check from time to time around the precincts, the firehalls, and the hospital emergency wards, and, at the end of my shift, send my stories downtown by cab, carbon copies to the *Star*. I was twenty-one.

That was, in many ways, a wonderful year for me. I straddled two worlds, and I revelled in their contrast. On campus, I turned my collar up, smoked out of the corner of my mouth, and took my lecture notes with thick 2B pencils on pads of *Tely* copy paper. Even on $55 a week, I had my own apartment, and, though it was only a dingy basement on Tranby Avenue, undergraduate women could sometimes be persuaded to visit it to further their research into the hard-bitten world of "*The Front Page.*" In the real newspaper world downtown, meantime, I was Leslie Howard, wan and dreamy, a volume of Dylan Thomas under my arm, willing to take my female colleagues from the court bureau to a higher plane.

I had also begun to learn to write. Just before I had dropped out of university a couple of years earlier, the man who had been teaching me English, Douglas Grant, called me aside to say that, though he didn't know what I planned to do for a living, he hoped it would have nothing to do with language. Now, after an apprenticeship on the Timmins *Daily Press*, I had picked up at least the ability to write sentences. The first English essay I handed in, pecked out on a police-bureau Underwood, and with moremoremore at the foot of each page, was read aloud to the class as an example of good academic prose.

Fulford was twenty-three, a veteran. He had dropped out of high school to follow in the footsteps of his father, Ab Fulford of the Canadian Press. He had been a copy-boy and a sportswriter (and a good one, too, I'm sure, although he is the worst athlete I have ever met, the only person I know to have sprained his ankle getting up to change television channels), but in the fall of 1955 he was covering night police for the *Globe and Mail*. The *Globe* being a morning paper, his shift was just ending when mine began, but more nights than not we would spend some time together before he turned over the office to me. We talked. If, as I believe, the single most important attribute of the aspiring journalist is curiosity, Fulford was a natural. Unlike my undergraduate friends, he loved ideas for their own beauty, loved discovering things, and figuring them out in new ways, loved sharing his discoveries with anyone who'd listen.

He is the most compulsive communicator I have ever met, and the habits I was impressed by then have stayed with him. Much later, in fact, his friends coined the verb "to fulford", meaning to be so determined to share your own delight in something that you spoil other people's pleasure. I remember, for instance, sitting through *Dr. Strangelove*, which Bob had of course seen first – he sees *everything* before I do – being reduced to groans as each fulforded joke rolled onto the screen; ah yes, I would say, this must be the place where Keenan Wynn says "pre-vert".

In the 1960s, Bob and I worked together at *Maclean's*, to which Lefolii and I lured him, and our young families were summer neighbours on Ward's Island. I remember riding with him in a Diamond cab – he never has learned how to drive, which is probably good for public safety – on our way to the Park Plaza for a drink, when he announced he had fallen in love with the woman to whom he is now married, and we have shared a lot of each other's passages over the years.

He was always the best writer and clearest thinker of us all. In 1960, *Maclean's* sent me to Montreal for a year, and while I was there I made the acquaintance of the distinguished American man of letters Edmund Wilson, who looked me up for some contacts for the work that became *O Canada*, his study of our literature. The next year, Wilson came to Toronto, and I arranged a small gathering for him in the roof of the Park Plaza–on the roof, as we always said: Lefolii, Fulford, Barbara Moon, and me. It was a memorable occasion, during which Wilson, then in his seventies, managed (a) to insult Serrell Hillman, the *Time* correspondent in Toronto and another roof habitué, who refused to leave without being introduced to the great man, (b) to astound us by having a lady waiting in his hotel room several floors below, whom he summoned after his fifth double Scotch (she turned out to be his wife), and (c) to outdrink us all. From the Park Plaza, we went back to Barbara's apartment, and the conversation waxed far into the night. Afterwards, Lefolii drove the Wilsons back to the Park Plaza, and the next morning reported the following conversation:

WILSON: Funny, that Fulford doesn't look Jewish.

LEFOLII: Well, sir, that might well be because he isn't.

WILSON: Don't be silly.

LEFOLII: ?

WILSON: Nobody can be that bright and that young without being Jewish.

We quit *Maclean's* together in 1964, along with Lefolii and Moon and Harry Bruce and David Lewis Stein, and, still later, worked together on the *Star*, I as entertainment editor, Fulford as a columnist. I called him at home when Ralph Allen died. Officially, I wanted to ask him to write something for that day's paper. But mostly I just wanted to talk.

For nineteen years now, Fulford has been the editor of *Saturday Night*. Although he's never been able to find anyone who can match his own nicely crafted writing, he's put his stamp on the magazine, and given it a stature it hasn't enjoyed since the days of B. K. Sandwell. In middle age, he's become distinguished. He is portly, and most of his hair has receded beyond his brow. But he has lost none of the joy of communication he had when he was a police reporter, and the recognition that has come to him still seems to surprise him. We were lunching in this same restaurant a couple of years ago when I burbled on about my still-confidential first honorary degree, and he waited until I'd finished before topping me with the news – also confidential, naturally – that a few days earlier, ahem, he'd been given the Order of Canada.

Over our broiled trout, we settle in to exchange some recent notes.

He wants the details of the Trudeau interview. How did it come about? Jim Coutts, I tell him, the Liberal insider who had been a *Morningside* contributor, had called me on Thursday, just after Trudeau had published his views on Meech Lake in *La Presse* and the *Toronto Star*, and said in his most conspiratorial tone, "I see my friend has been very frank." In my wisdom, I tell Fulford, I thought Coutts was talking about John Turner, who, even earlier in the week, had made some tough comments on *Morningside* about throwing some of his colleagues out of the caucus. Fortunately, I kept my lip buttoned, and the arrangements unfolded as they should. How did *The National* get a line into our studio? I don't know, I say, nor have I figured out how CTV led its Thursday night newscast with a taped excerpt from our exclusive interview. Do I think Trudeau really thought he could change anything with his salvos in the papers and on radio and television? No, but he is on the record now–for his children, as he said.

So much of what has attracted our professional attention over the years has concerned this man Trudeau. I wrote about him in *Maclean's*, in my year in Montreal. Even then, he seemed set apart from other people, as if his mind were focussed on more important things. He was disconcerting to interview. As part of my preparation for writing about him, I showed up at his mother's house in Outrement at ten in the morning. "Want a drink?" he said, and I, fresh from Toronto and thinking what a risqué bunch these French Canadians were, accepted. He poured me three fingers of Scotch, then sat sipping water under the original Braque on the mantelpiece, looking owlish as I drank myself stupid.

Later, at the *Star Weekly*, whose management had given me a mandate to attract "young adults", I sent a team of reporters across the country to look into the Liberal leadership campaign. Trudeau had become the rage of the readers we were after, and, just before the convention that chose him, we said so, loudly and on the cover. John Turner, I learned only last year, was sure I'd cooked some of that coverage; he bore a grudge for nearly twenty years, though now, he says, he has forgiven me–we finally cleared the air in Ottawa this season, when he lingered in the studio after a *Morningside* interview. Trudeau, so far as I know – and I've talked with him a few times since – didn't notice it at all.

Fulford's connection has been less personal. But his years at *Saturday Night* began at the same time Trudeau became prime minister, and throughout those years, whether you agreed with him or not (as Fulford, from at least the implementation of the War Measures Act in 1970, frequently did not), Trudeau set much of the tone and most of the agenda. Even in the seclusion he has chosen for himself since leaving office, he has remained more interesting than the politicians who now occupy the stage.

We turn to other matters, speaking in the shorthand of old friends. We note the passing of Paul Rimstead, a newspaperman of our generation who died of booze last week in Florida, and lament the way the *Toronto Sun*, which carried his daily column of personal misadventures, had overdone its tribute: "A legend dies." We talk about the curious side-effects that doing things in public has had on our own lives. "Doug Fisher said in his column last week," Fulford says, "that I'd turned down Charlotte Gray's piece on Geills Turner that appeared in *Chatelaine*. He said it was too tough for *Saturday Night*. That's nonsense. I hadn't even *seen* it before *Chatelaine* came out. But it proves how famous I am now; I don't have to *do* anything to get written about." I try to top him. In *Maclean's*, I say, Allan Fotheringham has decided he can convey what some waiter in England looks like just by naming him Peter Gzowski.

"I read that," says Fulford – of course, since he has read everything I've read before I've read it, and has been known to quote even my own material back to me after I've forgotten it. "Wasn't the waiter also surly and inefficient?"

Fulford is going on an extended trip to Asia in the fall, with his wife, Geraldine, who produces the CBC radio program *State of the Arts*. I'll miss him. Our lunches are rare interludes for me, chances to talk with someone who knew me before all this started and who shares my bemusement at how it's all turned out.

Geraldine is Jewish, by the way. I wonder what Edmund Wilson, long since dead, would make of that.

Tuesday, June 2, the apartment, Toronto, mid-morning: Ross McLean is dead.

Jesus.

I had no warning of his obituary in the *Globe*. Gill and I were out last night, and if Ross's death was on the news I missed it. There was nothing on the front page, either, and I'd made my way through most of the paper–the Blue Jay results, Jeff Simpson . . . even the cryptic crossword–before I found it, a two-column headline, way inside:

Blunt-spoken producer was television pioneer.

Try this instead:

"In the seven personality-spattered years of Canadian television, no personality has provoked more headlines, created more stars, stirred more anger, drawn more plaudits or launched more widely quoted epigrams than a tall, bespectacled, blue-jawed, aloof thirty-four-year-old who's . . ."

I wrote that about Ross in the winter of 1959, the first profile I ever did for *Maclean's*, the boy wonder of one medium, some would say, describing the *enfant terrible* of another. I've just read it again – obviously. I asked the young *Maclean's* reporter who called me for a comment to send it down. By today's standards, it's not very good. Aside from the breathless lead, a tone I managed to sustain for about four thousand words, there's one long passage where I quote some of Ross's one-liners. One CBC executive was "the bind that ties". Another was "so unpopular that even 7-Up dislikes him". A playwright known for recycling old material had "just written a new title". And so on. What I didn't say was that Ross had actually given me a list of his sayings, printed on a file card in his neat capital letters. He handed them to me at the end of our last formal interview – "just in case you need this stuff," as he said – and now, of course, with the hindsight of maturity, I realize that that act was more revealing of him than the pointedness of his wit.

He was a very complicated man, shy and wary, hard to be at ease with. He had a distinct manner of talking, which I described in my profile as sounding punctuated, as if he had written his material in advance.

Long after I wrote about him, he tried to add me to the long list of people he had already brought to television: Elaine Grand, Joyce Davidson, Dick MacDougal, Percy Saltzman, Max Ferguson, Pierre Berton, Charles Templeton, Barbara Frum – a slew of them, including, I see as I check my own wide-eyed list from 1959, quite a few you don't hear much of any more (where *is* Olga Kwasniak anyway?).

I was among his failures. In the mid-1960s, when I was free-lancing and Ross's fortunes at the CBC were beginning to fade, he was given a chance to develop a late-night talk show. He hired me to host the first four weeks, and I was awful–stumbling, hesitant, self-conscious: a preview of my celebrated debut on *90 Minutes Live* a decade later. Bobby Taylor, a football player of the time, took such umbrage at one of my questions that he did an end run off the set. I didn't know what to do–then or when my stint ended.

Part of my insecurity, I think I can say fairly, was Ross's fault. For all his deserved reputation as a Svengali of television personalities, he was not much of a coach. As a producer, he operated, as I heard Charles Templeton say on the radio today, by instinct rather than by analysis; he was supportive and helpful in meetings and on the set, but he did not tell you how to do things so much as encourage you to find them within yourself. Later, in his precise, unhurried way, he would tell you whether he liked them.

My time with him, however, came at the pinnacle of the career of the American talk-show star Dick Cavett, who, for a while at least, was a symbol of sophistication and wit on the tube. In spite of the fact that Cavett's background was categorically different from mine–he was a gag-writer for Johnny Carson while I was doing profiles for *Maclean's* –Ross thought he saw some similar possibilities in me. "Cavett wouldn't do that," he would say, or, ominously, just "Did you see Cavett last night?" The pressure didn't do much to reassure my already shaky self-confidence. And I raised my eyebrows years later when, after I had begun to catch on as host of *This Country in the Morning*, Marci McDonald, writing for *Chatelaine*, called Ross for a comment on why I was doing so well on radio when I had been such a disaster on TV. "On television," Ross said (among other things), "he tried too hard to be Dick Cavett."

I don't mean to make him sound small-minded. I think he enjoyed saying outrageous things–I guess I'm still remembering the list he handed me – and, Lord knows, he could be just as untrammelled in his praise as in his criticism. For the past few years, he's been writing a column in the *Globe's Broadcast Week*, and teaching at Ryerson Polytechnical Institute. I've visited Ryerson a couple of times–Alison was in one of his courses last year–and, whatever his failings as a coach on the job, I could tell that his students had been enlightened by his insights; he knew, and cared, more about television than anyone I've ever met.

He died alone, of a heart attack. He was sixty-two. In his late thirties, he had married Jean Templeton, a lovely and funny actress. They had three children before Jean died of leukemia, and Ross raised them on his own. One of the kids found his body last night. Today, phones are ringing all over town, and everyone I talk to is as shocked as I was when I read the *Globe*. I still don't know why he fell from grace at the CBC, how the young man of so much influence became, towards the end, so peripheral a figure. Too feisty, perhaps, or not good at learning survival skills. Or maybe he simply did his best work when he was young, and burned out. When he was hot, he had dozens of chances to go to the U.S., but he chose to remain here, to raise his kids and forge his epigrams. I think we kind of failed him. I have the feeling Ross grew up when we weren't paying attention, and that there was much he still had left to say and do.

Thursday, June 4, Lake Simcoe, 6 p.m.: Golf this morning. Still can't play. Lost four Dunlop Maxflis, none on my own property. Stopped keeping score at 100. Saw a grosbeak in the woods off the ninth fairway, though–*way* off the ninth fairway. Less adventurous shooters miss such pleasures, right, Gill?

GLORIA CALLED this afternoon, apologizing for interrupting my holiday so soon. Peter Puxley, one of our most valued producers, has announced he'll be leaving the unit. The news was expected, but it's still disappointing. Richard Handler, a brilliant and eccentric expatriate American who has produced the distinctive column we call "War and Peace" and given the program much of its intellectual fodder, left this spring to write a book on the peace movement. Jim Handman, who has developed a long list of contacts for international stories, is going to try free-lancing for a while. Glen Allen, a peripatetic print journalist who has been of immeasurable help to me and my passion for the listeners' mail, is moving to Kingston, to work on the *Whig-Standard* and be nearer his children in Montreal. And now, Puxley, a former

Alberta NDP-researcher, who has handled economics for us, has decided to accept an offer from a weekly program on business. Producers leave *Morningside* all the time, and I don't blame them. Their work is as gruelling as mine and less rewarding. But four in one short period – nearly half the producing staff and all but one of our males – is a record, I think, and disconcerting.

We probably need some new blood anyway; comfort is the enemy of energetic broadcasting. But, as Gloria sighed on the phone, there's a lot of rebuilding to do this summer.

Friday, June 5, late afternoon, still at the cottage: I have two tickets for a dinner honouring June Callwood in the city tonight. Four hundred dollars – and unbegrudged; the money goes to Casey House, a hospice for people with AIDS, one of June's causes. (Casey was June's fourth child, much younger than her other three, and for that reason a special joy. He was almost exactly the age of Maria, Jenny's and my third. He was killed in a motorcycle accident just before he turned twenty-one.) But I don't feel much like going. I've called Gloria and asked her to sit in.

I have a limited capacity for social engagements. Much as I like talking one-on-one to many of the people who'll be there tonight, I'm never comfortable with them all at once.

Partly, I'm just shy – much more so than you would expect from someone who struts his stuff in public every morning. But, more than that, if I went, I would almost certainly offend someone. Not on purpose. I may not always be as nice in private as I try to sound on the radio – in private, in fact, I am more given to waspish comments and pointed sarcasm than I ought to be – but, grounded by the Colonel, I am at least polite. I have, however, a world-class inability to remember names. I am to names – and faces, actually – what the tone-deaf are to music. Even watching movies, I am continually asking Gill if that's the woman who was in the bar scene earlier. In real life, where people know – and they do see through your cheery "Why, *hello*, there"'s – it's ten times worse.

In Edmonton, flogging a book, I once spent half an hour convincing a newspaper writer that the rudeness she had observed in me was in fact a ramification of this failing and then autographed her copy of my book – "Thanks for a conversation instead of an interview," I wrote emotionally – to somebody else.

At the race-track last week, I commiserated with a man in a pin-stripe suit about getting fired as a trustee of the Jockey Club, only to have Gill explain his puzzled expression by pointing out that the guy was a veterinarian I'd met two nights earlier at her father's house. I once made a ten-minute speech introducing the Toronto alderman Anne Johnston (believe me, I remember her name *now*) and then, at its climax, dried completely: "and so I give you . . . ah, er, ummmm . . ." The words I dread, when I see someone who looks familiar, are (this hurts just to think about it), "Bet you don't remember who *I* am?" The work I do makes it worse. People who spend twenty minutes in the *Morningside* studio tend to remember the experience – and me. They expect the favour to be returned; I seemed so nice at the time. Gill, who is much better (and thrives on the social circuit as much as I shrink from it), has become adept at whispering ID in my ear when she sees an approaching smile, like an anti-aircraft spotter picking out the Messerschmitts, or quickly introducing herself and waiting for the return. But even with the prospect of her at my side, it's easier to stay home.

Besides, I'm still no good at staying up after dark.

JUNE AND BILL (her husband, Trent Frayne, but no one who has known them as long as I have calls him Trent) are two more friends who go back to my early days at *Maclean's*, and the story I have sent in to be included in the program of tributes for this evening goes back to that time. Sadly, it also involves Ross McLean, whose death is still on everybody's mind, but I hope the people who read it tonight will realize that I wrote it a couple of weeks ago, and won't think I was being casual about his memory.

At least as much as I have, June Callwood has had to deal with a conflict between what she has always done for a living, which is to write about people who do interesting things, and having become, mostly through that work, the kind of person who used to be her subject. Her good works, and they are myriad, have brought her more attention than I imagine she wants, and she has accepted the accolades being poured on her this evening, for instance, only because the event will raise a lot of money for Casey House.

Before she became an activist, June was not just *a* magazine writer. To those of us around *Maclean's,* which is where she was selling most of her stuff, she was *the* writer: astute in concept (she was the first person in North America to write about thalidomide, to take just one example), painstaking in research, elegant in style. There were others who could do individual pieces better, perhaps–Sidney Katz on sociological stories, for instance, Fred Bodsworth on nature, Farley Mowat on the north, and a few others on other subjects (certainly Bill on sports)–but, fact for fact and phrase for phrase, Callwood was the queen. So one of my first acts, when the editors gave me the assignment to write about Ross, was to visit her. Formally, I wanted to talk about Ross's background in Brantford, Ontario, where they'd known each other as teenagers. But, more crucially, I wanted advice on how to write a profile.

I don't remember any of the anecdotes she gave me, although I'll bet about half the early stuff I was rereading the other day came from her. But I do remember the advice she offered on writing about people who worked in similar fields to your own and whom you'd be likely to see again. "You'll be very aware," she warned me, "that if you write about someone like Ross, he's going to read it. You can't help thinking about that; you'll see him looking over your shoulder. But you must ignore it – you have to. You have to forget about your friends."

We flash forward now, from the late 1950s to the early seventies. I am hosting *This Country in the Morning.* June is writing a column in the *Globe* called "The Informal . . .", and after a couple of seasons I qualify to be a . . . She comes to see me at the CBC, and we talk into her tape recorder for about an hour. Three weeks later, her portrait of me appears. It is, as I should have expected, brilliant: tough–heart-achingly so, if being accurate is being tough–but also gentle and affectionate, and, in the end, fair, by far the closest anyone has yet come to capturing me in print.

I don't see her for several weeks after that. Then one day she is in the CBC again, picking up a cheque. I scurry over to say how much I appreciated the piece, toughness and all.

"Thank heavens," she says. "I had a terrible time writing it. I was so conscious of you looking over my shoulder I couldn't even get started."

MORE DAMN GOLF THIS MORNING, by the way. Saw three gold-finches by the eighth green, and, on the back nine, a kingfisher diving the river. That was the closest I came to birdies of any sort. No pars, either.

I can't play this game any more, and the Gzowski Invitational is only a week away.

With the three boys at Maria's wedding, 1985. That's John at the left, Peter in front. Mickey, with his arm around Peter, was in a black-haired mode at the time.

With Jenny and the kids on Ward's Island, 1974. This photo was taken for the article in Chatelaine *in which Jenny said she felt sorry for anyone who had a crush on a radio guy.*

CHAPTER TWO

*On finding a cause . . . Social notes from the
Wedding of the Year . . . The most dedicated
father I know . . . The Leacock winner and
the goy Reuben sandwich . . . "A walking
case against inheritance taxes" . . . My three
sons . . . The end of a marriage*

Wednesday, June 10, the cottage, nearly midnight: The tournament
is only hours away now – a shotgun start at 8:30 – and the anticipation (or, more likely, the fear of things going wrong) is keeping
me awake.

I started all this about a year and a half ago. I don't know in
what order these things usually unfold, although I suspect most
of them start with a good cause and then come up with a way
to raise money. But mine went: (1) I'd like to have a golf tournament with my name on it so I could have some friends for a
day at the Briars; (2) if I raised some money by doing it I'd have
an excuse to turn down all the other charitable events I don't
want to do; and only then (3), so what about Frontier College?
Actually, I didn't even think of the college. I thought about
something that would be non-controversial enough not to raise
eyebrows at the CBC (Gzowski to Raise Funds for Morgentaler
Defence just wouldn't do) and yet would blend with the things
I believe in, and with *Morningside.* Literacy was perfect. Books,
as someone said, is my life. I couldn't see the CBC brass taking

offence at my cause ("It's not that we're *against* people reading, Peter, it's just that there's this group from Saskatchewan
who . . ."), and, to be honest, it was high on the list of things I
would scarcely have thought about if I weren't paid to poke into
public issues–it really is hard to believe that more than a million
adult Canadians can't read.

On *Morningside*, I had met a woman who'd grown up in the
Palestinian refugee camps and come to Canada as a teenager.
She was smart enough to bluff her way around her inability to
decipher letters. Among the jobs she had held before she came
out of the closet and took reading lessons (she has an MA now)
was a spell as a librarian at McGill, a feat she brought off by
memorizing the size and colour of the books on the shelves. Her
story made a profound impression on me. It also brought, as
Morningside subjects often do, a torrent of mail, among which
was a letter from John O'Leary of Frontier College, an organization I remembered as sending labourer-teachers out to the same
construction camps where I'd worked as a student. O'Leary suggested I recruit what he called "the *Morningside* army" to join
the college's more contemporary campaign against illiteracy. He
told me what they were doing in prisons and among street kids
and in some other unexpected places. I was intrigued. O'Leary,
as I have since learned, is a very persuasive man. I called him
to say the army idea was a little too ambitious, but how about
a golf tournament to raise a little money and generate some publicity? And here I am tonight, on the eve of the second.

Last year, we made $18,000. Seventy-two people paid $200
each, and O'Leary talked some corporate sponsors into picking
up tabs for lunch and the bar. David Peterson, who had been a
Frontier College labourer-teacher during his law-school summers,
arrived by helicopter to fire the shotgun, played three holes
(while CITY-TV's cameras followed, waiting for him to dub a
shot, which they showed on the news), and clattered back to
Queen's Park. Michael de Pencier, the president of Key Publishers, and Lorne Rubenstein, who writes on golf for the *Globe*, tied
at 76 for the best round of the day, and Michael won a thrilling
playoff to pick up a trip to Florida. Peter Downie, of CBC television's *Midday*, who'd shot about 126, won a weekend at the
Briars and an autographed copy of a poem. The poem was by
Dennis Lee. I had invited Dennis, who doesn't play, to come

and wander around for the day and write something on the spot. When he read his opus at the end of our closing ceremonies – we'd also had the Bowken trio playing flute, cello, and piano while we dined – I laughed with pleasure, and, if the truth be known, felt the sweet sting of tears, partly from exhaustion but also partly because everything had worked so well. I felt, simply, good about what we had done, and that evening, after a Scotch or two, wrote on a paper napkin my pledge to raise a million dollars for the college before I give up. I'm now a total convert to the cause.

The highlight of the day, though – for me at least – had been when Bill Buckner, a computer scientist, jazz musician, and Frontier College director, who arrived at the Briars in leathers and on a motorcycle for the first round of golf of his life, had finally hit a ball about a hundred and fifty yards down the fairway – he played in a group with Gill and Peter Sibbald-Brown – and cried aloud, so that all around could hear: "All *right*. . . . It's . . . *airborne*."

THAT WAS LAST year, and, contrary to what people have predicted – "It will look after itself the second time around" – I am not, now, convinced we can do it again so successfully.

My own game remains in disarray. Though I am not sure it would have done any good – I might just have grooved my erratic swing – I have not been able to practise. Too busy.

I have been (I don't skip *every* social occasion) to Janet Turnbull's wedding to John Irving (Wedding of the Year, Canadian publisher and American novelist: Bishop Strachan School chapel, security guards at door; Robertson Davies reads lesson; everyone watches Jack McClelland, who has been going through a rotten time, to make sure he is in shape to propose toast to the bride – he is; reception at the Badminton and Racquet Club, the B & R, my dears, where John, the groom, loses his place in the Yeats poem he recites for Janet and has to call on, of all people, John O'Leary – they have met through Janet's involvement in Frontier College and the tournament – to prompt him; Malcolm Fraser, father of John Fraser of the *Globe*, places his hands over his ears during the band's rendition of a Chubby Checker hit, and, when he catches Gill gawking at him, sticks his tongue out at her; and, so far as I know, I get away without forgetting anyone's name – I hadn't met E. L. Doctorow before anyway).

I have met with some people from CBC television and talked about working for them at the Calgary Olympics this winter (things look promising, although I'm worried about the director's admiration for *Entertainment Tonight*) and with the art department of McClelland and Stewart (where I still miss Jack) about the illustrations for *The New Morningside Papers*.

I have had drinks with Mordecai and Florence Richler and two of their kids. (Daniel, the eldest, announces he is leaving *The Journal*, where he has been the host of the Friday-night entertainment section; I admire his fortitude – every other aspiring broadcaster I know would sell his sister to get this job – and say I hope he'll make occasional appearances on *Morningside* when he's free; Mordecai is grumpy about *Morningside*'s not yet having broadcast the readings he has done for us of *Jacob Two-Two and the Dinosaur*, and concerned about his future at McClellandless McClelland and Stewart, but with proud paternal disinterest – he is the most dedicated father I know – does not interfere with my solicitations.) And I have been trying to find time to read the galleys of the book about gold Lefolii has at long last finished, and which he has left with me to look over – I am flattered to be asked, and pleased that he is writing again – while he travels to Asia. Ah, holidays!

As well, though, I've been popping in and out of Frontier College's headquarters to fuss over last-minute details for the tournament. In the eighteen months since I called O'Leary, we have assembled a happy but motley crew. People have stepped forward from the college's curious mix of students and street-workers and part-time teachers, from Gill's family, from *Morningside*, and from the ranks of our friends, to scavenge for prizes (there is a trip to the Olympics up for grabs this year), sell tickets, write letters, promote sponsorships, and look after the countless details of what amounts to throwing an all-day party for a hundred or so guests.

In practical terms, there is nothing left for me to do but enjoy myself and try to remember the golfers' names. But in spite of my faith in our ragtag organization, I can't keep my hands off things. I worry. I fret. I make a nuisance of myself. O'Leary, an unflappable, black-bearded ex-schoolteacher, has developed a catch-phrase to ward off my interference. Whenever I call to pester him about whether Labatt's is really going to come through with the tab for lunch, or whether the rent-a-cars are really available for the musicians, or whether he'll really insist on having one of the ex-cons who have put the fire into the college's Beat the Streets program tee off in front of the president of Mother Parker's Coffee, or on adding to the trip and books and sportswear a prize from the sex-shop Love Craft ("the owner is one of your greatest fans," he swears), he retreats into nonchalance and a phrase that has become the watchword of our cause: "Relax, Peter, we're in great shape."

Those words, stitched in red, emblazon the white sweat-shirt I wear now. The sweat-shirt was presented to me earlier this evening by the tournament volunteers. In return, I gave them official Gzowski Invitational T-shirts, stamped, by Mickey and some of his pale-complexioned friends from Queen Street, with the logo Peter Sibbald-Brown designed for me, a golf club and a quill. The presentations were a highlight of the pre-tournament party that ended a couple of hours ago: a bedlam of volunteers, pooh-bahs from the college, a sponsor or two, Peter and his companion Marion Kilger, some people from the Briars, and a surprising number of golfers who have decided to come up the night before. A merry time. Hamburgers from the barbecue, potato salad, fresh greens, cold beer, red plonk. Much laughter.

Like all good parties, the evening has had a life of its own, and there are moments to remember tomorrow. About nine o'clock, Martin O'Malley and Joey Slinger, two writers who are among my own favourite golfing companions, drifted in from the cottage they have rented from the Briars (David Cobb, who usually joins them, is in Italy this summer, pretending to write a book and living the life he has become entitled to since investing a couple of thousand dollars in Trivial Pursuit). Slinger, a columnist with the *Star*, a distinguished bird-watcher and sartorial exemplar (his tartan plus-fours won him the Best-Dressed trophy at the tournament last year), had an uncustomary ration of wine with his supper, I think, and arrived in full gregarious flight. Unfortunately, he decided to loose a loud and frequently profane (if funny) public critique of his meal at the Briars, not knowing that my guests included that distinguished resort's owner, John

Sibbald, whose family has occupied this part of the world since the time of John Graves Simcoe. As well, Slinger's vast historical knowledge may not have encompassed the Briars' sorry record– now long buried–of anti-Semitism; Jews are welcome at its facilities now, but in John's father's day (and indeed, in the days of my own grandparents, who signed a covenant not to sell their property to the unwanted) they were banned.

"How's your cottage?" I asked Slinger and O'Malley when they arrived. "The Briars treating you okay?"

"Sure," said O'Malley, an astute and tough-minded journalist who in real life seems to lower his standards and enjoy everything under the sun. (I once accused him of giving indiscriminate four-star ratings to everything he experienced except, perhaps, funerals, and he replied by giving me a rave review of a burial he had attended that morning.)

"I had a goy Reuben sandwich," announced Slinger, who is a Presbyterian from Guelph, Ontario. "A fucking goy Reuben sandwich. It didn't have any *sauerkraut* on it, for Chrissake."

I looked at John Sibbald. I wasn't sure whether he'd heard. I hoped not.

"Joey Slinger," I said.

"Oh," said John, who has the mien of a nineteenth-century squire.

"Won the Leacock Medal for humour last year," I said. Stephen Leacock is buried up the road, on the grounds of Sibbald Memorial Church.

"Really?"

"Oh, yes." I turned to Bob Duncan, a film-maker from Montreal who is our house guest tonight. "Say, Bob," I said, "did you know that Stephen Leacock . . ."

". . . with goy fucking french fries," I heard Slinger's voice booming.

"And Mazo de la Roche too," I told Duncan.

"And then I had some goy fucking *coffee*," Slinger seemed to shout.

"Joey," I said. "Why don't you turn the television on? The Blue Jays are playing."

Duncan began to steer John Sibbald out to the deck.

"Mazo de la Roche, eh?" I heard him murmur.

As Duncan and Sibbald exited though the sliding doors, Joey's voice seemed to echo across the room: "You'd think they could make . . ."

But someone got the Blue Jays on the television (they won), and the evening progressed.

IT'S QUIET NOW. The foursomes have been made up, the trios of good golfers seeded with tyros to keep everyone moving at an equal pace. Ninety-two people will fan out on the course to begin play when the shotgun fires. No enemies, so far as I know, will have to play together. The cornucopia of prizes has been split up under appropriate labels, some for real achievement on the golf course, some for laughs. Love Craft is not on the list. The only thing I can think of to worry about is rain. The sky was cloudy at dinner-time. Now, as I peer into the shatterproof glass, I see only darkness and, as on the first evening of this summer, my reflection.

Thursday, June 11, the Briars: No problem. The weather, though not perfect, is eminently golfable.

Everyone's here. The Great Lakes Brass Quintet, five attractive young people in a rainbow of costumes, who, like the workers of Frontier College, sometimes spread their light in prisons and other realms of darkness, fan out on the pro-shop lawn to favour the early arrivals with a burst of the *William Tell* Overture. Michael Ondaatje, this year's poet laureate, has begun taking notes.

With a swing that presages my round of hacking, I slice my first drive out of bounds. Who cares? It's my yard, and I can't win a prize anyway. Gill can, and does, taking the honours as most honest golfer with a cool 172, although I am told later that Diane Francis, the financial writer and *Morningside* regular (who has swollen our coffers with an anonymous donation), would have given her a run for her money but for the fact that in Diane's compassionate foursome the better golfers had insisted she write no higher than an eight on her score-card. Shooting better than Gill by about forty strokes, and after following our complicated equalization formula, Shelagh Rogers, who reads letters with me on the radio, picks up the trip to Calgary. Lorne Rubenstein, with a backswing as smooth as his elegant prose, shoots the lights out, as they say–72–and wins the trophy we have instituted this year for the lowest unedited score: an antique putter, donated by the man who beat Lorne in last year's playoff, Michael de Pencier. (Michael found it in a lake near his cottage, and has added a silver ring with his name on it, and succeeding champions will be urged to follow suit.) Joey Slinger, recuperated, nevertheless loses his best-dressed title to a distinguished box-holder from the race-track, who took the gold with floral Bermuda shorts and bright suspenders. Frank Mahovlich, a gentlemanly exception to my ban on hockey players (most of whom think it's your privilege to play with them and hear them say "fuck"), picks up a small prize. Scott Young wins a disputed award for oldest clubs. The Great Lakes kids get an ovation for their antiphonal concert over lunch. Michael Ondaatje brings the house down (and very nearly more tears to my eyes). And the college makes $25,000.

Only $957,000 to go.

Evening, the same day: That figure, as I think about it now, should really be $956,800. At the conclusion of our ceremonies, just after I had presented a bottle of premium rye whiskey to Bob Duncan for having been the first entrant to pay–he had plunked down $200 cash one night when we were working together on an episode in my now-departed TV series – Michel de Pencier rushed forward with a fistful of money to pay for next year in advance. It was a typical de Pencier gesture: impulsive, generous, good-humoured–and canny. "I wanted to make sure I got in early in case you raise the price," he said as he handed me his crumpled bills.

Michael is rich. He was born rich – his family goes back in Toronto to at least the days of Bishop Strachan, to whom he is vaguely related – and he married rich: Honour Bonnycastle de Pencier comes from the Winnipeg family that made a fortune from Harlequin romances. (Honour's mother, it's said, was the final editorial authority on every word of all the early stories.) But, silver spoon or not, he is a publishing genius, who has built a multi-million-dollar company largely from his own skills and intuition. He is also, along with Honour, a walking case against inheritance taxes, an unassuming, decent man, liked by the people who work for his enterprises (many of whom have their own nice little nest-eggs shares) and admired by pretty well everyone who knows him.

He serves a lot of good causes, some because they're a function of his position and his upbringing, but others because he just believes in them, or thinks they matter to the world. For years, for instance, the *Canadian Forum* was published out of premises he paid the rent for, and the National Magazine Awards–none of which, characteristically, he qualifies to win–are almost solely his creation. He lives in a comfortable Rosedale house now, replete with swimming-pool, but goes to work in a battered car or by bus and subway,and keeps the world's most cluttered open-door office. He still persists in the habit he developed as a philosophy student of writing down his inspirations on scraps of paper, which he stuffs into the pockets of his oddly assorted clothes (he is colour-blind, and Honour's system of annotating his wardrobe for co-ordination does not always work). Miraculously, he'll come up with them when he needs them. I'm very fond of him, as you can tell, and sometimes I wish I'd stayed in the magazine business with him after we started some ventures together long ago. I might be rich, too.

Wouldn't have my own golf tournament, though, for a cause that's so much fun to serve.

Monday, June 15, the University of Windsor, Windsor, Ontario: I wouldn't have been here, either. I am getting an honorary degree, a doctor of laws, and it isn't for my work in magazines.

This is my second. Three years ago, at the same time Fulford was being named an Officer of the Order of Canada, the University of New Brunswick made me a doctor of letters. Now I have the OC and Fulford has his first doctorate. Today puts me ahead, but only briefly. Next weekend, Fulford gets *his* second, from York, in Toronto.

"Do you mean you're accepting a degree from a university in a *suburb?*" I asked incredulously.

"And where's yours from?" he asked.

"Why, Windsor," I said.

"Oh," said Dr. Fulford, "do they have a university there?"

Wednesday, June 17, the cottage: A day to be cherished. The three boys, men, now, I should say, and me: Peter Casimir, the engineer, named for his triple-great-grandfather in whose professional footsteps he follows; John (John Paul McGregor, bearing names from both sides of his breeding, and studying and playing music with gifts he has not inherited from me), and Michael David, known to no one as anything but Mickey, the baby, but a deep-voiced and capable adult now, torn from the hammering and painting he is doing to fix up his own first pad in a warehouse downtown.

My sons.

In a perfect world, I would have had all of the kids to myself for a while, as I did the day I turned fifty. But that becomes more difficult every year, as the sprouts from this branch of the family tree grow ever stronger and more independent. I see Alison, who is working at the CBC this summer, all the time. But Maria is married, the mother of Stephanie Anne Gzowski Zufelt, aged five months now and the apple of my eye, and is living in our old summer place on Ward's Island and working on the stock market. All five live their own lives. I take what I can get, and today has been special: some bantering golf in the afternoon (Peter, baseball grip and all, better than his erratic father, Mickey surprisingly long off the tee, John late for the golf because he was rehearsing with a jazz band in the city, but here shortly after), some roast potatoes and garlic steaks at dinner, a beer or two, a couple of long games of hearts (won by Mickey), comfortable talk, easy laughter. I wonder if it meant as much to them as it did to me.

So many of the people around me have been separated, divorced, or remarried, or have otherwise had their lives realigned in the last couple of decades–Richler, de Pencier, and Harry Bruce are remarkable by their exception–that I have come to take split families, including my own, as normal. In theory, I guess the kids do too; Lord knows, their situation has been different from mine in Galt a generation ago, where, so far as I know, I was the only child of divorce in town. But that hasn't made the pain any less real – not for me and, I'm sure, not for them.

Until I die I will remember John, aged twelve, going upstairs to his room, fighting back silent tears, after Jenny and I gathered them all together to tell them we were breaking up; and I remember, too, going up to console him, running my hand through his blond hair and trying to tell him in words what I felt in my heart but what, in his eyes, my actions must have been denying: that

I loved him and would love him always. And, for all the comfort of an evening such as this, I am not sure yet that he believed me, or believes me now.

Know what's bullshit? That "quality time" – the time you spend with your attention focussed on the kids you don't live with – is better than "quantity time", the hours and days and weeks you spend reading the sports section or trying to figure out your income tax while your daughter tugs at your sleeve. I didn't hear that phrase until after Jenny and I had split. When I did hear it–a family-court judge used it, maybe even on some broadcast I was hosting–I clutched it to my bosom, gloating to myself that taking the kids bowling on Saturday afternoon (I actually did that, I and all the other separated fathers who keep the alleys open on weekends), or to Fran's, or to some second-rate movie, was better for them than nagging them about their homework every night, or having them see me in my dressing-gown, grumpy with their mother, shaggily hung over.

Wrong. I know that now, and they knew it then. After I moved down to a furnished, glass-wrapped bachelor pad on Yorkville and, later, to a building with a doorman, John kept a boa constrictor in his room; I have a phobia of snakes.

Oh, mind you, I've been there when they needed me, or when I thought they did: when Alison got picked up for shoplifting after she and a buddy from the Island played some silly games in a hardware store, when Maria was hurt in a car accident (Peter was driving), when John won a math prize, when Mick played drums in a concert. And I've been, or have tried to be, good (maybe even too good) about birthdays and Christmasses and other moments of passage. But I wasn't *there*, goddamit, to be called on when *they* decided the time was right, and the years when I might have been won't come around again. It's been a long, tough battle to hold their love and reacquire their friendship. I have struggled, not always successfully, for every inch, trying sometimes to make up in the intensity of my concern – quality nagging, perhaps – for its infrequency. And the times when we are at ease with each other, telling lies about our boyhoods, carefully noting (on my part at least) the similar shape of the hands that reach for cards, the same throaty chuckles, speaking in the codes that mark a family . . . not *trying* for anything . . . are moments that make a summer.

I was twenty-three when Jenny and I were married. Jenny was twenty-four. It's still easy to figure her age from mine, and to pinpoint the night of our first date. I was in Moose Jaw, where I had ventured after leaving university the second time. I saw her picture in the Regina *Leader-Post*. She had designed the set for a Regina Little Theatre production of *The Women*. With the excuse that I was trying to direct some theatre in Moose Jaw – I was, too, though nothing much came of it – I tracked her down; she was an interior designer for a firm of architects. I asked for a date, and suggested the following Friday, July 13, my birthday. "Why not?" she said. "It's my birthday too." We were married the subsequent February, and the kids came tumbling after: Peter, Alison, Maria, John, Mickey, all in seven years.

What went wrong is buried in what you already know about my life since then, and in the times. Jenny, the interior designer, should have been an architect, and in a different time, and maybe even a different place, would have been. She is the second of three daughters of Reg Lissaman, a taciturn building contractor from Brandon, Manitoba. (He was the MLA from Brandon, too, almost until his death, and a man of high principles.) She was the kid who puttered around after her father, learning how houses were built and, later, helping with the blueprints. But when the time came to apply for university, neither the authorities there nor her unbending father thought she should set her sights higher than the school of interior design.

She was a very good designer. She had done the library of the University of Saskatchewan by the time we met, for example. But at the time Jenny Lissaman became Jenny Gzowski, that mattered far less than that she was married. We didn't talk about the change in her role, any more than we talked about whether we'd have children. It was the 1950s. We just did things. And we did them in a way that suited my career. I had gone from Moose Jaw to Chatham, Ontario, by the time we were married, to work the daily paper there, wearing horn-rimmed glasses before I needed them. When Ralph Allen summoned me to *Maclean's*, Jenny, pregnant, resigned her job with a local architectural firm and we moved to Toronto. Young husband became, increasingly, rising young star of his profession. Rising young designer became, exclusively, mother and wife.

Even if I could get away with it, I wouldn't try to ascribe everything that went wrong to historical forces. Whatever the statistical toll in my own circle, too many other people held too many other marriages together for that. Furthermore, I didn't handle my part well; there were far too many late nights that didn't have to be late, too many important visitors from out of town, too much roof of the Park Plaza. I think, now (as, of course, I should have thought then), of what it must have been like for her, after a day of washing diapers, to hear the latest quip from the elegant Barbara Moon, or to wonder why I had to write a profile of Dinah Christie the same week Maria had been sick on her dress. I was, not to put too fine a point on it, a jerk about those things. But the forces of history were a part of it; it simply didn't occur to us – or at least to me, any more than it had occurred to her father or the admissions officer at the University of Manitoba–that there might be a different way of doing things. By the time it did, it was too late.

I don't want to make it sound as if it was all empty when we were together, or that Jenny was a sad, uncomprehending victim. It wasn't empty at all; there were good, rich, laughter-filled, family times: first teeth, last diapers, Saturday-morning hockey, summers at the Island (where the kids put down roots that still tug at them), the year in Montreal, theatre outings, Beatles records, noisy guitars, John's evolving talents, Maria's modelling, Mick's drums, Peter's chess, Alison's wit. And Jenny, five foot one and never losing her prettiness, was at the centre of the whole jumble of snapshots, running her house, raising her children, and keeping her mind alive.

I think, now, of what reading the first literature of the women's revolution must have meant to her, or what must have gone through her mind when she would hear me struggling, in my early days on CBC radio, with ideas that have come to change the world of men and women – the biggest social revolution of our time – and then welcome me home that evening (when I made it on time), when I would lift the pot lids like Ozzie Nelson to see what she had prepared for dinner.

I think that now, as I say, but I didn't think it then, or ask her about it. We weren't good at talking, she and I, the descendant of staunch prairie stock and the only child of a broken home who never did, as Alison wrote in a magazine piece a couple of years ago, figure out how to be a father.

To this day, I don't know if Jenny enjoyed my successes or not. I don't know whether she knew – it certainly would not have occurred to me to tell her–that at least some of the late nights inspired good magazine pieces, and at least some of the visitors really were from out of town, and that if she hadn't been doing the work of both parents at home, I might not have done what I did, or whether she just thought what I did when I was out of the house, or locked in my study brooding–"and please can't you tell those kids to keep it down"–was something independent of her, and that the only times I needed her were as a sounding-board for my manuscripts or, when things had messed up, to help me lick my wounds.

I wonder. Or did she resent the attention that came to me because of what I was doing away from home? Would it occur to her to contemplate, I wonder, that, if I had done my share, she too might have had her name in the paper, and come to know the waiters on the roof by their first names? Marci McDonald, preparing the same magazine article she called Ross McLean for, asked Jenny what she made of the fact that a lot of housewives seemed infatuated with me. "I guess I feel sorry for them," Jenny said, "if their lives are so empty they have to fall in love with someone on the radio."

Jenny is okay now, if I may presume. Better off, I think–and she agrees–than if we'd tried to hold our marriage together. She stayed on in the house we bought in North Toronto and saw the children through to adulthood. Along the way, she picked up her old profession, and, although she can never make up for all the years she missed of changing fashions and technological improvements, she's doing well. In ten years of separation, we became the kind of friends we never really were as husband and wife, sometimes talking on the phone as we hadn't been able to in person, and keeping the lawyers at bay by working out our own arrangements, I agreeing she should continue to write cheques on our common bank account, she in turn reducing her requirements as her own income increased and as the kids left the nest. We spent Christmasses together, too, and often in the years I was away from Toronto she let me sleep on the couch while Santa hung the presents. But on Boxing Day mornings, I went somewhere else.

Our friendship is being tested this summer. Jenny has filed for divorce. She wants to sell the big house in North Toronto and settle into something smaller, which might give her an income for the old age she now faces more wisely than I. For my part, I've had a hard time realizing that no part of the house belongs to me. The lawyers, at last, are in on the action. We're communicating by writ. There is tension. I'll give in to her, of course; if nothing else, writing this down now, with the time I've just spent with our three splendid sons still fresh in my mind, reminds me how much she is the good guy in our story and I the villain, and how lucky I was that it lasted eighteen years before it burned out.

No, I don't wish it had turned out otherwise. The wounds have healed now, and the scar tissue is stronger than the original flesh. Life is better for us both. Common birthday or not, we were doomed, Jenny Lissaman and I, by the point in history at which we met and by the backgrounds we brought even to that first birthday dinner, and we are fortunate to have come out of the time we shared with as many good memories as we have, and with the five young people who bear mixtures of our genes.

But that doesn't bring back the years I could have shared with the kids, or mean that, even during the moments I spend most intimately with them now, there aren't still subjects we avoid, and things among us left unsaid.

And, oh, John, I wish it hadn't hurt so much.

*Saying goodbye to Maclean's, 1964. Ken Lefolii, back to camera,
works on opening the champagne, while Bob Fulford and
I look on. After the toasts, we smashed our glasses.*

CHAPTER THREE

*A Black day for Saturday Night . . .
"Sorry, I'm a Canadian" . . . Northrop Frye
and the answer interviewers dread . . . The
great Maclean's walkout of 1964 . . . When
the Schick hit the fan. . . . On hummingbirds
and new beginnings*

Thursday, June 18, Ridley College, St. Catharines, Ontario: I am deep in the bowels of the Ridley archives, thumbing through dusty prints and glass negatives for the book Peter Sibbald-Brown and I are just beginning to work on, when I am summoned to the phone.

"I think it's the *Globe and Mail*," says the librarian.

"Wonder what they could want."

What they want is my comment on the most astonishing news: Conrad Black has bought *Saturday Night*.

"Really?" I say. "Whatever for?"

"That's what we'd hoped you might be able to tell us," says the *Globe* reporter.

I repeat only that I'm dumbfounded. The magazine has been losing a lot of money for a long time, I know, and I have wondered from time to time when its latest owner, Norman Webster, who is both the editor of the *Globe and Mail* and the heir to a substantial fortune, would grow tired of subsidizing it. But Conrad Black? He has bought a newspaper in England, and has some background in publishing in Canada. But if the views he espouses in the column he writes for the *Globe*'s business magazine are any indication, he stands almost exactly opposite to most of what the magazine–meaning Fulford–has come to represent: a liberal, tolerant, unbiased forum of opinion, and graceful, independent journalism.

"How much did he pay?" I ask the reporter who has called to hear my views.

"Our story says several million."

"And what are his plans?"

"He's not saying. We wondered if you had any thoughts on what he should do with it. What should he keep, for instance?"

"Fulford," I say, and suspect I have made tomorrow's paper.

Friday, June 19, the apartment, Toronto, 6 a.m.: I have. The more prominent parts of the *Globe* story in which I am quoted are, fortunately, more interesting. Black has indeed bought the magazine, though he is still not saying what he plans to do with it. John Macfarlane, apparently, is out as publisher, which is disconcerting. John is a rarity in the ranks of senior magazine executives in that his background is editorial, like Fulford's and mine, rather than in advertising or circulation, or, as with Michael de Pencier, simply entrepreneurial. Before he became a publisher, his career hopscotched almost like my own and, indeed, has occasionally followed the same path as mine. I first spotted him at a Canadian University Press conference Fulford and I addressed in the 1960s, an articulate and presentable young editor from McMaster. In 1970, I lured him away from the *Star* to *Maclean's*, and he moved into his office there, as he has often reminded me, just after I, the man who had hired him, had left. Not long afterward, I lured him again, this time from *Maclean's*, to take over the editorship of *Toronto Life*, where I was involved. Later he ran *Weekend Magazine*, the last of the national weekly newspaper supplements, and, as I had with the *Star Weekly*, went through the heartbreak of seeing a magazine he had brought editorially to life folded by its owners. At *Saturday Night*, I know from Fulford, he has been the kind of publisher editors dream of, asking, as Bob has said, not how they could do things more cheaply or less controversially, but how they could do things better. This may, of course, have been his downfall, but it is an enviable thought for a magazine guy to have on his epitaph.

9:30: A remarkably unbowed Fulford returns the call I placed to him yesterday from St. Catharines. The news has come as a total shock to him, he says, and, no, he has not yet heard from Conrad Black. He had been out getting his degree from York – "I think I'm going to hire the guy who wrote my citation to run around after me and read it wherever I go," he says in a jolly aside – and when he arrived back at the office the magazine he had been editing for nineteen years had been sold out from under him. We are just moving on to some deeper analysis when I hear him become distracted.

"Excuse me," he says, "there's a Mr. Black on the other line."

When we talk later in the morning, he and Black have made a date for lunch. "I have only one question for him," he says, "and that's about who'll be deciding what goes in the magazine. If it's Conrad Black, I won't want to work here any more. If he says it's still me, maybe we can work something out."

Monday, June 22, the Briars, afternoon: O'Malley for golf. What a pleasure to play with he is! He is as bad as I am – why *can't* I play this game any more? – though with reason to be much worse, since he didn't play as a kid. But he is unruffled by his scores. He just *likes* being out here, and his enthusiasms, for the cedared beauty of this lovely course, the warm massage of the sun on his neck, the soaring arc of his occasional good drive, are infectious. He brought Karen to play with him today – Karen O'Reilly, who lives with him in Aurora – and the two of them and Gill and I had one of the season's happiest rounds.

I was playing with Martin here three years ago when he said something that has stuck in my mind. We were on the tenth tee, just outside the pro shop. Someone in a foursome setting off down the first fairway ran over his foot with a golf cart. O'Malley, in excruciating pain, raised his head, saw them staring, and said, "Oh, sorry." Then he looked back at me and, with a wry grin, said, "Holy Christ, am I ever a Canadian!"

I noted the moment then, and, in the time since, it has become the nucleus of a snowball rolling down a hill, picking up weight with every turn. In Edmonton, at the race-track, I walked behind a successful bettor – she was a schoolteacher, I learned later, taking part in what was presumably a research project with a group of her colleagues – and when she dropped a ten-dollar bill from her pocket I tapped her on the shoulder to say I'd retrieved it. "Oh," she said, "sorry." Across the road from our condominium in Toronto, I held the door for a young woman entering a convenience store. She made her purchase before I made mine and, on the way out, returned the favour. Unfortunately, the sidewalk was icy. She lost her footing and crumpled to the frozen ground. I bent over her in concern. She looked up and said – you will have guessed it – "Gee, sorry."

And so on. The show-piece of my collection, I think, stars Northrop Frye, the renowned Canadian literary scholar – there are people who have heard of him who haven't heard of Wayne Gretzky – who made a rare appearance on *Morningside* last season.

Frye is agonizingly shy and a very sweet man, but he intimidates the hell out of me. One night the year before our interview, I was invited to the head table of Massey College, in Toronto. After dinner, we all retired to a basement study for port and brandy (passed to the left, of course) and walnuts and conversation. To my chagrin, I was given the place of honour, next to Frye. What, I wondered, did a man who had been so ignominiously sent on his way from the study of first-year English say to the author of the century's most celebrated critiques of the Bible and Shakespeare? "Read any good Book lately?"

Somehow I made it through that evening (we ended up swapping yarns on the tyranny of word processors), but when Frye showed up for his *Morningside* chat, to talk about the collection of essays on Shakespeare he had assembled from his lecture notes, I was less than confident. I had arranged to pre-record our session in the afternoon, and, to avoid the torture of small talk, hustled him directly to the studio when he arrived.

I had, to be sure, boned up. Hal Wake, our producer of literary matters, had written me his usual eloquent background memo and supplied me with a fat file of articles from the accessible press, and I had sat up the night before, puzzling my way through his complex thoughts. But I was still overwhelmed.

When we rolled the tape, it quickly became clear to me that Frye had the disconcerting habit of simply answering the questions. This is a much rarer conversational quality than people who don't have to do interviews for a living probably realize. Being interviewed in public, most people – certainly those who appear on radio and television and get categorized as "good talkers" – do much more than respond to what you have asked them. They expand on it, or qualify it, or use it as the base from which to make another point. They may even try to dodge around it – to avoid the heart of the question they have been posed. But the task of the interviewer remains the same: to guide rather than to motivate. The subject paddles, the interviewer steers.

The ability to steer – even when it involves staying in the same place and rephrasing the still-unanswered thought – is the ultimate achievement of the craft. To master it, you must first learn to listen, to follow every turn of your subject's phrase, and to use the energy that comes from it to take him down the course you want him to follow; to be in control all the time, in other words, while maintaining the illusion that you are just along for the ride. But what can stump you in trying to practise this part of the craft is . . . well, Northrop Frye. Trying to make a strength out of my own feeling of awkwardness (another trick of the trade), I began on a note I had picked out of Hal's extensive background. I confessed to my own discomfiture in his intellectually intimidating presence, and asked if, as I had read in a magazine article, it was a common phenomenon.

He gave me the answer interviewers dread:

"Yes."

And so it went. I asked. He answered. If I posed a reasonable question, he gave me a reasonable and intelligent answer – never less, but certainly never more. If I didn't, he smiled benignly. On an exam, he'd have scored a hundred. But in a radio interview, he was close to failing. And, to save the piece, I was labouring. Rather than steering a boat, I was crossing a stream on stepping-stones, barely getting my balance on one before it was time – "Yes, that's what I meant about Hamlet" – to leap for the slippery surface of the next.

And then I started to cough. Partly from tension, partly from a sip of cafeteria coffee that went down the wrong way, but mostly, I know, from thirty-five years of unfiltered Buckinghams, I dissolved into paroxysms of hacking and spluttering.

Thank heavens this isn't happening live in the morning, I thought, as my lungs heaved and I reached futilely for more coffee.

I couldn't go on. I signalled to Hal in the control room to stop the tape. Through streaming eyes, I looked helplessly across the table. The world's pre-eminent scholar of Shakespeare, the Bible, and Blake peered back at me through his rimless glasses.

I coughed again, uncontrollably.

"Oh dear," said Northrop Frye, "I'm sorry."

8:30, the dinner table: On the eighteenth tee this afternoon, Gill spotted a pileated woodpecker, and for a few moments in the soft summer light, she and O'Malley and Karen and I watched it flutter among the trees.

"Too bad he's not an ivory-bill," Gill said. "We could have made Peter Whelan's column in the *Globe*."

O'Malley, of course, is undeterred. After dinner, and a Scotch or two, he insists on calling Whelan at home to report our find. Whelan is grateful, he reports, and says hello. (Whelan appears on *Morningside* from time to time.)

"He still won't put it in his column," Gill laughs. "Only an ivory-bill could get us in the paper."

O'Malley thinks she's being too cynical. He offers to bet me his golf winnings from this afternoon, five dollars, double or nothing, that we'll make the paper.

"Okay," I say. "But if you're right won't you be embarrassed by the fame?"

"I'm not *that* Canadian," he says.

Wednesday, June 24, the cottage, morning: Fulford is finished at *Saturday Night*.

I have called for an account of his lunch with Conrad Black. An awful experience, he says. Black brought along Peter White, an executive who works for him on this kind of deal ("I wondered if we should get Herb Gray to write our political column," Fulford says, "and maybe Ian Brown to do the cover stories"–"And Red Kelly for sports," I add, at last getting it), and together they made the wrong impression on him.

"So there's no hope?"

"None."

I don't have to ask him if he got the answer to the only question he had said would matter, whether it would be he or Black who would decide what went into the magazine. Sometimes, I know, it's not that simple; sometimes there are just situations you know you can't handle. Fulford is in one now. If it's over for him, it's over. Too bad.

THE GROUP OF US WHO QUIT *MACLEAN'S* together in 1964 were, I suppose, a pretty feisty bunch. For two years, with Lefolii as editor, we had been striving to be fresh, topical, and challenging. Though the magazine we had been putting out was much tamer than the kind of journalism that, even in the early 1960s, was showing up in the alternate press and on the campuses that some of us had left so recently, we tried our best, as we used to say, to call things as we saw them. We raised some tempers. Before we left, we had managed to attract libel suits that totalled, in their claims, nine million dollars. None of them, so far as I know, was settled for more than the dollar that was paid to Frank Cotroni for the damage the court found *Maclean's* had done to his reputation in Montreal by reporting his connections with the Mafia. But – and while I am not among those who think a journalist's success can be measured by the number of people suing him – it was a mark of our editorial direction in those days that we had attracted them.

Among the people who disliked the magazine most, we often felt, were those who paid our salaries, the senior management and board of directors of Maclean-Hunter Publishing Co. Ltd. Even in retrospect, it is hard to put my finger on exactly why this should have been. We were not, in that most dreaded of words, "socialists"; we preached no revolution. We ran some stories on alcoholism that may have upset some of the liquor advertisers who paid so many of our bills (though I can't remember any on lung cancer, which might have looked after our second-biggest category), and occasionally took on causes that might have upset some other sectors of the economy. Sid Katz did some remarkable reporting on the drug industry, for example, and June Callwood, as I've said elsewhere, broke the thalidomide story in our pages. But we were a long way from being, in the phrase that would have doomed us among our superiors, "anti-business".

Were we "controversial"? I hope so. Alan Phillips, who had taken on the Mafia for us, wrote a piece about physiology called "Is the Negro a better man?" I went back to Saskatchewan after a bunch of white men had trampled an Indian tent on the fairgrounds at Glaslyn, near the Battlefords, killing a young man who had been asleep inside; we labelled my report "This is our Alabama", and copies of the magazine were burned in some nearby towns. Mordecai Richler went to Israel, reported that all was not perfect, and had to defend himself against subsequent charges of anti-Semitism. But "controversy" had always been a part of *Maclean's*–as, surely, it is a part of all journalism worthy of the name. This was the magazine, after all, where George Drew had exposed the scandal of the Bren gun, where Blair Fraser had told the world about Mackenzie King's spiritualism, where Ralph Allen, stepping aside from his editor's post, had written, under the rubric "For the sake of argument", "What if Herbert Norman *had* been a communist?", and had admitted, during the height of McCarthyism in the U.S., that he had once voted communist himself.

The trouble may have started with our personal styles. Maclean-Hunter had what business analysts of a later day would call a strong corporate culture. In the fall, for instance, the day after Donald F. Hunter, scion of one of the founding families, wore a hat to work, the elevators would be full of advertising salesmen and executives of the profitable business-magazine division all decked out in the same model of headwear; vice versa in the spring. Lefolii, who to this day, so far as I know, has never owned a blue suit, let alone a fedora, just didn't fit in.

He is an auto-didact, the son of an Icelandic carpenter. At a time when other people went to college, Ken (as he has written in his book on gold) worked on sailing ships and in mining camps from Hong Kong to Australia. Some of the rough edges have not rubbed off. Though he has a precise sense of language, and, as he used to demonstrate to me during some late nights in our *Maclean's* days, is one of the great Scrabble players of the western world, he still pronounces some words the way he picked them up from the printed page–he says add-a-kit, for example, for adequate. He has innate good manners and a built-in gentility, but, in the 1960s at least, was not sure about which fork to eat the Dover sole with, a trait that did not help him in the Maclean-Hunter executive dining-room. When Floyd Chalmers, the distinguished chairman of the Maclean-Hunter board, called Ken "Ken", Ken called Mr. Chalmers "Floyd", which raised some eyebrows around our bi-weekly meetings.

There were, however, more serious problems. One was the

financial health of the magazine. In different times, the owners might have delighted in Ken's independence of mind and style. But in the early 1960s, general magazines were in trouble everywhere. *Life, Look, Collier's, The Saturday Evening Post* – all of whose roles *Maclean's* filled in Canada – were floundering, their readers deserting them for television. The day of the "vertical" magazines, aimed at specific sections of the population, had not yet arrived. *Maclean's'* difficulties, furthermore, were compounded by what continued to be unfair competition from American imports, who were selling space to Canadian advertisers in publications whose editorial costs had already been paid by their American editions – what in any other business would have been called dumping. We had been able to hold our readership at a comfortable half-million or so, but the advertising salesmen had an uphill battle selling the space around our articles. *Maclean's*, to be succinct, was losing its owners' neatly pressed shirts.

Then, too, there was the matter of the Vanguard – or the Viscount: I will never be able to sort them out. They were both airplanes. One was coming into service on the air lines; one was already there. One had some safety problems; the other didn't. In a piece he had written just before he became managing editor, Lefolii had confused them, ascribing to the trouble-free aircraft (whichever it was) the flaws of the other. The clanger, if human, was unforgivable. According to the ad department, the piece ("Is air travel obsolete?") resulted in some fifty thousand dollars in cancelled income, and, although no one felt worse about it than Ken – I can still get a rise out of him by suggesting he has remained in the "viscount of his profession" – its memory hung over all his subsequent years at *Maclean's* like the black cloud over Li'l Abner's Joe Btfsplk.

The unhealthy tension between the owners of the magazine and its editors first came to a head in the summer of 1963. The issue was a piece by Pierre Berton. After leaving *Maclean's* in 1958, Berton had been writing for the *Toronto Star* – setting a standard for newspaper columns not matched before or since. When he stopped doing that, we offered him our back page to fill in any way he chose, for the then-astronomical sum of $1,000 an issue. In a June issue he wrote a piece we called "It's time we stopped hoaxing the kids about sex", in which he argued – how tame all this seems now – that if one of his daughters was going to lose her virginity, he would rather it be in a comfortable bed than in the back seat of a car. Although I, as Berton has reminded me since, assured him that the column would cause little trouble ("We've already lost all those subscribers," I told him), there was a chorus of complaint from readers who felt he was encouraging licentiousness. Management appeared to agree. We weathered the storm, or so we thought, but when Berton, a couple of issues later, submitted a column that answered his critics and raised the whole matter again, they hit the roof. Not only would that particular column not run, Berton himself was to be *non grata*, then and forever. We knuckled under, for the time being, and Berton, who often manages to have the last word, sent his offending piece to the *Telegram*, which published it with much fanfare as "the column *Maclean's* wouldn't run".

Even when it wasn't making headlines in rival publications, the feeling of antagonism between owners and editors carried on. To deal with it, the owners appointed R. A. McEachern as executive vice-president in charge of magazines – which meant, effectively, Lefolii's overseer. The move was a disaster. Ron McEachern, who had enjoyed a brilliant career as editor and publisher of *The Financial Post*, had a different view of what the magazine should be than we did. He also had the diplomatic skills of Genghis Khan. Upon his appointment, Peter C. Newman, who had worked for the *Post* before ever joining *Maclean's*, resigned. McEachern proceeded to bombard Lefolii with memos about possible stories and criticisms of what he once called the "ego-ramblings" we were already running.

From the trenches, the warfare often appeared to reach ludicrous dimensions. One case in point was a piece of mine called "The Maple Leaf money machine", about Toronto's NHL hockey team and the building they played in. The piece included some conversation with Punch Imlach, the Leafs' coach and general manager. Imlach, as you may recall, swore a lot, and sprinkled his conversation with a word I decided to transcribe as " – – – – ing". Lefolii passed it that way, and the article was set in type. I had a call from Gerry Brander, a gentle and congenial former ad salesman, who, as publisher of *Maclean's*, had the difficult job of trying to mediate between Lefolii and McEachern. He was bothered by " – – – – ing".

"What's wrong?" I said.

"It means 'fucking', doesn't it?" Brander said.

"Yes, Gerry."

"Well, we shouldn't put that in *Maclean's*."

"We're not," I said. "We're putting in '----ing'."

"Well," said Gerry, "everyone who reads it will say, you know, 'fucking' to himself."

In the end, I lost. We replated, at some expense, four pages of the magazine, substituting "----" for "----ing". I don't know what people said to themselves when they read my account. The whole thing, as Lefolii said, was a "----ing fuck-up".

In the same piece, trying to make a point about the commercialization of an old Canadian institution, I described an advertisement that was then running in the Toronto subway system. The ad showed sixteen of the Maple Leafs, and claimed that all of them had shaved with a single Schick razor-blade. While I admired the advertising agency's ingenuity, I pointed out in *Maclean's* that it was unlikely that all sixteen players had in fact used the same blade, inasmuch as two of them, Andy Bathgate and Don McKenney, had been playing for other teams when the group picture was taken. I suggested–nay, said–that it was highly improbable that when Bathgate had checked into his new team the first words the trainer spoke to him were, "Hi, Andy, you'll be number 9, and would you mind shaving with this razor-blade we've been keeping for six months?"

The agency was not amused. Our own ad department reported that they had just been on the verge of landing the Schick account themselves. A lawsuit was mentioned. The next week, in Montreal, I found myself in the curious position of having to track down Andy Bathgate in the lobby of the Mount Royal hotel, where the Leafs were staying before a game with the Canadiens, and asking him if, by any chance, some version of the scene I had imagined had taken place. He said, of course, no.

Not long after that, I was in Montreal again, covering the Canadian Open golf tournament. Lefolii tracked me down by phone. Things had come to a head, he said, and perhaps I should come back to Toronto.

The last straw was a piece Harry Bruce had written about the International Typographical Union strike at the Toronto newspapers. Although Fulford, Ken, and I had all read the piece and passed it, the page proofs that came back from the printing plant had not carried it. Ken had called to see what had happened and had been told that Ron McEachern had killed it. It was "unfair to both sides," McEachern said later. Lefolii, as he said, no longer felt like the editor. He resigned. On my return, I sent in my own note. Fulford, Harry, Barbara Moon, and Dave Stein soon followed.

On the Friday before Labour Day, 1964, we ordered a jeroboam of champagne into Ralph Allen's old office. The staff rented some glasses. Lefolii proposed a toast to our days at *Maclean's*, drank it, and hurled his empty glass against the wall. Then, seeing the dismay on the face of the person who'd put up the deposit, he placed fifty cents in change on the desk. I followed suit, and, before the afternoon ended and we retired one final time to the roof of the Park Plaza, so did everyone else.

Much later, I learned from Floyd Chalmers' autobiography that Lefolii's eventual resignation had been neither unexpected by the owners nor unwelcome. I don't know if they thought all of us would go with him, in what *Time*, on one of its Canadian pages, called a demonstration of "college paper loyalty".

To us, though, there didn't seem to be any choice. Though the circumstances are much different, I imagine Fulford feels the same way now.

4:30 in the afternoon: While I sip an iced tea in the summer sun, and work on the last few clues in this morning's *Globe* cryptic, an iridescent hummingbird hovers at the young honeysuckle vine Gill has planted on the trellis at the edge of the deck. It – she, for there is no ruby throat – pauses at each orange-red cluster, darting the needle of her bill into the sweetness of each individual flower.

A female hummingbird – maybe this one – got trapped in the house this spring, when Jack and the Finnish artisans he had hired were putting the finishing touches on their reconstruction. She must have come in through the still-unscreened verandah. When we tried to steer her out, she fled to the height of the clerestory, a glass-walled cupola that rises over the centre of the main room, sixteen feet above the floor. Gill climbed on the exposed beam, reaching high above her head to wind open a window and remove the screen. For nearly an hour we tried to usher the bird out, fashioning a makeshift net out of a bedsheet and two long boards left over from the pine siding.

No luck. Gill kept probing into the dark of the clerestory after I had gone to bed, but the bird huddled on a sill, misunderstanding, presumably, our good intentions. She was still there when we rose in the morning. But when we came back from golf that afternoon, she had found her own way to freedom.

FULFORD, when I talked to him this morning, said that the whole affair of *Saturday Night* was, for all its wrenching emotionalism, exhilarating. I know what he means. At whatever age, there's something exciting about starting on something new.

With Denise Fergusson at the Timmins Little Theatre, 1954. I think this is from "Springtime for Henry", which I also reviewed.

CHAPTER FOUR

*Defending the CBC . . . The librarian's
son . . . Studying draft at the KCR . . .
North to Timmins . . . The worst ad
salesman in the history of Thomson
newspapers . . . Award-winning photo
exposed . . . Confessions of a music
critic . . . Growing up British, learning
American . . . The indelible lessons of*
Stage 54

Thursday, July 9, the cottage: I've been coasting for a while. The page proofs of *The New Morningside Papers* are under control. The incomparable Lynda–Lynda Hanrahan, my assistant, who's been holding the fort for me while I'm away–has sent out permission letters to the contributors, and I can do nothing until I hear back from them over the next couple of weeks. The Ridley book is proceeding apace, and there's nothing on my calendar until the Winnipeg Folk Festival next week. Some mornings, I even sleep in (if seven o'clock is sleeping in), and no one–not even me–has dinged a window on the cottage yet. I was just puttering this morning, in fact, trying to thread some vagrant strands of honeysuckle through the trellis Jack has installed, when Donna Logan called with an extraordinary request.

CBC radio will appear this fall before the Canadian Radio-television and Telecommunications Commission–the CRTC–to apply to have its licence renewed. Donna's idea is that we take *Morningside* to Ottawa that day and broadcast some of our own appearance. By doing that, she says, we can show the commission what we do and, at the same time, make our listeners aware of some of the points we want to make. She is not yet sure precisely how it should work, but she has had a brief huddle with Gloria – Gloria is in Montreal, in a heart-rending death-watch at her mother's bedside – and if it's okay with me, they have agreed, we can start making plans.

I am intrigued. In ordinary times, I forswear as many of these bureaucratic rituals as I can, and, though I don't know the details, hearings at which a fifty-year-old institution applies hat in hand for permission to keep going seem to me patently silly. But these are not ordinary times. The CBC is being squeezed. Now is the time, surely, for all good men to come to its aid.

I am pleased, moreover, that Logan is willing to entrust me with the task, for she realizes that while I'll be carrying the CBC's colours in public, I'll speak for myself, too. I can't promise, as I have told her, to hide my dissatisfactions with the way things are now.

This is a dilemma I face all the time. I hold the idea of public broadcasting to be essential to this country's existence, and am proud to be a part of its tradition. But I am sometimes less than enthusiastic about the practices of the people who now manage it. In the current climate, I am reluctant to air my views. I don't want my complaints about *how* the CBC is run added to the ammunition of people who don't think it should be run at all.

My most ardent criticisms, to be sure, are directed at television. It seems to me simply wrong, for instance, that the CBC continues to carry *any* American programs. When the corporation first went into television, in the early 1950s, it had to deliver *Ed Sullivan* to Moose Jaw; no one else could. But in the 1980s, *everyone* carries *Ed Sullivan* – or its descendants, say *Three's Company* – to Moose Jaw and everywhere else. The CBC exists, or ought to exist, as the alternative. There are a lot of reasons, of course (nearly all involving money), why there are still some imports on the public air, and every year the TV executives promise fewer of them. But I'd say the hell with it: it's time for a hundred per cent.

I'm not alone in these sentiments. In Ottawa a couple of years ago, on one of the rare occasions I did win an ACTRA award, I followed Pierre Juneau to the podium. In his remarks, the president had proudly announced that there'd be one week that fall in which all of the prime-time programs on CBC TV would be Canadian. He was given a warm reception. I was given a warmer one when I cheekily congratulated the network for doing in one week's evenings what CBC radio does all day every day of the year. It was an easy shot, I know, but I often think the bureaucrats get so bogged down in house-keeping practicalities–bean-counting–that they lose sight of the vision.

I am also not always in total agreement with the way radio is run, which Donna knows even better. Last June, she invited me to make a luncheon speech to the Radio Group, several dozen CBC managers from all over the country who gathered in Toronto. I spoke frankly. I made the usual obeisance–and meant it–to the long and worthy tradition we all served. I said–and meant it–how grateful I was to be able to do *Morningside*. But then I slapped the managers' wrists for the fact that not a single one of them had ever come down to peek at the volumes of mail that *Morningside* gets; I suggested they were wacky to spend hundreds of thousands of dollars on surveys trying to figure out why we can't reach a younger audience when the network crawls with young producers who feel shut out from programming decisions; and I lambasted them for trying to lure those younger listeners from commercial radio by offering them more of the music that's already all over the dial. "If they want UB-40," I said, "they know where to find it."

To wrap things up on what I thought was a positive note, I said that CBC radio should get out of sports altogether, that we should make radical changes in our drama ("which a friend of mine has described as theatre for people who don't want to go out, rather than a true use of radio"), and that we should, in these impoverished times, re-evaluate the money that subsidizes musical institutions across the country but doesn't provide much radio. I drew some applause. But I have, shall we say, been more enthusiastically received.

Margaret Lyons, then the vice-president in charge of radio (she's in England now, keeping the CBC's presence alive), was scheduled to thank me. She chose instead to respond to some of my criticisms and, if time had not been so short–I had gone on for nearly an hour–I think she would cheerfully have driven a dessert fork through my larynx. On the way out, I shared an elevator with the head of radio sports, who smiled coolly all the way to the ground.

What Donna obviously understands, though–and I am grateful to her – is that it is possible to voice these objections and still believe with all one's heart that CBC radio is a great institution, nearly always greatly served. I love it, I sometimes think, not in spite of its flaws but because of them, for they are flaws not of villainy but of misdirected zeal. So, if the brass think it's appropriate, I will be honoured to argue its case before the CRTC.

MY FEELINGS ABOUT THE CBC –about radio, at least, which I take to be a different case from television – are inseparable not only from what I do for a living, but from where and when I'm from, and how I came to this career. This summer afternoon, with the breeze feathering the cedars on the golf course, and my fifty-third birthday approaching, my mind goes back.

I was born in 1934, in Toronto, where both sides of my family had roots. My parents were divorced soon after I arrived. My father, the Colonel's first child and only son, went wandering until war broke out, and my mother, the daughter of a successful and well-connected lawyer, remarried. Her new husband was Reginald W. Brown, sales manager of the Narrow Fabrics Weaving and Dyeing Company of Galt, Ontario, and for the years I lived in Galt I was Peter Brown – or, as my grandmother would address her letters to me, Peter John Gzowski Brown.

My mother was a stylish woman, educated at Toronto private schools and in Switzerland and with an MA from St. Andrew's University in Scotland, which she acquired when she was nineteen. She was quite beautiful, too, or so I remember, tall and tranquil, given to the big, floppy hats of the time, with a taste for the verse of Dorothy Parker and the music of her jazz-age youth. In Galt, she became the children's librarian, and a minor star of the Little Theatre, but her life was not happy. She chafed and strained in her confining marriage. The tension affected me as well. My school marks, which had been respectable in the early grades–I could read before I went to kindergarten, thanks to her–plummeted in my teens. I developed terminal acne.

On the day after Christmas, 1949, when I was fifteen, I left

Galt to visit my Gzowski family, who had continued to play a central part in my life. I never went back. The Colonel and my father, who had settled in Toronto for a while after the war, arranged for me to go to Ridley. I took back my patronym, and, under the discipline of a private school, my marks picked up enough for me to win a couple of scholarships to university, where I proceeded in the fall of 1952. In the meantime, my mother died, aged thirty-nine.

I don't mean to be terse about this. Tension in the home or not, I had a good, solid, small-town Canadian childhood, thanks to my mother's decision to marry Reg and take me with her. But her death, and the years of loneliness and unfulfilment that led up to it, scarred my soul more than the acne marked my skin. I miss her still. As a perceptive piece about me in *Saturday Night* last season pointed out, it remains a sorrow of my life that I have not been able to talk with her about what has happened to me since—she would have made a lovely luncheon date. I condense her story here, and gloss over my father's entirely, only because they deserve more than I can give them in these pages. Some day they will have a book of their own, I have vowed, and I feel better equipped to write it with every year that passes in my life, as I gain more understanding of what went wrong with each of theirs.

The university scholarships didn't work out. I couldn't decide what I wanted to study. I enrolled in arts but, free from the obligatory routines of Ridley I studied fraternities at Zeta Psi, and draft beer at "the KCR"—the King Cole Room of the Park Plaza. A couple of months into my second year, I realized I was going nowhere and dropped out. With some summer experience in heavy construction in Labrador and B.C. under my belt, I tried some surveying with half a mind to return to study the family profession of engineering—one of my scholarships had been in maths and physics—and then took off for Timmins.

That was the autumn of 1954. I can mark it by the descent of Hurricane Hazel on Toronto. I can still remember huddling in my grandparents' attic apartment on the night before I left, listening to the emergency on the radio and wondering what it would be like to be out there with a notebook, asking questions, jotting down history as it occurred, maybe even helping to rescue survivors – "Young Reporter's Courage Saves Child's Life". I remember, too, the devastation of the countryside outside the train windows the next morning.

In Timmins, I was a long way from writing for the front page.

I'm still not sure what pulled me into the career I chose, even though, now, I can't imagine having done anything else. Mostly, I think I wanted to be a writer, or at least to try it for a while. In spite of Douglas Grant's assessment of my academic inclinations, I'd written a bit as a student, mostly bad poems and clumsy short stories. I read voraciously, if not well, and many of the people whose work I enjoyed – Hemingway , Lardner, Runyon – had come from newspaper backgrounds. In Toronto, I had looked up Ed Mannion, an ad salesman who played badminton with my mother in Galt and who had been promoted to the national office of the Thomson chain. There was an opening in Timmins, he said, where Roy Thomson had started. It wasn't a reporter's job, but if I was prepared to sell ads for a few months–and who knows whether that might lead to something?–maybe I could move to the newsroom later on.

I was, I think, the worst salesman in Thomson history – an ambitious claim, I realize, in a chain where the news was often regarded as grey material to separate the ads, but one I'm prepared to justify. I couldn't sell anything. As the new boy on the block, I was given as my list of prospects everyone else's leavings, the deadbeats and the grouches, the merchants whose sisters-in-law's picture had been out of focus on last week's women's page. On top of that, I didn't believe in what I was selling. I was sure I'd never bought anything from an advertisement in my life, and I couldn't see how anyone else could have, either. Though I worked diligently with the Thomson training manuals and with books on salesmanship – "don't sell the steak sell the sizzle" – I couldn't subdue my doubts. Instead of applying the tricks, I used to *believe* the excuses my prospective clients offered. One haberdasher on Pine Street so overwhelmed me with his tales of woe that, instead of convincing him, as the manuals suggested, that the worse his business was going the more he ought to advertise, I bought a hat from him, a black homburg that set me back about a week's salary (forty dollars). I wonder now what a picture I must have presented in the weeks that followed, a weed of twenty, still not over the ravages of acne, pounding the pavements of the Porcupine in headgear that would have looked too pompous on Louis St. Laurent.

At nights and on weekends, and over drafts in the Double L –the Lady Laurier hotel, across the street from the *Daily Press*– I pestered the reporters and editors from the newsroom for a chance to show my stuff.

Some stuff. The first published piece in the oeuvre of Peter Gzowski, OC, DLitt, LLD (Hon. Caus.), is a five-paragraph account of a speech given to the Beaver Club of Timmins, Ontario, by someone whose name has mercifully been lost to history. In spite of the fact, however, that the putative author slaved for several hours over those paragraphs, pecking laboriously with the beginnings of the four-finger system that serves him still, the truth is that nearly every word in them was dictated –or typed impatiently while I looked on–by Robert Reguly, a rough-hewn ex-smoke-eater from Saskatchewan, who had worked on the *Winnipeg Free Press* before drifting in to Timmins, and who went on from there to win fame and national awards at the *Toronto Star* by tracking down Gerda Munsinger in Munich and Hal Banks on the docks of the eastern seaboard. I thought of that last spring, in fact, when I found myself presenting a writing award in Calgary to Bob's son, Eric, a rising star of the press.

Timmins. Thomson. The days of setting out.

In certain circles, it is fashionable to decry the papers of the Thomson chain as, on the one hand, exploiters of young talent and, on the other, graveyards for the old. To a large extent, they are, or have been, both those things. In my own days in Timmins –and, later, in Moose Jaw and Chatham–I worked in newsrooms made up of odd mixtures of the unprepared young and the washed-up old, many of the latter the dry drunks Sandy Ross described in the report he wrote for Keith Davey's royal commission into newspapers, men with broken dreams, working their weary way around the country, from city room to city room. In between, on every paper where I worked, was a smattering of home-grown journeymen (the women were pretty well confined to the church socials and wedding announcements), capable enough, but uninspired and uninspiring.

But there was another pool on every paper as well: aspiring Ring Lardners like myself, starry-eyed and awkward at the typewriter, or immigrants from the British Isles or Australia or New Zealand, many of them graduates of the strict apprentice programs of their homelands, or good young pros like Reguly, putting the finishing touches on their own experience.

We were, all of us, studying a craft. From the veterans and the vagabonds, we picked up what we could in anecdote and experience. We read everything about newspapers we could put our hands on. We devoured magazines, and, in our spare moments, sent them overreaching queries, double-spaced and with self-addressed, stamped return envelopes, as we were told to do by *Writer's Digest*. We conducted post-mortems on each other's copy. We memorized the Canadian Press Style Book (you can spot us still, by our ability to spell accommodate or to differentiate between imply and infer). We worked long hours and talked longer ones. And, when we were ready, we moved on.

Sure, the Thomson stories were true, or most of them: of pencil stubs that had to be turned in to justify a new issue, of bus tickets handed out grudgingly to dispatch reporters to fast-breaking news (I actually know a man that happened to, on the Quebec *Chronicle Telegraph*, when a ship was burning off the ramparts), and of coolies' wages and butlers' hours. But on daily newspapers that might not have stayed alive in a couple of dozen small Canadian cities without the Thompson parsimony, and in the days before journalism schools, hundreds and hundreds of us got a chance to try our hands. Under-trained, under-rewarded, and far, far under-qualified for what we were doing, we were, nevertheless *reporters*. We sat in at the places where the news was made. We knew the heady thrill of spilling the inside stuff. And the intoxication of that feeling is with many of us still. It lingers every day for me as I make my way to *Morningside*, and numbers high among the reasons that, tired or not, I like to come to work.

I remember my first by-line, some weeks after my Beaver Club report. To the relief of the advertising department, I'm sure, I had finally badgered my way onto the reportorial staff, and I occupied a desk in the city room, right next to Austin Jelbert, who knew every cop in the Porcupine by his first name. I wrote obituaries and service-club announcements, accident round-ups, and, when Jelbert was too busy, courtoom briefs. Tie loosened, a cigarette turning to ash against the gunmetal grey of the desk top, I rattled the keys of my Underwood with increasing speed, and learned how to take a story on the typewriter with the phone cradled against my neck. And then, one day, I saw the city editor pencil my name in capitals across the first take of my copy:

By PETER GZOWSKI
Daily Press staff

The paper closed at eleven in the morning in those days–only the laity would have said "went to bed"–and it was our ritual to retire to a coffee shop on the main street after we'd wrapped it up. On the day I awaited seeing my name in print, we sat at a round table, and the waitress–whom our news editor later ran away with to San Francisco–came to take our orders.

"Coffee and french fries," said Reguly.

"Just coffee," said Jelbert.

"Chocolate milkshake," said Chris Salzen, now a news executive on the prairies.

And so it went until she came to me.

"Yes?" she said expectantly.

"Peter Gzowski," I said, then changed it to a coffee and two doughnuts before I could add, "of the *Daily Press* staff."

Timmins.

I joined the Little Theatre, played the male lead in *Springtime for Henry*, opposite Denise Fergusson, who lives and works at Stratford now, and, when no one else was available, wrote the *Daily Press* review myself, finding myself adequate, but Denise (thank heaven, as I read the clipping now) much better. With growing confidence in my critical faculties, and, of course, a year and two months of higher education, I took over much of the cultural beat for the *Press*. This made me responsible for covering the occasional concert given by touring classical ensembles. The secret of my ability to carry off this chore was a pretty piano teacher, whose name I remember as clearly as a Northern Ontario sky, but which I will keep to myself now for the sake of her dignity and her four children. She would accompany me to whatever concert I was required to cover, and, afterward, usually in the Ladies and Escorts lounge of the Empire Hotel, we would go over the program, piece by piece, while she dictated scholarly adjectives to my waiting ear.

One night, however, we decided to meet at the Empire first, and together enjoyed its congenial atmosphere until well past curtain time for the evening's performance by a group from Jeu-

67

nesses Musicales. Never mind, I said, we have the program, and we settled in to another couple of O'Keefe's. Later, when I walked her home through the clear and searing cold, she gave me some appropriately scholarly words–none too critical, mind you–and, after returning to the office, I pounded out my review of the concert.

Next morning, a couple of hours before the paper went to press, I answered a call at my desk.

"Can you tell me," said a plaintive voice, "why the Jeunesses Musicales were cancelled last night?"

"Not right now," I snapped, and, practically before my phone was back in its cradle, I scurried to the front of the office. There, pretending other business, I managed to find my fraudulent manuscript in the city editor's still-unread in-basket, and withdraw it from publication.

Maybe I shouldn't tell these stories. But their memory has helped when I've been beaten up by critics. Maybe, I tell myself, they were at the Empire Hotel, too.

While I'm on the subject, here's another self-exposé: the confessions of an award-winning spot-news photographer, a scandal of journalism never before revealed.

I won my photography award one weekend, when more senior reporters had better things to do. It was the spring of 1955. Forest fires were scorching Northern Ontario, and I was in charge not only of covering for emergencies, but of running around in the *Daily Press*'s fire-engine-red panel truck and taking pictures with the office Speed Graphic, which all of us had to master. I drove to the edge of a terrifying blaze. At its perimeter, I found a tree bearing a sign warning of the dangers of forest fire. On a second tree, not far away, was a second sign, this one on the dangers of smoking.

Aha! There was no one around, and, though the fire was licking steadily closer, I had time to remove the sign about cigarettes and tack it carefully just below the general warning: a matched pair framed on the trunk of a symmetrical spruce. I put a fresh four-by-five slide into the Speed Graphic and stood back.

Nothing.

The spruce stood unscathed.

I ran to the truck, and moved it away from the encroaching

wall of flame. I could see brown scorch marks on the red paint. I parked the truck in what appeared to be a safe spot, and returned to my vigil.

Setting myself in position, I raised the Speed Graphic again, and squinted into the view-finder.

Nothing again. My spruce stood in unspoiled symmetry, a cool green sentinel amid the onrushing inferno.

"Catch *fire!*" I screamed at it against the roar of the wind.

It stood.

The world grew hotter. The roar grew louder.

Every tree in creation seemed to be aflame. Except mine. I put the Speed Graphic on the ground, ran desperately to the very edge of the surrounding fire, ripped a small branch from a jack-pine, and plunged it into the flaming underbrush till it caught. Then I sprinted with my torch back to the tree I had prepared for fame and – how good it feels to tell the truth at last! – I set the perfect spruce alight myself.

The picture, with flames framing the warning signs in terrible irony, won the Canadian Press Photo of the Month Award for May 1955, and made, as I recall it, five columns that Monday on the front page of the *Telegram* in Toronto, the big time.

BUT THERE WAS MORE THAN THAT to be learned in Timmins, and, as my mind turns over Donna Logan's call and what I would like to say to the pooh-bahs of broadcasting this autumn, it goes even further back.

Like everyone else who was born in English Canada when I was, or who came here as a child, I was schooled to be British. I sang for God to save the King in the morning and studied his ancestry in the afternoon. Galt was Scottish, as it happened, home of the Highland Light Infantry, but there were touches of England everywhere too: Manchester School, Victoria Park, the fish and chips store near the corner of Main and Water streets –the corner itself marked by four staid banks–or the overcooked mutton that even my mother prepared at home. I went to Cubs in the basement of the Church of England, and studied the gospel of Baden-Powell. At Christmas, if I was lucky, I got *Chums* or *The Boy's Own Annual*. My first war hero was Dave Dawson of the RAF, fighting for king and country with his side-kick Freddy

Farmer. I went from the *Just So Stories* of Kipling to the novels of Dickens and Scott, from the verse of A. A. Milne to the poems of Wordsworth, both of which I can–and do–still quote. There were exceptions, of course–"Along the line of smoky hills"–but they were oddities; the only Canadian writer I saw in the flesh was William Drummond, who came one afternoon to Galt Collegiate when I was in grade nine, to spout his racist doggerel to our assembly.

But if I was being schooled to be a young Englishman, I was being acculturized to be an American: Abbott and Costello at the Grand, the *Saturday Evening Post* in our mailbox, Glenn Miller, when I was at last allowed to go, at Teen Canteen. Gradually, as I grew older, the extra-curricular influences grew stronger; the residue of my academic brainwashing and childhood reading weaker. The red of Empire receded in the landscape of my mind, and the Stars and Stripes marched in. Their principal route was the radio. The movies were Saturday afternoons, the big bands were Friday evenings, and the magazines were for grown-ups. But the radio was everywhere, all the time. American radio. On Mondays, while she ironed, my mother listened to *Lux Radio Theatre* (or *Theater*, as I'm sure they spelled it) with Cecil B. DeMille. On Sunday evenings, prime time, we gathered around the pulsing green eye of our living-room console to listen to Jack Benny, Fred Allen, and Charlie McCarthy, from Lucky Strike to Maxwell House, LSMFT to Good to the Last Drop. I heard Bob Hope and *Fibber McGee & Molly*, *Amos 'n' Andy*, *The Thin Man*, *The Whistler* (I can still whistle the theme), *The Lone Ranger*, *The Shadow*, *Dragnet*, *The Green Hornet*, and *Mr. Keene, Tracer of Lost Persons*. On Saturday mornings, where I lived, it was *Uncle Ben's Club*, from WBEN in Buffalo; I joined. When I was sick, and allowed to take the kitchen radio to bed, I could catch up on *Ma Perkins* and *Pepper Young's Family*, *Big Sister* and –a touch of England here, to make me feel at home–*Our Gal Sunday*. Eighty per cent of the programs that were broadcast in Canada when I was a kid were American, I read somewhere not long ago, but at the time I would have told you all of them were, except of course for *Hockey Night in Canada*, with Foster Hewitt from the gondola, broadcasting to hockey fans in Canada, the United States, and Newfoundland, but most of all to me.

Hockey aside (which I have written about elsewhere), I was

70

American too – an American kid who knew some British history and said "out of the house" differently from Uncle Ben, who did Hirohito imitations and scribbled Kilroy Was Here in his notebooks (while the father he scarcely remembered slogged through the mud of Italy, saving, as I believed, the Empire), who thought Bing Crosby was the greatest singer in the world, had a crush on Jeanne Crain, and wanted to grow up to be Tyrone Power. I knew the words to "The Maple Leaf Forever", but sang "The Marine Hymn" to myself. The HLI was in Europe, distinguishing itself in battle, a regiment of neighbours, but, as I pictured them in my mind, I saw the kid from Brooklyn who would die in the second reel, and the white southerner who would at last make friends with, as I learned to call him, the Negro. In Galt, Ontario, I read the same comics, sang the same songs, laughed at the same jokes, and worshipped the same heroes as any kid in Akron, Ohio, or Corpus Christi, Texas.

Then, slowly, slowly, something else began to creep in to the culture that enveloped me. Right between Benny and Allen ("You were expecting maybe Tallulah Bankhead?") on Sunday evenings came L for Lanky , which turned out to be, if you listened closely, about the RCAF. At noon, if my mother had the day off from the library, there would be on the kitchen radio – "Knock, knock." "Who's there?" – The Happy Gang, which came from, of all places, Toronto, where my grandparents lived. If I lingered, I could hear the homey conversations of a farm family called the Craigs, whose adventures lacked the high drama of Our Gal Sunday – "Can a girl from Wyoming find happiness in the stately homes of England?" – but who sounded curiously like the people we bought tomatoes from, over on the Blair Road. Sometimes, at night, my mother would swirl to the strains of Mart Kenney and his Western Gentlemen, from Vancouver. And for news, as the war wore on, she seemed to turn more and more to the sepulchral tones of Lorne Greene and the vivid front-line reports of Matthew Halton, coming to us from CBL Toronto, on the Dominion Network of the Canadian Broadcasting Corporation.

Preoccupied with growing up, I scarcely noticed.

I went away to Ridley, spent summers on construction sites beyond the reach of radio. Television came when I didn't live at home, and flickered on the edge of my life: *Ed Sullivan*, *Your*

Show of Shows, Life With Elizabeth, I Led Three Lives. I didn't pay much attention. Radio faded too, the Hit Parade in the background. I can't even tell you what stations I listened to.

And then, in Timmins, I found *Stage 54*, bearing, as the series did, the number of its year.

1954.

Sitting here now, with a landslide of galley proofs already piling up at *Morningside* for the launch of their authors' fall tours, with this year's Berton nearly in the stores, this year's Mowat on its way, with last year's Davies and last year's Atwood still perking from their solid run at the Booker prize, with Gallant and Newman and Richler and Hood all nearing completion of new projects, with Laurence and Engel (Marian) sadly gone, but Munro still here and in her prime, and with Sandra Birdsell and Sharon Bhutala and Heather Robertson and Isabel Huggan and Susan Kerslake and Audrey Thomas and Joy Kogawa and Katherine Govier and Bharati Mukherjee and Jane Rule and a host of others all following in their footsteps, and with Findley travelling, Rooke spieling, Hodgins residing, Mitchell teaching, Kinsella talking baseball on the radio, but all busily writing too, with MacLennan resting on his laurels for a while, but Callaghan still churning it out, and Matt Cohen and David Adams Richards and Austin Clarke and John Metcalf and Scott Symons and W. D. Valgardson and Andreas Schroeder and Edward Phillips and Michael Ondaatje and Lesley Choyce and Graeme Gibson and David Lewis Stein and Ray Smith and Robert Kroetsch and Clark Blaise and another host of others all hot on their heels. . . .

Sitting here now, in 1987 – and I have just run that list from my memory of writers who've been on *Morningside* in the last few years – it's hard to remember how rare a creature the Canadian writer was then. MacLennan had published *Barometer Rising* in 1941, and, seven years after that, Mitchell had brought out *Who Has Seen the Wind*. I'd heard about them in 1954, but mostly as curiosities. I couldn't believe they were any good. They were, for heaven's sake, Canadian. I'd relished Leacock, knew Frederick Philip Grove's name, and, as a kid, had browsed through the Glengarry novels of Ralph Connor and gobbled up the lore of Ernest Thompson Seton – had played, in fact, *Two Little Savages* in our duplex apartment's living-room. Other than that, and if you didn't count Robert Service, the words "Canadian" and "writer" didn't seem to belong in the same sentence.

Yet there, on the radio, *Stage 54* was putting on plays, some of them classics (and wonderful productions they were), but a great many of them written by Canadian writers–*Canadian writers!*–performed by Canadian actors, and telling Canadian stories.

By 1954, the *Stage* series was ten years old. It had started in 1944, under the direction of Andrew Allan, and was to run, virtually every week, for another seven years after I left Timmins, until 1961. In that time, Allan, and the equally important Esse W. Ljungh–it was nearly twenty years before I learned his name was not Young–put on six thousand radio plays, almost exactly half of them Canadian originals. The writers whose works were produced included Lister Sinclair, Joseph Schull, Mavor Moore, Fletcher Markle, Tommy Tweed, and Len Peterson, and the actors who appeared in them included, among many scores of others, Lloyd Bochner, Budd Knapp, Don Harron, Jane Mallett, and the incomparable John Drainie, whose work even now–we played some samples on *Morningside* last season, as part of our tribute to the CBC's first fifty years–can raise the hair on the back of my neck. Before I met the cast of the Canadian Players' *Saint Joan*, who played Timmins, I had probably heard all of them on the radio.

The *Stage* series was not the first radio drama in Canada; Rupert Caplan had produced some plays on the old CNR station in Montreal in the early 1930s (Tyrone Guthrie directed a number of them), and there was drama on CKUA in Edmonton. But it was the best, and it was heard everywhere. In Timmins, some of the young reporters with whom I was working used to make a weekly pilgrimage to the listening-room of CKCL, a CBC affiliate in the second storey of the *Daily Press*'s comfortable art deco building. They would light cigarettes and drink coffee out of cardboard cups while they sprawled on stuffed green-leather couches to listen to the magic from Toronto. They initiated me into the ritual. I was entranced.

It is possible to make too much out of this memory, I know, as if it were Keats discovering Chapman's *Homer*. And, to be sure, there was no moment – or I can recall none – at which I leaped from the green leather and snapped my fingers in epiphany. But it was a revelation for me, a signal that people could make drama and literature out of the same experiences that had formed me, that Canadians had something to say that was worth listening to, and I began to wonder if there wasn't something more I could write about than forest fires or service clubs. I wouldn't have said it then, and have some difficulty with its pretentious overtones now–Martin O'Malley would know what I mean–but I was beginning to think of myself as a Canadian. And the instrument through which the discovery arrived was CBC radio.

I'd like to tell the CRTC about that, and to suggest to them that in other ways and other places the same thing might be happening now.

YEARS LATER, after I had succeeded Bruno Gerussi on the air and helped to launch *This Country in the Morning*, I came to know Andrew Allan. His glory days were gone by then. He had not managed to translate his radio skills for television. He had survived a difficult marriage and an affair or two with the bottle. He came into Studio F twice a week to sit across the desk from me and read short, elegant essays, which he would type out impeccably the night before, some of them autobiographical, though never about the days of his triumphs, and some just filigreed exercises in urbane wit. In spite of his formal bearing–he wore a suit, a white shirt, and a tie every day–I called him by his first name both on and off the air, as the custom had become, and only afterwards came to wonder if that had irritated him.

He was a formal man. Lorne Greene, reminiscing, once told a story about having come back from Hollywood to appear in a radio play Andrew was directing. From the studio, he said, he had asked several questions about his lines and wondered aloud if he was doing them the way "Andrew" would want them. Over the public-address system from the control room, a voice had suggested that Mr. Greene was doing it exactly as Mr. Allen wished, and if he would get on with it, after they were finished "Andrew will buy Lorne a drink."

For the first several weeks of his appearances on *This Country*, the producers allowed some time after his essays for us to banter about what he'd said, but I had difficulty wrapping him up, and after a while we stopped. I'd just say, "Andrew Allan," or "Thank you," and he'd be gone. One awful morning in the winter of 1973, he did not show up for his scheduled spot. We sent a messenger to his apartment. He had had a stroke. For some

74

time he lay in hospital, immobile and unable to speak. He died that winter. He was sixty-seven. I wish one morning I had told him how much what he had put on the radio had meant to me, as it must have meant to so many thousands of others.

When I went just now to look up his birthdate in the *Canadian Encyclopedia*, I found this quotation in his entry: "Robert Fulford has observed that Allan's CBC Stage 'gave many of us . . . our first hint that there were Canadian writers who had something interesting to say.' "

And I don't think Fulford and I even talked about that on the midnight shift at the cop shop.

Moose Jaw, 1957. Murray Burt, my star reporter-photographer,
was so tired of taking cheque-presentation pictures of
other people that he and I posed for our own.

CHAPTER FIVE

*Notes of an aging folkie . . . A slice of family
life . . . Boy publisher runs aground . . .
Alison in her father's footsteps . . . The
soiled doves of Kapuskasing . . . Golden days
at* The Varsity *. . . Fired from the*
Tely! *. . . Hooked on politics in the land of*
Jake and the Kid

Friday, July 10, the Airport Hotel, Winnipeg, 1:30 a.m.: Another
long, music-drenched evening in the fields of Bird's Hill Park is
over, and I huddle in my room. The concert was rain-drenched
this year, too, as it seems to be so often. If drought ever returns
to the prairies, as someone said tonight, they could take this show
on the road – a rain-dance for the 1980s, with guitars.

I go a long way back at the Winnipeg Folk Festival. In 1974,
when *This Country in the Morning* was coming to an end, Mitch
Podolak, a burly, darkly hirsute former Trotskyite, invited me to
help with the first edition of his idea. I caught the bug, and
returned for a lot of years, introducing the artists from the main
stage, proudly wearing my "performer" badge to the parties
(where else can a guy my age get a sign that certifies *that*?), mercifully refraining from adding my off-key baritone to the midnight
hootenannies.

As I lobby-sat this morning (another phrase I picked up from
hockey players), watching the folkies trek in for their fourteenth
reunion, memories came rushing back: smoky spare-ribs and

backstage rye; trooping through the Bird's Hill woods for a celebratory barbecue where Bruce Cockburn, Ian and Sylvia, Colleen Peterson, Valdy (who's here tonight), and Joni Mitchell, among others, left their instruments under cover from the rain and sang together all the songs the rest of us knew, "Michael, Row the Boat Ashore", and "Cumbaya", and, with their arms intertwined and their bodies swaying, "Will the Circle Be Unbroken?"; Leon Redbone in his rocking chair, recreating Fats Waller songs so well that, as someone else said, you could hear the scratches on the old 78s; Steve Goodman making up songs on the spot; having to tell the crowd that the Mounties had issued a tornado warning and understanding when no one budged from their stake-outs in front of the stage; John Hartford, the crowd in his hand, refusing to get off the stage until I almost wrested the microphone away; Doc Watson demanding cash on the barrelhead from Mitch before he walked on; Duck Donald and Cathy Fink; Utah Phillips; Bryan Brown and his autoharp; Mimi Farina's eyes; Debbie McCaslim singing Robert Service in a Tennessee accent; Sonny Terry and Brownie McGee not speaking to each other but making unforgettable music together; John Hammond Jr., the stammering son of one of the great figures in all popular music, losing his stammer when he picked up his guitar and singing traditional blues so well you could confuse him – as an eminent New York critic once did – with Sonny and Brownie both; Stan Rogers, big, hearty Stan, rolling out endless verses of "Barrett's Privateers" on the bus back to the hotel – "God damn them all," the men from Bard would join in – or standing on the main stage, his pate glistening as the sun broke through a stormy horizon, charmed from the darkness, as it seemed, by the power of his voice; and, perhaps most vividly of all, big, gruff, autocratic Mitch walking right out into the audience while Pete Seeger sang "The Internationale" at the tenth festival, throwing his battered felt hat on the ground and stamping in joy, "Goddamit, *this* is what I started the festival for." Good times.

Even in my bad years – during *90 Minutes Live*, or the long, dreary spell after I left broadcasting–I would pull myself together in July and come to Winnipeg. But I feel out of place now. I brought John and Mickey to the tenth festival and glowed with pleasure when they sat in with Taj Mahal on guitar and drums. But my sons have gone on to music of their own choosing now, and I find myself listening to Bach instead of Baez. I am too old for all-night parties, too settled to fall in love with long-haired gypies, too sedate to hoot. Two weeks ago, Rosalie Goldstein, to whom Mitch has passed the torch, called to ask me to come for the opening ceremonies. She wanted, she said, my imprimatur on the new era, and here I am. But Stan Rogers is dead, leaving only the glory of a voice that still moves me, and Steve Goodman and Duck Donald, and Sonny or Brownie or both. The beautiful young woman with Valdy tonight is his daughter.

At the post-concert party downstairs, everyone was eating deli sandwiches and drinking beer, and, I'm sure, having a happy evening. It's still going on. But the parties used to be the place you went for the impromptu concerts on banjos and guitars and Celtic drums and washtub basses. Tonight, the only music came from a stage where four or five young men–John's and Mickey's ages, actually–pranced about with electric guitars. They were playing rock and roll.

Time to go home, I think.

Sunday, July 12, the Briars, afternoon: As my cousins Jack and Patrick Madden and I waited to tee off for a family golf game this morning, a man asked if he could join us. Knowing the club prefers foursomes on a weekend, I said sure. I was certain I recognized him from my tournament, anyway – Jack Leone, who owns a travel agency, and, in fact, donated the prize that Michael de Pencier won the first year. I introduced him to the Maddens.

In spite of some confusion over two Jacks in our group – "Whose ball is that, Patrick? " "I think it's Jack's"–the round seemed to be going smoothly. But after nine holes, our new friend dropped out. I followed him into the pro shop to buy some more balls (we don't have to ask why). The young woman behind the counter greeted him warmly.

"Hi, Murray," she said.

Captain Memory strikes again.

I ENJOY THESE FAMILY GAMES, though my scores remain astronomical. Jack, the man who rebuilt the cottage for Gill and me

– he seems to have inherited all the Gzowski practical abilities that passed me by – is a schoolteacher by profession. Patrick is a civil servant. They're both amiable, pleasant men, good company on the golf course, and wild enough off the tee to convince us all that slices are genetic. (My son Peter, playing with us on another occasion, hooked one so far to the left that Jack questioned his parentage.)

As usual, and even with a stranger in our midst, we told tales all the way around of the Colonel, our common grandfather (and, like *his* grandfather, an engineer): his knee socks and pressed khaki shorts; the box of wooden matches that fell out of his shirt pocket every time he planted a tee; his refusal to believe that each of us in turn could grow to outdrive him – "Hit the ball, goddamit," he would say as we waited for the foursome ahead to get out of range (until the day I plonked a dentist friend of his on the shoulder) – and, of course, his hole-in-one, scored, when he was in his seventies, on the Briars' 110-yard par three. We used to keep his score-card with the circled single digit tacked to the wall of Betlyn, the cottage he bought here after the war and where I spent so many summers. My own best card, the family record 38 for nine, hung beside it for years. Now it takes me thirty-eight strokes just to reach the fifth tee.

Jack, with his wife Mary, and their beautiful red-haired daughter Stacey, who's testing the waters of a modelling career, own Betlyn now, and Jack, a consummate architectural tinkerer, is gradually changing its interior. But the memories linger for all of us, of dinners of roast lamb and new potatoes with a sauce from the mint in my grandmother's garden, with the family stretched out along the plywood table the Colonel built on the screened verandah, of eight-handed Canasta or rubbers of kitchen bridge (the Colonel had a bidding system he called "Massey-Harris" – three no-trump in response to anything), or of the men, including, on occasion, my own shaky-handed father, teaching us the dart games they'd learned in the pubs of wartime England.

The darts come out now, when Gill and I and whichever of my kids are visiting go to Betlyn, and so do the fading photos and the well-worn stories. I am only beginning to realize, I think, how deeply my roots are planted in this neck of the woods, and how much, in the years I haven't been here, I have missed the sense of family these summer evenings bring.

THE LAST FULL SUMMER I spent at Betlyn was in 1956.

Timmins was long behind me. After less than a year on the *Daily Press*, Thomson had sent me to Kapuskasing, from where I sent copy to the daily paper and edited a weekly supplement. I began filing stories to the Toronto papers, mostly the *Tely*. "Two soiled doves were escorted out of town . . ." I remember one lead going, until Ed Monteith, the Ontario editor, who apparently didn't share my grandmother's catch-phrase for prostitutes, cabled back in confusion. But, flowery language or not, I was edging in.

I was also learning how much I had to learn. When the Canadian Players had brought their *Saint Joan* to Northern Ontario, one of them – it may well have been Bruno Gerussi, whom I was later to succeed on morning radio – asked me what playwrights I was interested in. I answered with a man I called See-an O'Casey. The next fall, Monteith worked out the deal that landed me at police headquarters, and I went back to school.

At the end of the academic year, I was elected editor of *The Varsity*, the student daily. The *Varsity* job, which would begin in the autumn, would give me pocket money, but to raise some cash for tuition fees, I decided to become an entrepreneur. I looked up Clyde Batten, an earlier editor of *The Varsity*, and proposed that we start a weekly paper in the area I knew from my childhood summers. Clyde agreed. Our paper would be a giveaway – a pioneer version of what the modern marketeers call "controlled circulation" – and we would make our living from the ads. *The South Shore Holiday*, we would call it, after the cottage country of Lake Simcoe that stretches from Beaverton to Brown's Landing. When the school year ended, Clyde and his wife and small children moved into a housekeeping cabin at Jackson's Point and I settled in at the family cottage. Clyde and I pooled our capital to make the down payment on a used Hillman Minx, and flung ourselves into business.

It was a busy summer. Through the week, the two of us would run around to pick up whatever news we could find, supplement that by scalping the Toronto papers for anything that had to do with cottages or Lake Simcoe, write the stories, editorials, headlines, and picture captions, design the ads and sell them (Clyde, even without a homburg, was much better at that than I), and try to avoid calls from our creditors. On Thursdays, we would pile our copy into the Hillman, drive down to the North Toronto

Herald on Yonge Street, wait till the printer had turned our material into a sixteen-page tabloid, reload the Hillman, and drive back up to distribute stacks of papers at various country crossroads.

I think I had more fun than Clyde. As the unmarried partner and a veteran of the Timmins cultural scene, I shouldered the responsibility for the summer-theatre beat, reviewing every production at the Red Barn, and making sure the publicity stills of the prettiest actresses made our front page. The rest of the writing, which we shared, was more notable for quantity than quality, and sometimes, I'm afraid, our casual research showed through. We used to slug the stories we lifted from other publications C & S, which sounded, we thought, like an important international agency, but in fact stood for Clip and Set, which is what we did. Once I took a story George Bryant had written for the *Star*, rewriting his lead to disguise my theft and pasting the rest of the clipping onto copy paper. The next day, our exclusive story appeared with George's closing by-line still intact.

If Bryant had wanted to sue, though, there weren't enough profits to attach–or to look after both the Battens and me. Before summer's end, I handed over my share of the *Holiday* to Clyde, and scampered off to the St. Lawrence Seaway to earn the money for my tuition. Until *Toronto Life* and the beginning of Key Publishers, that was the end of my capitalistic career, although Clyde stayed on and parlayed our summer throwaway into a small string of local weekly newspapers, before moving on to the greener pastures of public relations.

Monday, July 13, the cottage: My birthday, and the kids all phone with greetings (it was Jenny's turn to have them for dinner on our mutual anniversary). In her call, Alison has some news. She may, at last, have landed a job at CBC radio, where she'd very much like to work.

She's had a hard time breaking in. Everyone likes her, and agrees she has a future, and, with a degree in English and two years at Ryerson, she's certainly qualified. Last winter, while she finished her broadcast-journalism course, she went into *As It Happens* at dawn to rip the wire copy off the teletype and distribute it on the producers' desks. And this summer she's been working there as a fill-in. But no one will give her that all-important first full-time job. For one thing, she has a habit of being too frank with the interview boards she has to pass before she can join the ranks. She was doing well at one for *Midday*, I've been told, until someone asked her if it wasn't true she liked radio more than television. "Sure," she said. "There's more room to do serious things." Goodbye TV. The real problem, though, is her last name. She's ruled out at *Morningside*, of course, but even at programs I have nothing to do with she has to be much better than the competition so no one can make accusations of favouritism. It's reverse nepotism, and it's been getting her down. Earlier in the summer, she told Gill she's been thinking of changing her name. But she's kept plugging, and this week she's been offered an associate producer's spot on the morning show in St. John's, Newfoundland. I've urged her to take it. It's a long way from Queen Street and the movies she loves, but it's a foot in the door.

THINGS WERE CERTAINLY EASIER in my day.

My time at *The Varsity*, from the fall of 1956 to May of '57, was as happy a sojourn as I've ever spent, a medley of golden autumn, frothy beer, *Caraban* weekends in Montreal, Belafonte songs, happily quarrelsome editorial conferences, self-indulgent crusades, carefree editorials, and, at last, the glorious release of spring. On the university rolls, I was a third-year student in General Arts, headed for a degree, but in practice I went to no classes and wrote no essays. I was the editor of the student paper, and that was my life.

The Varsity of the time, a tabloid which appeared on campus every weekday morning, was the largest student daily, as we used to say, in the British Commonwealth. It had a long and distinguished tradition, having published, over the years, the early writings of Stephen Leacock, C. P. Stacey, Andrew Allan, and Johnny Wayne and Frank Shuster, among others. For all the past glories, though, it's hard to imagine that any editor could have walked into as promising a nest of aspiring journalists as I did. John Gray and Elizabeth Binks were junior reporters when I took over as editor; John is now the national editor of the *Globe and Mail*, and Elizabeth, who married him after graduation, is now the Liz Gray who has regularly beaten me for ACTRA awards at the CBC – even though a couple of years ago, when she and the producer of *As It Happens*, which she had been hosting, came to loggerheads, the brass unwisely dropped her. Cathy Breslin, an American who was studying at St. Michael's College and who wrote a column for us, hit the best-seller ranks a while ago with a novel about, I think, the rape of a nun. John Brooks, who was the sports editor, is now an executive at the *Toronto Star*. Bill Eppridge, who walked into the office one day and offered to take pictures, went on to *Life* magazine and won honours for his work in Viet Nam. And so on. Other people who worked on *The Varsity* when I did excelled later in other fields – most notably, I suppose, Michael Cassidy, the NDP MP from Ottawa – but it is the journalists I remember, and the excitement of trying our wings together.

We were creatures of our time. Not many years after we moved on, the university press turned earnest and political, and on many campuses, including Toronto's, the newspapers were focal points of what came to be called the New Left. But we were there in the fifties, when the world looked bright and secure. With rare exceptions – I remember, for example, a front-page editorial I wrote about the Soviet invasion of Hungary, which I entitled "Our Generation's Spain", and in which I urged my contemporaries to go overseas and fight to defend my freedom – the issues we tackled were mundane or callow. Canadian politics, with Uncle Louis at the helm, seemed dull to us, and, 1956 being an election year in the U.S., we took part in a campaign to run Pogo for president. We opposed student apathy and censorship in the rare-books room and stood foursquare for more parking and lower fees. We ran football stories on the front page and news of our own doings inside; Cathy Breslin, for heaven's sake, wrote one of her most memorable columns about *me*. But we got the paper out every night, even when one of us had to sit in our basement office making a column out of nothing while the rest stalled the printer's courier with the offer of an extra beer. We learned as we went, not only the seductive thrill of having a forum in which to speak our minds, but the effect of what we wrote on the life around us, and many of us, not only from *The Varsity*, have stayed in the business we discovered at school.

The generation that has followed us is far better trained. Alison, for instance, despite her inability to crack the CBC, knows more about the profession we now share than I did when I became managing editor of *Maclean's*. From the perspective of age, I sometimes wonder if I would have done things differently if I'd had more background than I had picked up in Timmins or at the *Tely* or in the basement of *The Varsity* before I assumed my first real command. But even in my most sombre moods, I know I wouldn't trade those heady days for anything. There is much to be said for learning by doing, and having a place to make mistakes on your own.

Besides which, I don't think I've ever had such fun.

TO SUPPLEMENT MY INCOME at *The Varsity* – I was making about $35 a week–I had continued to string for the *Tely*, sending downtown, at a fee per inch of copy used, whatever stories from the campus I thought they would be interested in.

In the spring, there was a terrible rape-murder in a Toronto ravine, just the kind of stuff the *Tely* thrived on in its circulation battles with the *Star*. The *Tely* editors, in fact, went a little berserk in their coverage, and when the police arrested a young newsboy who had been seen going into the ravine on his bicycle on the day of the murder, they ran his picture on the front page, bicycle and all. From my ivory tower – well, basement hideout – I decided to bring them to justice. I borrowed a bicycle, rolled up my pant-legs, and had Bill Eppridge take my picture in the same pose as that of the accused. I ran the result in the campus paper and, in an accompanying editorial, suggested that if the witnesses who would be asked to pick the young man out of a line-up were *Varsity* readers, they could identify me as easily as *Telegram* readers could now identify the newsboy. Art Cole, the *Tely*'s city editor, fired me from my stringer's post the next day.

At almost the same time, *The Varsity* wrapped up its publishing season. With both my jobs coming to an end, and with no hope of passing any exams, I looked around for something to do. Ron Brownridge, the managing editor of Thomson's Moose Jaw *Times-Herald*, was in the east looking for a city editor. He had heard of my squabble with the *Tely*, but was less interested in that than in my previous Thomson experience. That May, aged twenty-two, and after one last beery dinner with my undergraduate colleagues, I took the train out of Union Station, and headed for the prairie.

That decision–the fact, as I say in speeches, that when all the people I had known at university went to London and Paris and Zagreb, I went to Moose Jaw, Saskatchewan–was to be of seminal importance to me, and I cannot think now of what my life would have been like if I hadn't made it. But at the time, I decided to go there because I was broke and out of work.

NOT LONG AFTER I arrived in Moose Jaw, I decided to do something about my baby-faced appearance. Feigning eye-strain–"I just *read* from morning till night, doctor"–I talked my way into a pair of horn-rimmed glasses. My success may have accelerated my real need for spectacles, which I have worn full-time since I was about thirty (I sport bifocals now), but it did little more to add to my maturity than the homburg I'd worn in Timmins a few years earlier. I still looked, I'm sure, like what I was: a twenty-two-year-old greenhorn fresh from college, trying to run the local news department of a daily paper.

Fortunately for my job security, there wasn't anyone around to see through my lack of qualifications. Ron Brownridge, who had hired me – he left newspapering a few years later to do public relations for doctors – was concerned largely that the paper get out on time, and, as in Timmins, the rest of the staff was split about equally between people who knew the community and were quite capable of doing what they'd always been doing and youngsters who lacked even my experience.

The reporter I made the closest friends with, for example, was Murray Burt. In the years since, Murray has done very well in Canadian journalism and is now the managing editor of the *Winnipeg Free Press*. But when I first knew him, in 1957, he was as raw to both print and the prairies as I was. After a brief apprenticeship in the newspaper business in his native New Zealand, he'd been a deck-ape in the Mediterranean, and a charter skipper in the Caribbean. Somewhere in his travels, he'd met a Thomson executive, and when he was dry-docked in North America he had taken advantage of that connection, as I had with my mother's friend from Galt, and been assigned to the first available opening. In the mornings, after he'd finished his writing chores, he would sit at the back of the city room and close his eyes; you could see him swaying on his typist's chair and, if you were close enough, you could have heard the lapping of the ocean waves inside his mind. Compared to Murray, I was an encyclopedia of Canadian prairie lore, and he happily and unquestioningly charged into the assignments I gave him.

By contrast, there was a senior reporter named Harold Davies. Harold had been covering local news in Moose Jaw, I'm sure, since before Murray and I were born. He was an inaccurate two-fingered typist, a creative speller, and a writer of untrammelled prolixity. But he knew the city and its habits as Dickens knew London. By the time I became his boss, his contributions included a bi-weekly report on what he heard over his daily coffee break on Main Street, complete with the names of his friends and acquaintances in bold-face, the news of who'd said what, who was in town and who was leaving, and all the gossip that was fit to print. With the wisdom of my years, I looked on this sort of reportage with condescension, and, gritting my teeth, pushed it as far back in the paper as I could. For some reason, though, I didn't kill it, and Harold's columns stayed at the *Times-Herald* as long as I did.

If I'd had any brains, I realize now, I'd have run them on the front page; for those columns were the real news, much closer to people's lives than the service-club reports and the endless debates at city hall we covered instead. As well, I'd have strip-mined their author's knowledge of the city and its past. Years later, when James Gray included some of Moose Jaw's colourful history in such works as *Booze* or *Red Lights on the Prairie*, I discovered some of what I missed while I was there—a secret tunnel, for instance, where bootleggers used to hide on storied River Street, and a bar that was once the longest in the world. But at the time I was too busy trying to run a paper that might have impressed my friends back in Toronto. If youth but knew, as someone said, or age but could.

I'm not as rueful about all this as I may sound. Having my first professional command so young gave me experience I couldn't have acquired elsewhere, and, heaven knows, the old youngest-city-editor-in-Canada line has adorned my c.v. over the years (as has the fact, as I say, that "in my graduating year I was editor of *The Varsity*," conveniently leaving out the fact that I failed to graduate). But the truth is, when I was running the *Times-Herald*'s city desk, I had neither the skills to impart to young reporters nor the wisdom to learn from old ones. The system that had given me the job so young also made sure that there was no one looking over my shoulder while I did it. I think of that as I contemplate Alison's future in St. John's. For, leaving aside the obvious comments about how badly the readers of the *Times-Herald* were served by my inadequacies, what Moose Jaw gave me professionally was, in the end, an opportunity to implant my bad habits irreversibly, and I am lucky, I think, that I escaped from the Thomson machine before that happened.

I fell, in 1957, upon interesting days. John Diefenbaker, the populist from Prince Albert – PA, as I learned to call it – had taken charge of the Conservative party the year before, and was thundering toward the election that would topple the only party I could ever remember having ruled Canada. Still closer to what was now my home, Ross Thatcher, the Moose Jaw hardware merchant who had sat in the House of Commons for the CCF, had crossed the floor, and was girding up to take on his old seatmate and ex-friend, Hazen Argue, in Argue's riding of Assiniboia. With the self-assurance of youth, I assigned myself the juiciest stories, driving south to watch Thatcher and Argue hurl vitriol at each other (I can still see Ross, as everyone called him, standing at the front of a Legion Hall in Old Wives, a fat cigar jutting from his mouth, growling, "I changed my mind," as he faced down the calls of "turncoat" from his old supporters), and, later, to Mossbank to cover the historic debate on Crown corporations between Tommy Douglas, the premier, and Thatcher, who had suddenly become the spokesman for Liberalism and free enterprise.

Heady times. Clenched fists and smoke-filled midnights, snarled insults and belly-shaking repartee–politics that was close to the people, that *mattered* in their daily lives. And, furthermore, fun–the Thatcher-Douglas debate alone, in which, to everyone's surprise, Ross Thatcher's bulldog mustering of the facts somehow blunted Tommy Douglas's rapier brilliance (and which, some historians now figure, marked the beginning of the end of the CCF's rule in Saskatchewan), was as exciting as any sporting event I had ever seen. As a reporter, I had a ringside seat. What had seemed so irrelevant from the perspective of Toronto became, on the prairie, vibrant and alive, and I was hooked on politics for life.

Moose Jaw was not my first time out of Toronto. Even before

I started newspapering in Timmins, I had seen some country. In the summers, I had earned tuition fees at construction projects in, first, Labrador, where I worked on a survey crew for the Quebec North Shore and Labrador Railway, headed for the iron ore of Knob Lake, and, later, northern B.C., where I helped muck out the foundations for the towers that would carry the power lines between Kemano and Kitimat. In both places, I had been surrounded by majestic landscape, and the landscape had had an impact on me – almost, though not quite, as strong as the impact of the blackflies and no-see-ums. But the rain-washed mountains of the coastal range and the jagged, rusty rocks of the the land God gave to Cain were landscapes without people; until the power or the minerals in their rocks drew the men and machines from the south, even the native populations that ringed their borders had been unable to wrest life from their wilderness.

The prairie, by contrast, was civilized. Yet that civilization seemed inextricably bound to the land it was based on, as Galt or Toronto or Lake Simcoe were not – the people were *of* the land. The men I met, outside the newspaper office, had powerful hands, sun-dark faces with white foreheads, and indelible memories of the dust that had drifted over Moose Jaw less than twenty years before. The women were stoic and strong. Even in the political wrangling, there was a transcendent sense of decency in the way things were done, of people with a common purpose, with common enemies, not only in the uncaring east but in the relentless weather. The institutions the *Times-Herald* covered – the co-ops and the churches, the women's groups and the ethnic fellowships, even the CCF itself, which had grown out of the prairie soil – had been built by people huddling together against the bald, forbidding land. To the kid from Toronto, it was both exotic and revealing. But it was also a part of me, as the worlds my friends from university were discovering overseas could not have been a part of them.

On my way west that spring, I had sat in the dining-car with a British immigrant who stared steadily out the window, chin in hand. Somewhere west of Brandon, I asked him what he thought. "It's the biggest expanse of bugger-all I've ever seen in my life," he said. At first, I had thought so too. But in Moose Jaw, in partnership with Household Finance, I bought a used Austin convertible, green as the spring wheat. Behind its wheel, I drove the slick blacktop to Regina to court Jenny, holding the Austin's wheel steady all the way—except for the single curve near Avon-lea where the Trans-Canada bent to change lanes, as it were, with the CPR. Sometimes with Jenny but more often by myself, I patrolled the dusty sideroads, staring at the land. I learned what coulees were, and sloughs. What had at first seemed one monot-onous colour gradually took on life for me, in shifting shades of gentle greens and browns and mauves and yellows under the end-less blue of the great, high sky. I felt the fearsome power of a prairie thunderstorm, saw meadowlarks and crocuses, and heard the magic singing of the wires.

Especially when I travelled by myself, my guide on these excur-sions, as the echoes in my prose still show, was W. O. Mitchell. I read *Who Has Seen the Wind* in Moose Jaw and, on the radio –CBK, with studios in Regina and transmitter in Watrous, as every prairie gopher knows–I listened to *Jake and the Kid.* The words I read and the sounds I heard reverberated in the land that lay around me. The notion that had begun to dawn on me in Timmins as I listened to the plays of Andrew Allan–that there were stories worth telling and writing and editing that grew out of the Canadian experience–grew deeper all the time.

I WRITE ALL THIS, of course, with hindsight. Thirty years later, on the edge of a golf course where the shadows of the cedars lengthen as I stare into my past, I find strains of cultural enlight-enment that would not have been evident to me then. At the time, I would have told you I was absorbing other things. On Saturdays, when the paper had gone to press, I would walk three blocks to the Horwood Hotel, find the massed tables of com-positors and reporters, and throw my two dollars into the pot that brought a steady flow of beer and tomato juice till closing-time, when we would buy more beer at the off-sale counter and lurch off to find a dance. I watched the Regina Roughriders in a pouring rain, swam at the Natatorium, drank lemon gin in an open field at midnight, trying (unsuccessfully) to tumble the assistant women's editor among the stubble, learned, if not to hunt, then how to pick buckshot from feathers, dabbled in the Little Theatre, read much and widely, courted Jenny, and, from Murray Burt, who had scrounged the local Sea Scouts' clumsy dinghy for experiments on Buffalo Pound Lake, learned to sail.

But it is the land that has stayed with me, the land and its hold on life. In the next decade, when the CCF – the NDP, as it had become – finally fell, *Maclean's* sent me back to Saskatchewan to try to find some patterns. The most Canadian of provinces, I called it then, and, though that phrase may have been too glib, I know now what I meant – a place where people tried to hold together in a harsh climate, and weave a social fabric in answer to their common needs.

I remained in Moose Jaw much less than a calendar year. When winter settled in, I headed back east. Since then, though – and it still happens occasionally – people who have listened to me on the radio have told me they were convinced I came from the prairie. I've never been sure why this should be. Jenny has a lot to do with it, I guess – I may have mentioned my western relatives – and my admiration for Ralph Allen and Bill Mitchell and Paul Hiebert and others of my heroes who came from the country they wrote about. Whatever the reason, the misconception pleases me, as if it proves that I learned something while I was there. For Alison, soon heading off in the other direction to find her own corner of this varied land, I wish the same.

Thursday, July 16, the cottage, 10 a.m.: Gloria calls to say there are rumours that Alex Frame, who has been working in the bureaucracy of television, will be returning to radio this fall as head of current affairs – nominally, her boss. The prospect is a bright one. Until last spring, the department to which we belong has been headed by Andrew Simon, a prototypical manager, who has moved on to other chores. Andrew had his good points. After I lost the last couple of ACTRA awards I was nominated for, he sent me a bottle of champagne and a note that said simply, "Fuck them." But in the inevitable friction between those of us at *Morningside* who were always trying to test the limits of the CBC's resources and the man whose job it was to embody the corporation ("the company", as I'm afraid he called it), there were more thorns than were healthy.

Frame, by contrast, is a broadcaster, as well as a man whose career has been inextricably tied up with mine. He hired me for *This Country in the Morning*, where he was the executive producer, and his genius was behind whatever success I enjoyed there.

Later, he was also the producer of the biggest disaster of my life, the television program *90 Minutes Live*. After I left to lick my wounds, and the CBC's late-night experiment folded, he stayed on in TV. I've lost track of him in the last few years – he is a Baha'i and lives a very different extra-curricular life from mine – but my admiration for his undertanding of radio remains undiminished. *Morningside* has to answer to *somebody*, and I can't think of a better choice. But, so far, his appointment is only a rumour. I'll wait for firmer news. Right now, amid the hummingbirds and the cedar trees, I am content to live a writer's life.

*Ralph Allen at Maclean's, 1960. This photo was one of a series
taken as reference for the portrait we commissioned
when Ralph resigned.*

CHAPTER SIX

All is not a dishwasher detergent . . . Picking
winners at the Plate . . . Chatham, Ontario,
and the "good news" paper . . . "A school of
writing with Ralph Allen as the faculty" . . .
"A nation of dental cripples" and other
memorable titles . . . My career as a song-
writer . . . Death of a mentor

Sunday, July 19, the cottage, 11 a.m.:   Queen's Plate day, and we
have gathered our team of racing partners for our excursion. Peter
(my son) and Heather Black arrived last night, all atingle. Peter
and Heather, engineers who met at Queen's, are *ferocious* racing
fans. They discovered the sport while I was researching my book
about thoroughbreds. Peter has written a computer program to
help his handicapping, but mostly they enjoy the scene and the
people, and today, the 126th running of everyone's favourite race
and spectacle (founded, as we like to remind ourselves, by Sir
Casimir Stanislaus Gzowski) is a highlight of their summer.
Heather has brought a hat to wear to the clubhouse this afternoon, and they have, of course, brought *Racing Forms* for the
whole party. Their excitement is infectious.

Just as pleasantly for me, Lefolii has shown up, my friend now
for nearly thirty years–I must have given him the first cigar when
Peter was born.

11:30:   Everyone's raring to go. Gill, already behatted, leaves in
her car to join her family at their house near Woodbridge.

12 o'clock: Peter and Heather, who have gone out to their car while Ken and I do some last minute cleaning up, return with the annoying news that my BMW, parked in the driveway, sports a flat tire. We send the impatient kids off to the races and tell them not to worry: experience in these matters is more important than energy. Lefolii goes to put on the spare while I throw the last of the breakfast dishes into the dishwasher and add a cup of All.

12:10: All isn't dishwasher detergent. All – Concentrates on Clean! – is for laundry. When you put laundry detergent into a dishwasher, it turns out, you make foam. A lot of foam. Now, while Lefolii, his hands covered in grime, tries to figure out how to stop the BMW's jack from sinking into the gravel driveway outside, I swab the pine floor, trying to keep up with the suds. I'm losing. The machine churns out bubbles the way the magic bowl in the fairy story churned out porridge.

12:12: Lefolii appears at the doorway. He is about to seek my advice on jacking up cars when he sees me playing King Canute at the dishwasher.

"Wow," he says, helpfully.

"All isn't for dishes," I explain.

"Why don't you turn the dishwasher *off?*" he says.

"Why don't you call the bloody *garage?*" I reply.

We dissolve into helpless laughter. Another Gzowski-Lefolii production is under way.

Once, years ago, we bought a boat together, a twenty-seven-foot graceful wooden-hulled yawl called the *Tim-Tam*. Before we handed over our certified cheque, we called Lloyd's of London, asked them who did their survey work in Toronto, called that firm, hired them, had the *Tim-Tam* hauled out of the water, and received a five-page detailed report on such matters as a missing screw in a hinge on the door of the head. Other than that, we assumed, she was sound. Then, when we were sailing our new purchase from the yacht club where we'd bought it across Toronto harbour to a smaller club we wanted to join, it sank.

A lot of years after that, while I was researching my book on the race-track, we bought a horse together, a shining yearling we paid $10,000 for. We called him Johnny Canuck, got Gill's brother Ian to train him, turned down $20,000 from someone who'd seen one of his brilliant workouts before he got to the track and then . . . well, in a way, Johnny Canuck sank, too. You could claim him now at Fort Erie, if you had $2,500 you wanted to invest in a good-looking gelding with no heart.

5 p.m., Woodbine Racetrack, Toronto: Floor dry, tire changed, we have made it, scarcely missing a race on the card. I don't know what number Queen's Plate this is for Lefolii and me. We used to come with our wives in the *Maclean's* days, picnicking in the parking lot before we made our way up to the grandstand. I remember Jenny, pregnant–it must have been with Alison–the year Caledon Beau won. I had thought a horse called Eskimo Flyer would come in first, but since both he and Caledon Beau were owned by Conn Smythe, a bet on one had been a bet on the other. I had cashed a ticket big enough to buy us dinner. Now, as then, we are caught up in the pageantry and the tradition, and we delight as much in the swirling crowd as in our fruitless attempts to out-handicap Nancy Howard. The sun shines, the wine flows, the women in their hats stroll by.

For the Plate, I wisely throw out the favourite, Afleet (no favourite has won the Queen's Plate for ten years), and decide to back a ten-to-one shot called Steady Effort, which I have seen run as a two-year-old. Lefolii takes the Sam-Son entry of four horses for the price of one, and various Howards and the kids make other selections. The race is a thriller, and we are all on our feet in excitement. In the last few strides, a colt called Market Control bounds out of the pack and beats Afleet by a nose. I check my program. Market Control is owned by the same stable as Steady Effort.

Dinner is on me again.

I ask Lefolii if he has noticed that the Sam-Son entry is owned by Ernie Samuel, the man from whom we bought *Tim-Tam* so many years ago.

THE ROUTE THAT LED ME TO *MACLEAN'S* and my friendship with Lefolii (along with so much else) took me first to Chatham, in southwestern Ontario. Not directly. When I left the prairies, I had a vague idea of going into the weekly business with Clyde Batten. I took Jenny with me in the Austin, stopping to meet her family in Manitoba–her father, who didn't believe in leaving home, later sent us five hundred dollars in lieu of coming to our wedding–and then, in Ontario, introducing her to mine. Some time while we were en route, Clyde's plans fell through, and I ended up in Toronto again, unemployed. Ah, well. Good old Thomson needed a city editor at the *Chatham Daily News*, and though they were disappointed by the fickleness I'd shown in the west they gave me another try.

The managing editor of the *Daily News* was Ray Munro, already (I learned later) a legend in the business. He'd been a decorated fighter pilot in the war, and had taken up peacetime newspapering in Vancouver with the same zeal he must have applied to gunning down the Luftwaffe. He had captured a rapist in Stanley Park after persuading a copy-boy to sit, in drag, in the front seat of his car. He had claimed to have been shot at in the *Vancouver Sun*'s plane while he flew over a Japanese ship in the harbour, and produced photos of the bullet holes to prove it. (It dismayed him not at all, apparently, that the bullets seemed to have been fired from inside the cockpit.) Still working on the *Sun*, he had uncovered (genuine) evidence of corruption in the Vancouver police department, and, when the established papers refused to carry his material, he resigned and published it in the tabloid *Flash*.

How he had arrived in the comfortable little city of Chatham, I have no idea. Somewhere between newspaper jobs, he had taken up hypnosis, and, though he had been good at it, he left that line of work after people who had volunteered to come on stage with him began to show strange symptoms after his departure–they sang "O Canada" whenever they saw the jack of diamonds, or something. But there in Chatham he was, with the fire in his eyes still smouldering, delighting in the stories of his past achievements.

The news in Chatham, a bland diet of farm developments, fires, accidents, news from city hall or the Kent County council – and, of course, the inevitable service-club speeches – was too tame for him. In various ways, he had been trying to spruce it up. At one point, he decided that too much of what went into the paper was bad news: deaths, robberies, car crashes. Sooner or later, I think, this observation comes home to everyone in the business – it bothers me now, in a different way, and I struggle with it on *Morningside*—but I have never known anyone to fight against it as boldly as Ray Munro did. For one brief, happy time, the *Chatham Daily News* became the "good news" paper. The switchboard answered the phone that way, and, in the paper itself, all unpleasant developments were banished to the back pages or the waste-basket, while in their place ran birth announcements, graduations, upsurges in the market for sugar beets, or features from nations where there was no war.

Laudable as it was, the experiment did not last long. Its highlight came at its outset. On the day the policy was inaugurated, Ray sent wires to the White House and to 24 Sussex Drive, outlining his plans, and then had reporters track down unsuspecting press officers for a reaction. When, presumably, they had allowed that it sounded fine to them, the paper carried a screaming headline, DIEF, IKE, ENDORSE "GOOD NEWS", along with three-column pictures of each of the two leaders.

When even his own enthusiasm for the good-news paper ebbed, Ray still couldn't settle for the events his reporters turned up on their beats or that came over the wire. He was living in the lovely little village of Blenheim, about ten miles from Chatham, and one morning not long after I had taken over the city desk, he rushed into the newsroom with the report that a farmer out his way had seen a mysterious, glowing circular object land on a field the night before. Fortunately, Ray knew exactly which field, and, at his urging, I dispatched a reporter and a photographer to have a look. Soon they called in to say that, sure enough, they had found a circular burn of the appropriate diameter. Both they and I were skeptical. They agreed to keep poking around. It didn't take long to turn up a witness to the previous night's events. What he had seen, it developed, was not an unidentified flying object settling on earth but a not-quite-identifiable well-dressed man stopping his car to put a blowtorch to some hay.

Was it Ray? I could never prove it. But when the reporter and the photographer returned to the office with news of their exposé, he quickly lost interest in the story.

That reporter, by the way, was John Morgan. Some time after his fruitless pursuit of the UFO, he moved on to other interests. Now he's a member of the Royal Canadian Air Farce, which, I imagine, seems at least as sane to him as his early days in the news game.

THAT SPRING, Ray was elected Kent County's Man of the Year in a contest the *Daily News* sponsored with much flourish, and in which more ballots came from Blenheim than from anywhere else in the county. But, inevitably, he came to a parting of the ways with the local Thomson management, and I succeeded him as managing editor. I was twenty-three, newly married, and an expectant father.

Meanwhile, back in Toronto, *Maclean's* had launched a new department–eight pages of yellow stock wrapped inside the covers, and carrying short, bright, topical material with a more immediate deadline than the major articles. Ralph Allen, whose eye had been caught by my scrap with the *Tely* the previous year, and whom I had been bombarding with story ideas from both the west and Ontario, called to ask if I'd be interested in a reporting job. I leaped at the chance. Though Thomson offered me a hundred and twenty dollars a week to stay on in Chatham, the nation's youngest managing editor quickly became its youngest ex-managing editor. On the day after Labour Day, 1958, I started my real education in journalism, as a bright-eyed, six-thousand-dollar-a-year assistant on Ralph Allen's *Maclean's*.

RALPH WAS FORTY-FIVE when I met him, two years younger than my father, a rumpled, red-haired, freckled, gruff, sardonic, irascible, passionate, shy, erudite, complex, curiously prudish man. He was a demanding editor who somehow convinced you that you could do better work than you had ever done before, and a brilliant writer who was never satisfied with his own work – he would scribble all over his own finished manuscripts and then, when they were set in type, scribble all over the galley proofs, too. He hated sham and pretence, cared passionately about what he did but not a whit for the honours it brought him, was uncomfortable with women, gambled for small stakes as if his life depended on the outcome, drank prodigiously and not always well, read voraciously and seemed to remember every telling phrase (he could quote from everyone from St. Augustine to St. Vincent Millay and appeared to have memorized the works of Shakespeare), overestimated his skills as a fisherman, loved all sports and many of the characters in them but was bored by mediocrity, was subject to black moods and towering rages, but was also, with his stories, his enthusiasms, and his wry observations, the best company anyone who ever knew him ever had. But, as Christina McCall (Newman then) wrote of another list of his qualities she set down in a memoir published after Ralph's death, "all of these things are true, but they do not add up to the ultimate truth about Ralph." Maybe no simple list of characteristics ever could. As Christina's lovely book demonstrated, everyone who knew Ralph or worked for him had a special and private sense of him – a feeling that he belonged to them. Christina wrote (and I can do no better):

> he had the quality of making nearly every man he met think that he alone understood and appreciated the true Ralph, that he was probably the only one who could comprehend what went on under the sometimes puzzling façade Allen presented to the world. Just how this empathy was achieved is hard to analyse since Ralph was never known to have said to anybody: Look, you and I understand each other; or even obliquely, you and I are friends. But if you were fat and shy and tongue-tied, he had a way of letting you know that he sometimes felt fat and shy and tongue-tied too. And if you tried in halting or in flowing sentences to let him know you had stumbled in your unusual sensitivity on some truth about existence, he would indicate that truth had hit him too.

He was born in Winnipeg, but, as the son of a CPR agent, grew up mainly in Oxbow, Saskatchewan. He left home at sixteen to write sports on the *Winnipeg Tribune*. In 1938, when he was twenty-five and already married to the only woman he ever loved, a beautiful former nurse named Birdeen, he was hired away by the *Globe and Mail*. Even his first piece for the *Globe*, an account of the theft of his wallet from the hotel he had checked into, is regarded as a classic of his style. (The thief had *not* stolen Allen's coonskin coat, and Allen wanted to know why not. "That was a mighty fine coat, smart guy," he wrote. ". . . Long nights since I knew I was coming to work for *The Globe and Mail*, I have dreamed of sauntering easily into the press box at Maple Leaf Gardens, parading its prehensile glory while the ushers whispered to distinguished visitors, 'That's that new sports writer at the *Globe*, Allen. Snappy dresser, what? They say he makes two hundred bucks a week.' ")

When war broke out, the snappy dresser signed on as a gunner in the artillery. Overseas, he became a sergeant with Conn Smythe's famous sportsmen's brigade, and, eventually, a war correspondent, renowned among his peers for his yellow corduroy trousers, his dogged bravery under fire, and his honest and perceptive prose. He was awarded an MBE, an honour he always pooh-poohed. ("They gave everyone one of those," he would say, wrongly.) In peacetime, he became a novelist, a sportswriter again, briefly (the trouble with that job, he once told Trent Frayne, was that "you have to go to all those goddam games"), and, under W. Arthur Irwin, an assistant editor at *Maclean's*. In 1950, when Irwin went on to become commissioner of the National Film Board, Ralph took over as editor.

He hired Scott Young and Pierre Berton (actually, he sent Young to Vancouver to hire Berton, and Pierre still delights in telling the story of how, when Scott said, "I've been told to offer you between $4,000 and $4,500," he replied "I'll take the $4,500") and Sid Katz and Lefolii and Christina McCall and Barbara Moon and Peter Newman and McKenzie Porter and, for a while, W. O. Mitchell to oversee the fiction. He continued to publish from Ottawa the impeccable prose of Blair Fraser, and from elsewhere the offerings of Robert Thomas Allen, Fred Bodsworth, Morley Callaghan, June Callwood, Trent Frayne, Bruce Hutchison, Hugh MacLennan, Farley Mowat, his old war-correspondent crony Lionel Shapiro, and a host of other Canadian writers whose works now fill our libraries and illuminate our visions of ourselves. As well, in the crowded sixth-floor editorial offices of the old Maclean-Hunter building at University and Dundas, he built a team of journeymen who formed the backbone of his staff, highly regarded craftsmen who could churn out pieces under their own names or, as they often did, shape the writings of others to meet the standards Allen set: Leslie Hannon, a New Zealander who oversaw the copy desk; Eric Hutton, a gigantic rewrite man who must have filled two airplane seats when he set off on his own assignments, but who could also take home a shapeless manuscript and show up the next morning with neatly tailored prose; and Ian Sclanders, a crusty old CP hand from the Maritimes who could find the proper lead in a hopelessly jumbled article the way Glenn Gould could find middle C.

When they came to *Maclean's*, or sent in their first submissions, none of these men or women knew the first thing about magazines. Most had newspaper backgrounds, although Lefolii, for instance, had worked at an advertising agency (as well as *Liberty*), and Katz, who made his mark at *Maclean's* by taking LSD before anyone else had heard of it and by ferreting out the story that became *The Three Faces of Eve*, had been a social worker. But at University and Dundas, they all—we all—signed on for the course in what Pierre Berton once described as "a school of writing with Ralph Allen as the faculty".

The most important part of that course consisted of sending your work, as the office phrase had it, "up the line". The line was a route-list of initials. For most of the 1950s, when Berton was the managing editor, it had been some version of LFH (Hannon was the copy editor), IS (Sclanders was articles editor), PB, and RA. But when I arrived, which was the week Berton left, it was KL (Lefolii had taken Hannon's job as Hannon became managing editor) IS, LFH, RA. No matter. The system remained. Even before your research began, your outline went up the route list, and then back down to you, with comments and suggestions about who you should see, what dangers you should avoid, and what approach you should take. Early drafts of the pieces themselves went first to Sclanders, who would read them over and then take you to lunch next door at the old Sea-Hi, where, over green tea and egg foo-yung, he would give you the bad news ("There's some good material here, much of it well handled") or the good. It was almost never good. Occasionally the old pros – Bruce Hutchison most of the time, I think, and Blair Fraser almost always–got their first drafts into the editing process without having to do a major rewrite first, and there was a story, which Christina McCall repeats in her memoir of Ralph, that Barbara Moon, the most meticulous of us all, once had a profile of Nathan Cohen published with only one word changed. But for the rest of us, it was fix, fix, fix. No one knew what the record was. Peter Newman, I think, has claimed eight rewrites. But I'm sure others did more. Fred Bodsworth, who went on to fame as the author of *The Last of the Curlews*, among other works, is said to have had seventy outlines rejected before he was given his first go-ahead for a full article.

When Sclanders was satisfied, the manuscript would go up the line to Hannon for some careful prodding ("could use a bit more detail here"), and, finally, to Ralph's eyes. He was not gentle. "Oh, for Christ's sake," I can still remember one of his inky marginal comments chastising me, or, on another occasion, "This is bullshit." But he could encourage you, too. A little "nice touch" in the margin, became, in the light of his immutable standards, more important than the Pulitzer prize.

Somehow, too, he managed to make it clear that his criticism was not of you but of your work; he was not so much angry as disappointed that you, of all people, could hand in such shoddy stuff. The editor, he used to say, is a referee between writer and reader.

Because he wrote so well himself, and cared so much about his own standards, he could make you feel part of a tradition. Once, after I had handed in what I thought was a satisfactory draft of an early piece, I rode the elevator down to Dundas Street after work, shaken and upset over the editorial bruising my master-piece had been given up the line. Ralph, carrying the swollen briefcase he always took home, stepped in after me. "How many marginal notes did you get?" he asked just as we reached the ground.

"About fifty."

"I had eighty-seven on my first piece," he said, and strode off into the winter night.

THERE WAS MUCH, to be sure, wrong with the system Ralph implanted in us. For one thing, it smacked too much of formula. You wrote your lead, anecdotal if possible, and then your sub-lead, designed to convince the reader that the rest of the piece was important ("However absent-minded, this unassuming New Brunswick beekeeper has revolutionized the way the world looks at . . ."). After the sub-lead, you assembled the rest of your mate-rial as if by blue-print: anecdote, exposition, anecdote, exposi-tion. For each transition, you fashioned what we called a "link" – a phrase that cleverly shifted the mood. In biographical sketches, or "profiles" as *The New Yorker* had taught us to call them, you stopped about halfway through, cleared your throat, and began at your subject's nativity, always using his full name ("Robert Marvin Hull was born in the village of St. Anne. . . ."). Finally, you wrapped your conclusions in a succinct and tangy "tail-piece".

For another thing, much of what we wrote suffered from simple-, or perhaps single-, mindedness. If you didn't have a working title, ran one of our beliefs, you didn't have a piece. As a result, once you had found your angle, you tended to select the facts and anecdotes that buttressed it and ignore those that didn't. In our view, the worst sort of writing was what we labelled (the phrase was A.J. Liebling's) "on the one hand this, on the other hand that". This wasn't dishonest; all journalism sooner or later is a process of over-simplification, and there was no greater sin at the *Maclean's* of the 1950s than to make up a quote or to offer a fact the checking department couldn't confirm. But it still made what we wrote somewhat less than the truth, which often *does* consist of "on the one hand this, on the other hand the exact opposite". We were not, as they say, willing to let reality stand in the way of a good story.

Even our titles came dangerously close to self-parody. We favoured alliterative adjectives ("The gay and gutsy world of . . .") and vivid nouns: trials and triumphs, crises and booms – stark and dramatic statements. My own all-time favourite from this school, which I may well have written myself, appeared over an article by Sidney Katz, quite a nice piece of reporting on its own, but labelled, I'm afraid, "Canada's a nation of dental cripples".

But all that, in the end, is surely less important than what Ralph Allen's *Maclean's* meant to its readers and to the people who worked for it. In the days before television, *Maclean's* was the window on Canada. For the generation of writers and editors who learned their craft under Ralph and tried, after his departure, to maintain the standards he had set, it meant at least as much. It taught us how hard it was to write well, but how worth while it was to try. It made what we were doing seem to matter. It was an enriching place to be.

AFTER MY APPRENTICESHIP on the yellow pages, I moved to the copy desk, which Lefolii had vacated. There, I relied on the skills of the two editorial assistants, Shirley Mair and Carol Lindsay, to cover for my greenness. (Carol Lindsay eventually left *Maclean's* to go to library school and is now the chief librarian at the *Toronto Star*; Shirley Mair married a lawyer and left the business altogether. Other women replaced them, and, over the years, broke in other copy editors who made more money than they did.) At the same time, being on the copy desk made me privy to all the fix notes and marginal comments that stayed affixed to every manuscript until it finally came down the line. It was the most intense course available at the Ralph Allen school. I saw the way each individual writer worked within the format. I helped repair the imaginative spelling and carefree typing in which Farley Mowat submitted his vibrant, shining prose, and received a lecture from Barbara Moon after having presumed to change a "which" of hers to "that". I saw how Sid Katz first typed out all his notes, cut them up and pasted them on reams of brown wrapping-paper, then went painstakingly through draft after draft of condensation, how Bruce Hutchison's majestic prose seemed to roll effortlessly from his typewriter onto three-quarter sheets of newsroom copy paper, and how Robert Thomas Allen spent days over his typewriter composing endless run-on sentences that somehow, when he was finished, sang.

After months and months of being convinced I could never learn the trade and that I would have to go back to Thomson again, homburg in hand, I began to write articles myself, at first mining the familiar territory of my family's past ("What it's like to have a famous but forgotten ancestor") or the undergraduate press, and then, gradually and tentatively, venturing into the unknown. I wrote about bridge, hockey, politics, women. With Peter Newman, I prepared a cover package on young Canadians, including a short story by the hitherto unpublished Adrienne Poy (she is Adrienne Clarkson now) and a political panel that starred Brian Mulroney, a promising young Tory from Laval. After the copy desk, I took over the yellow pages, and masterminded, among other triumphs, a special section that welcomed the 1960s and featured drawings of domed cities and one-man helicopters and other developments we haven't quite seen yet.

Mistakes and all, I was, as the hockey players might have said, turning pro.

RALPH LEFT in 1960. For some time he had been struggling with the commercial difficulties of the magazine. In the early years of his editorship, *Maclean's'* circulation had soared–to nearly triple the quarter-million it had been after the war. "The magazine that can't stop growing," the promotion department crowed. The dollars rolled in. Then, quite suddenly, everything turned around. Although circulation didn't fall, it failed to make the increase the ad salesmen had guaranteed. The troubles that were to continue to beset *Maclean's* through Lefolii's years and beyond – television, a changing audience, and, of course, the unfair competition from the south – were taking their toll. Money had to be refunded to advertisers – the kiss of death for "the magazine that . . . etc.". The momentum swung; *Maclean's* was cold.

From time to time in Ralph's last months at *Maclean's*, the strain would show. We used to meet regularly over lunch in a private dining-room at the back of Little Denmark, a licensed – this was crucial then – restaurant on Bay Street. After a gin and tonic or two, we would take our places at the assembled tables, and Ralph, seated, would give a kind of state-of-the-magazine report to the whole staff, on advertising and circulation and other, for him, increasingly depressing news, and then throw the floor open for editorial ideas and discussion. These sessions were important, not only for the story suggestions they engendered, but for the magazine's *esprit de corps*. They made us all feel a part of things, although, as Ralph would remind us when he felt some ideas with which he disagreed had been given adequate airing, "*Maclean's* is not a democracy."

The meeting I remember most clearly never reached the stage of open discussion. Ralph began proceedings with his usual remarks on the business side, and then, without pause, began talking about editorial standards. The more he talked, the angrier he got. "We're getting manuscripts in here," he said, "that would be rejected by the *Brandon Sun*." His face grew redder and redder, and no one dared to speak. When he was finished, he rose, slammed his chair back into place, and strode off belligerently towards the door, still fuming. The exit he had picked, however, had been locked from the other side. Temples throbbing and eyes downcast, he threaded his way back among the tables of the crowded room and, wordlessly, out the door that led to the street.

He felt alone, I think. Although he would cheerfully enter football parlays with such acolytes as Lefolii and me (he lost interest in me after I picked eight straight five-dollar losers on a single Sunday) or sit in with his insatiable gusto on our poker and bridge entertainments, his true friends were the men he had shared the war with. On appropriate occasions, he and Birdeen would entertain the staff in their duplex in Moore Park, and he was a gracious and generous host, even though, when it was time to go to bed, he would clear the house with recorded bagpipe music. But he was becoming a kind of elder statesman, and I don't think he knew how to handle that. Once, when he was on holidays, Lefolii and Hannon bought a manuscript from Mordecai Richler (who had already sold us a piece called "How I became an unknown with my first novel"), and Ralph, with his prairie puritanism, was offended by its references to teenage sexual fantasies. He was angry about it, as if he'd been betrayed.

I came in one Sunday to catch up on some extra work, and he was in his office, his door closed. There were a lot of doors closed for the next few days, and a lot of comings and goings, as the news spread that Ralph had handed in his resignation. For a while, there was a rumour that Hannon, a good pro but no leader of men, would succeed him. The rest of us–certainly the younger ones–would have preferred Lefolii, but since Ken was barely in his thirties, there was little hope. Behind more closed doors, a call was made to India, where Blair Fraser was on assignment. Finally, word came down: Blair, reluctantly, had agreed to leave his beloved Ottawa beat for two years and assume the chair while, we all hoped, Lefolii, who would now become managing editor, picked up the experience that might persuade the owners to give him a chance at the editorship. The staff chipped in to commission a Franklin Arbuckle painting of Ralph in his office, feet on desk, and, with lumps in our throats, we determined to carry on.

I WAS TO WORK FOR RALPH one more time.

After my departure from *Maclean's*, in 1964, I free-lanced for nearly two years. I wrote for *Saturday Night*, where Jack Batten and, later, Harry Bruce worked as editors (Fulford had gone back to the *Star*), for the *Star Weekly*, *Sports Illustrated*, *Weekend*, and almost anyone who would have me. I helped Bill Frayne put together a book on sports for the Canadian Centennial Library (Lefolii was managing editor), and wrote, among other things, a pamphlet for the government on how tax dollars were spent (leaving out, as it happened, how much went for pamphlets on how . . . etc.). I also found myself writing the captions for some exhibits in the Centennial Train, and the lyrics for a song, entitled "Song for Canada", by Ian Tyson.

I was spreading myself, in other words, pretty thin. In the first months after I left *Maclean's*, my by-line had been anathema to management, and Borden Spears, the gentlemanly former newspaperman who stepped into the breach after Lefolii's departure, and who was desperate for reliable writers, had resorted to subterfuge to buy my wares. For some time I was the pseudonymous Strabo (the squinter), who wrote about television for the yellow pages. In time, the ban had been relaxed, but so, I felt, had the standards of the editors, and the work I was selling them, while helping to pay the bills for our growing family – John was born in 1964 and Mickey in '65 – was, shall we say, of the minimum quality I could get away with. I wrote, for example, a profile of Genevieve Bujold, whose picture they wanted for the cover, on the basis of one interview and a stack of old newspaper clippings – as dumb a piece as I've put my name to, but the source of the same six hundred bucks I'd have earned if I'd worked six weeks.

Ralph, meanwhile, another novel and a book of history behind him, had become managing editor of the *Toronto Star*. He asked me to take over the entertainment section. Delighted at the prospect of returning to both a salary and his aegis, I agreed instantly. For most of 1966, under his watchful eye, I handled the copy of Fulford, Nathan Cohen, and William Littler, who, as one of my first acts, I pried away from the *Vancouver Sun*.

That winter, Ralph went into hospital with what turned out to be cancer. On December 2, to everyone's shock, he died. I stayed at the *Star* for a little while after, but quickly realized that, salary or not, I had gone to work not so much for the paper as for the man. I turned to other things.

Twenty-one years later, I cannot write a paragraph or consider how to cover a story without thinking he might be looking over my shoulder, trying to make sure I do it as well as I can.

Dalton Camp (RIGHT), Stephen Lewis, and Eric Kierans on one of the rare occasions they were all in Morningside's Toronto studio. More frequently, Dalton was in Fredericton and Eric in Halifax.

CHAPTER SEVEN

*Friendly invasions . . . A history of our
history . . . Life after Lynda? . . . How to
read an entire book in two hours or less and
remember almost nothing . . . Budgets and
bean-counters . . . Morningside's wise
men . . . Scribe of the Quiet Revolution . . .
Speaking* joual in la ville en bas *. . .
Fulford goes to academe*

Sunday, August 2, the cottage, 11 a.m.: I am sitting at the word processor, wrestling with my memories, when someone – a guest from the Briars, it turns out – taps on the front door and asks if I will autograph the two copies of the first *Morningside Papers* she has under her arm. When Gill, shrugging, invites her in, she brings them to the table where I'm working.

"Gee," she says. "Hope I'm not disturbing you."

Hrumph.

Last week, the Briars' social director, a lady who organizes what she calls "literary walks" for the guests, which I'd always thought were ambles past the graves of Stephen Leacock and Mazo de la Roche, told me proudly how large she has concluded the *Morningside* audience must be. "When I point out where you live," she said, "four out of five people say they listen to you on the radio."

"When you point out where I . . . ?"

I bit my tongue. She meant no harm. Still . . .

OCCASIONAL INTRUSIONS aside, I've had a more productive summer than I might have dared to hope. The *New Papers* are on the press now; the final editing done; the illustrations arranged; and the permissions negotiated (the glee with which the authors agree to my requests to anthologize their works continues to delight me). The Ridley book is still making good progress, thanks, I quickly concede, more to Peter Sibbald-Brown's energies than to my own.

That project arose in a roundabout way. Last year a committee approached me about writing a book to celebrate the school's centennial. I pleaded, truthfully, no time, and said no one reads official histories anyway; they should do a scrapbook instead: old photos, report cards, letters home – all the things people who wouldn't read the history would pore over with nostalgia. Good idea, they said. Would I do it?

Without Peter, I wouldn't have. Ever since I met him–he came round to introduce himself the first summer I came back up here –I've wanted to work with him. Though he's younger than I am, he's an old-fashioned bibliophile, given to cravats and the sipping of sherry. He works away in his studio in the manse of St. George's Church, a couple of miles along the Hedge Road (where Leacock and Ms. de la Roche are buried), designing his elegant books (he's Charles Bukowski's publisher, among other things) and letting the world go by. Now, with Lucinda Vardey, a literary agent we both like, we've set up a little company, the Hedge Road Press, and moved dozens of cartons of Ridley memorabilia into the old manse. Peter, and Marion Kilger, who shares his life, sort, catalogue, and pan for gold, and between sessions on this journal, I scribble. It's pleasant and absorbing work, and sometimes I think I could build my life around it. But we're in August now. The summer is drifting by, and *Morningside* looms.

Thursday, August 6, 2 p.m.: Lynda, my invaluable assistant, calls. She's had to screw up her courage to do it, she says, but didn't want me to learn from someone else. She'll be leaving me this winter. Her husband will be taking an MBA in Australia, and perhaps banking his future on a career in Asia. They'll leave just after Christmas.

I'm happy–or try to be–for her. But her departure is bad news. Lynda has been with me two years now, getting half her pay from me and half from the CBC. She organizes my life, handles my travel, keeps up with the mail, and looks after a hundred other details (including, for example, the administration of *The New Morningside Papers*), all with unflappable good spirits. The office joke that I'd be helpless without her is not far from the truth.

This winter, I guess, I'll find out how close it is.

Damn.

Tuesday, August 11, the cottage, 10 a.m.: A courier from the city (arranged, of course, by Lynda) brings me the first sign of the impending autumn, a batch of galley proofs collected by *Morningside*'s literary producer, Hal Wake, from the season's upcoming books.

It's a helpful gesture. There are more authors lining up for interviews every season, and this year, from late September until well into November, when the pre-Christmas rush is in full flight, there'll be close to an author a day trudging into the studio. Since I like to boast that I've never interviewed a writer whose work I haven't read, I'll have my hands–and my evenings–full. The galleys are a nuisance to read, big, bulky sheets that inevitably spread themselves around the cottage and are especially hard to get through in bed, but having them now, in August, gives me the chance for a head start.

I wish it were that simple–that I could make my leisurely way now through books whose authors I won't meet till October and then, when they appear, astound them with my intimate knowledge of their work. It isn't and I can't. In truth, the way I prepare for author interviews is a technique all to itself, and my braggadocio about reading every book in advance, while not really a lie, is, shall we say, coloured by wishful thinking.

I read like lightning. I can make my way through a thick volume in an hour or two, a thin one in even less, and, when I'm finished, have the gist of it in my head. It's not "speed reading" –not in the sense that I've ever taken a course. But, probably from my years as an editor, I've learned how to skim over a manuscript like a motorboat planing across the open sea.

Ideally, for *Morningside*, a producer will have read the book first, and given me a chart. But even without that, I've learned how to look for the most productive parts. In non-fiction, I read introductions and conclusions, the first sentences of a lot of paragraphs, and, always, the last few pages of all – there are few writers, thank heavens, who can resist telling you what they've told you. I love indices, and photographs with long captions. Fiction is harder. I pay scant attention to plot, which is probably too complicated to convey on radio anyway (and is usually the last thing the author wants to give away free), or, indeed, to character (unless there are overt symptoms of the *roman à clef*), and concentrate instead on, first, getting a sense of style – writers love to talk about how they write – and, then, finding the descriptive passages. I am partial to descriptions of place, or of how things work; there is much reportage in modern fiction, and it lends itself to the same re-creation in an interview as non-fiction. Poetry, unless there are passages of obvious autobiography, is the hardest of all.

In any mode, I slow down at least once or twice and dive in. I pick up one or more anecdotes, images, characters, or sets of facts in detail. I make notes on them (usually, to the distress of future readers, on the end-papers), and, in the interview itself, make sure to show off my specific knowledge early.

I learned long ago how valuable it is to convince the author that you know his work well. Writers – especially those who have been through a mill of interviewers who rely on a quick survey of the dust jacket or a glimpse at the publisher's summary press release – quickly develop a canned pitch about their books, which many of them learn to deliver no matter what questions they are asked. It may sell their work for them, but it makes for dreary radio. An early and detailed demonstration of precise knowledge ("I was wondering why the Ford convertible in chapter eleven was purple . . .") quickly shakes them out of it. A comparable trick, which I also learned long ago, is to say the book's title and, if possible, publisher early in the conversation myself, thereby relieving the author's compulsion, implanted firmly by his publicity department, to mention the commercial data as often and as clearly as he can. This is particularly useful when what you really want to talk to an author about is something quite outside the venue of his most recent work – with some of the Canadian politicians, for example, who have recently made themselves available for interviews so they can hawk their wares. (We beat our heads against the wall trying to get René Lévesque when he was in power, but almost had to fight him off last season after he released his memoirs, and Peter Lougheed, who finally came in to talk when a book about him was published, apparently was angry at me because, on that occasion, I scarely mentioned its title.) If you get the book-flogging out of the way early, you can move quickly to the questions you wanted to ask your subject before he decided to be an author.

For all these reasons, I read to prepare for an interview much differently than I read for pleasure. It serves my purposes, though when I come across a book I'd read even if no one was paying me, I have to force myself to keep skimming. I am the radio equivalent of a university student who, having slept through every lecture in a course, is able to ace an exam by staying up all through the night before.

But a corollary of my ability is that, like the student who memorized the causes of the War of 1812 on No-Doze, I retain nothing over the long term. I could read all the galleys Hal has gathered, in other words, but when their authors come around to be interviewed, I'd have to read their work again.

I'll set them aside.

Saturday, August 15, a park in Old Strathcona, Edmonton, 11:30 a.m.: Proudly bedecked in my number oo Edmonton Oilers sweater–presented by the team after I wrote a book that chronicled their season of 1980-81–I have the honour, along with the mayor and other dignitaries, of opening the sixth season of the Edmonton Fringe Festival.

I have mixed motives for being here. I like this city–aside from the time I spent with the Oilers, I holed up here the summer between my two disastrous seasons of *90 Minutes Live*–and have a number of friends here. As well, and in spite of being able to stay for only a couple of days, I'm looking forward to sampling the theatre this festival offers: more than a hundred and fifty plays, if you can believe it, at fourteen locations, all competing to sell five-dollar tickets in a rough-and-tumble competitive market. Their titles, which range from *My Boyfriend's Back and There's Going To Be Laundry* all the way to *Ilsa, Queen of the Nazi Love Camp*, promise exactly the kind of fare I often wish we had on *Morningside* – cheeky, fresh, experimental. If we can't broadcast it, at least we should know about it.

Mostly, though, I just needed to get back on the road for a bit.

I've had a seductive summer, and some mornings, when I've taken my coffee and the cryptic crossword out behind the honey-suckle, I could practically feel the roots taking hold of the cedar decking. But there'll be enough sitting still when the season begins next month, and to do *Morningside* properly I have to keep prowling—especially outside Toronto. It's one thing, for instance, to read or hear about the dreadful damage the tornado that struck here wreaked (and Linda Goyette, one of our Alberta columnists, did a powerful job of describing it on the air last week), and quite another to see it for yourself. I'll store that up.

12 o'clock: Through some confusion on the printed program, so many people have shown up after we've declared the festival open that Brian Paisley, the long-haired genius who runs the show (it's a long time since I've seen a man who knots his hair behind his head), wants to do the whole ceremony again.

Why not?

A couple of springs ago, I hauled my dinner jacket to Yellowknife to help declare the Arts and Culture Centre open. There, too, though for different reasons – everyone in town wanted to go–they had to do the ceremonies twice. The native chief who'd chanted a moving prayer on the first night, however, was reluctant.

"It's already blessed," he said.

More malleable, the dignitaries and I cut a second ribbon.

Wednesday, August 19, the cottage, 9 a.m.: The season's first meeting begins, Gloria presiding at one end of the butternut table, I at the other, near the open door to the deck to which, when my addiction calls, I can slip for a cigarette. Elsewhere around the room, where they have drawn the furniture into the semblance of a circle, the rest of the *Morningside* unit settles in.

We've held this session, or a similar one, every summer since I returned to radio: gathered away from the office to go over the program inch by inch, assessing the strengths and weaknesses of the season that's gone by and pooling our ideas for the next one. The last couple of times we've met in hotel suites downtown, but this year, not unselfishly, I've invited them all here. Last night, before everyone slipped off to their rooms at the Briars, we gorged ourselves on spare-ribs, corn, and my celebrated gazpacho (which even the redoubtable Talin Vartanian declared palatable), and drank more wine than was good for us. But this morning, though nearly all the participants are in shorts and T-shirts – many of them looking uncustomarily tanned – it's all business.

Despite the changes of last spring, there are a lot of familiar faces around the room. My friendship with the laconic Dave Amer, who picks the records we play among the interviews (and until his recent conversion to good sense could have been counted on to join me on my smoking trips to the deck), dates back to well before even *This Country in the Morning*, where we also worked together, and I have known Patsy Pehlman, our senior producer now, almost as long. She was just breaking into radio in Thunder Bay when we took *This Country* there in the early 1970s. Janet Russell, our quiet and efficient script assistant, has been at *Morningside* longer than I have – she was the script, as they say, in Don Harron's day as well–and Carol Wells, slim and athletic (she's a threat on the base paths in our annual softball games), joined about the same time. (Carol's title is production assistant, but in fact she runs much of the office paperwork.) Talin, too – her name is pronounced Tah-*leen* – pre-dates me, though she spent a year working at Erika Ritter's *Dayshift* and is now in her second term as a producer. Talin is dark, occasionally naughty, and always ebullient, the unofficial puncturer of office egos, sometimes (perhaps most frequently) including mine.

The other producers all signed on at *Morningside* after me. Hal Wake, prematurely silver-haired (his neatly trimmed beard, more fittingly, is still dark), who handles our literary matters and grows stronger in all dimensions every year, came to us from Vancouver in Nicole Bélanger's time. The rest have all arrived since: Nancy Watson, a tough-minded pixie from the Maritimes with the world's most expressive face (the look of pain that crosses it when I ask a dumb question has caused me anxious moments in the studio); Bev Reed, a hard-digging professional who came to us from *Sunday Morning*; Susan Rogers, a deceptively modish recent mother (she has the mind of a prosecuting attorney and the tenacity of a bulldog) who's worked in print and broadcasting from Yellowknife to Halifax; and Carole Warren, a former professional musician (but more recently journalism graduate and veteran of TV) who's taken over the parts of the program involving live music and its performers.

Despite her title and the length of time I've known her, not to mention her considerable broadcasting experience, Pat Pehlman is a relative newcomer. She came to us from *The Journal* last season to take over the thankless but vital role we call "the desk". More properly, this is the "assignment desk", a sort of quarterback's position (Gloria being the coach) where the grinding routine and the incessant pressures had defeated a string of her predecessors. So far, to everyone's relief, Patsy is thriving on it, and her combination of professional seasoning and practical wisdom – she's a working-class kid from Red Lake, Ontario, she likes to boast – have made all of our lives easier.

Rounding out the returning cast this morning, as they round out our meetings through the year, are our two regular technicians, tiny Carol Ito – a three-year veteran now – and handsome Jim Summerfield (who, I suddenly realize, also dates back to the days of Don Harron), our over-qualified receptionist Sue Kilburn, and, of course (I'm still having trouble facing life without her), Lynda.

There are, in addition, this year's rookies: three, so far, as Gloria continues her search. Ken Wolff is a promising young journeyman who was working on local programming in Halifax. (We're lucky to have him; with Toronto's house prices, it's getting harder and harder to attract people from the regions.) David Langille, seated now at the table, notepad at the ready, is a bright PhD candidate who has been working in the peace movement and wants to give broadcasting a whirl. The third, still making her way from her own family cottage (she and Gloria have just concluded their negotiations), is Janet Enright, an experienced journalist with a lot of magazine experience. Janet is married to Michael Enright, the new host of *As It Happens*, which, given the rivalry between the two programs, ought to make for some interesting dinner-table talk this season. More troubling to her, and one of the reasons she needed to think a long time before joining us, is the fact that she is also the sister of Barbara McDougall, the Tory cabinet minister. While anyone who knows either of them will realize this won't make a whit of difference to her work, she's been worried about perceptions.

Janet's connections aside, I don't envy the tenderfeet their next few weeks. The *Morningside* unit is a tough club to crack, as much like a family as a working assemblage, with all of a family's inside jokes, unwritten ordinances, and volatile politics. Over the years, I'm sure, we've bruised some sensitivities. Since a principal weapon for the bruising has often been my own unthinking snappishness, I make a note this morning to try to mend my ways.

Good luck, I can hear Talin saying, to us all.

10 a.m.: After some opening remarks – the rumours about Alex Frame are true, by the way, and there is general approval, even though most people have to take my word for his record on radio – we have dived into the budget. As usual, it's depressing. By my arithmetic, we have $718 more to spend this year than last – not much on a budget of just under $900,000. But the built-in costs, especially unionized salaries, have risen at a much higher rate, so, once again, we have to cut. Since what we pay contributors (shockingly little) is now at an immutable bottom, we're forced to shave from such expenses as the newspapers and magazines we buy, the travel we undertake (there's $100 a week this year, to account for all of us), and, most painfully of all since they are our lifeline, the phone calls we make. Gloria is a wizard at masterminding these matters, but it's enervating. The cuts at the CBC, in radio at least, have long since sliced away the fat. Now they're scraping bone.

11 a.m.: Cheerier news. Gloria has invited a vivacious young woman named Christine Wilson from the CBC's research department to attend upon us, and, while I remain disdainful of bean-counting, I am transported by some of her figures. *Morningside* is up in all the important categories: ratings (we're well over a million in total every week now – people who have listened at least once), "share" (even in the best of times the CBC rarely goes over ten per cent of the sets in use, and we have solid eights and nines), and so on. Furthermore, those who listen continue to like us: among the people who filled out a questionnaire on their favourite CBC radio programs, we led the league. Ratings are like best-seller lists. If they're good, you believe them. These are obviously solid.

11:15: Oh-oh. Spoke too soon. To buttress her analysis–which contains some useful information about people's preferences (they think we should do more on health, for instance, and play less rock and roll)–Christine has distributed some documents. Among them is a collection of comments from the people who filled out the questionnaire–seven pages of them, each coded with the respondent's sex, age level, and home town. As she talks, I browse, magnetized (wouldn't you be?) by my own name. Although most of the comments are favourable ("Gzowski is admirable and entertaining," says the perceptive F60 + of London, Ontario), it's not the compliments that catch my eye. *"Morningside* would be my favourite show if it had a different host," says M60 + , of Ottawa. ". . . boring . . ."–F25-34, Prince George, B.C. . . . "inaudible . . ."–M25-34, Grimsby, Ontario. And M35-49, of Salisbury, New Brunswick, has "stopped listening since Gzowski took over." Stupid bean-counters. What can we learn from them anyway?

1 p.m.: Lunch bolted, we get down to the serious stuff.

The most pressing problems concern three of our show-piece features. Our business column, which leads the program every Wednesday, has lost two of it three regulars over the last couple of months: Christopher Waddell of the *Globe and Mail* has been transferred to his paper's Ottawa bureau, and Richard Osler, the Calgary-based stockbroker who's been a mainstay from the column's outset, has been made a vice-president of his company and, regretfully, feels he can no longer find the time.

Our Ottawa column, which leads Fridays, has been limping; we've had a hard time finding anyone who can slug it out with Mike Duffy, the CBC's irrepressible television correspondent. Like almost everyone who knows him, I love Duff, both on and off the air, and, in turn, he loves doing the radio, where he can use all the information (and sometimes loose the opinions) that he can't squeeze onto TV. But he's a hard man to get the mike from. One time, when we had him paired with Jeff Sallott of the *Globe,* a good reporter and a natural broadcaster, Mike decided the *Globe* was going too far in its front-page exposés of Sinclair Stevens, and he just *steam-rolled* Sallott–it was tough to listen to. Lately, we've been using Deborah McGregor of the *Financial Times*–a real find–but maybe we should tinker some more.

After some talk, the solutions to those two seem straightforward: Add Chris Waddell to our Ottawa coverage, keeping Duffy and McGregor–three voices will give us more texture, anyway –and build a new business column around Diane Francis, who's been emerging as a star.

The third of our pressing problems requires more thought: Tuesdays.

Tuesday mornings, when we've run the column we call "national affairs", have become such a hallmark of *Morningside* that it's hard to remember how long it took to find the right formula. Even the most astute historians of the program, I imagine, would be hard-pressed to recall that we started with Roy Romanow, Doris Anderson, and Dalton Camp before we hit on the combination that became our most celebrated feature (it actually used to show a bulge in the ratings): Camp, Eric Kierans, and Stephen Lewis–the three wise men. For more than three seasons, under Talin's proud guidance, they swapped their views and their wit, on everything from international crises to the politics of smoking, enjoying the sessions and each other as much as the listener (and I).

When Stephen was named ambassador to the UN (he said later that his major reservation about taking the post was that he'd miss his sessions on *Morningside*), we replaced him with Dave Barrett from B.C., who used to get up at five in the morning to take part, and our sessions gained in dramatic tension what they lost in polish. At the beginning of last season, however, when Dalton was appointed to the Prime Minister's Office, we decided, perhaps wrongly, to start again from scratch. Since then, we've run through a quorum of distinguished politically affiliated figures, from the Tory Eddie Goodman to the labour leader Bob White–it's through this column, in fact, that I know Jim Coutts, who brought us Trudeau in the spring. But we've never recaptured the flavour that made KCL, as we called them, such a hit. Their secret, I think, was that they listened to each other, and each was less interested in making his own points than in adding to the general conversation. Such civility is hard to find.

Now, as much in sorrow as in frustration, we've decided to give up. In the Tuesday spot this autumn, we'll launch an idea we've been playing with for some time: three provincial attorneys general, a different combination each week, talking from their own capitals. There's a wide enough political spectrum to draw from, heaven knows, from the staunch conservatism of Brian Smith in B.C. to the prairie radicalism of Roland Penner in Manitoba, and the AGs' portfolios cover a wide variety of subjects.

We'll see.

7 p.m.: Everyone's gone; I have the cottage to myself again.

The rest of the day was fruitful: new ideas for some regional columnists, a renewed determination (though who knows how successful we'll be?) to get more native voices on the air and more accents, some pleasant surprises from the new producers. Janet Enright, for instance, who showed up before lunch, has an interest in the visual arts (an area we've been weak in), and Ken Wolff, to my delight, has said he'd like to dig into the mail, a gold mine of material that Glen Allen mined last year with much profit. As the meeting broke up, there was a feeling of optimism and a sense of new opportunity.

As well, though, some familiar themes raised their heads, and I wondered what the rookie producers were thinking as groans echoed around the room. How do we get more women on the air? Why can't we develop more people like Stuart McLean? What to do about Ontario, with its several regions under the rubric of one province? Shouldn't we have more/less sports/popular culture/live music/real people/famous names/ this, that, and the other thing?

Mostly, of course, that's what summer meetings are for. But tonight, as I replay the long session and look over the pages I've filled with doodles, one subject sticks in my mind: Quebec. We spent even more time on it than usual this year, discussing our columnists, wondering whether to continue the regular interviews with cultural figures we call *"Pause Café"*, generally trying to figure out how to keep in touch. By and large, we're proud of what we've done over the years. But we're never sure. Our two executive producers, each from Montreal, have had conflicting ideas about how to cover their native province. Nicole felt the only way to reflect its reality was to hear almost solely from francophones – to remind the rest of the country how French it is. Gloria has been equally adamant about giving a voice to the minority. They're both right, I think – and probably both wrong, too. Everyone who knows Quebec has his or her own certainty about its truths, and Janet Enright, who has volunteered to step into the role vacated by the fluently French-speaking Glen Allen – Talin has offered to help as well – has a tough row to hoe.

IN THE SUMMER of 1961, Jenny and I, with Peter and Alison and the baby Maria, moved to Montreal. Lefolii had been running a bureau there for *Maclean's*, and when he returned to Toronto as managing editor, I was named to succeed him. The job entailed acting as a liaison with the magazine's new French edition – called, unfortunately, *Le Magazine Maclean* (it's *L'Actualité* now) – and covering Quebec affairs for the national anglophone audience.

I had fallen onto rich ground. The Liberals were still fresh in power in Quebec, having toppled the Union Nationale only the year before, and the province was in turmoil. The church, the school system, the universities, the role of women, journalism, the language itself – everything was up for re-examination and reform. I plunged so quickly into stories of the "Quiet Revolution" and wrote so much about it over the succeeding months that, later, at least one authority claimed I had invented the phrase. (I hadn't, as a grumpy letter to the *Canadian Forum*, where the claim had appeared, made clear.) I wrote about politicians and clerics, singers and poets, union leaders and intellectuals, including Pierre Elliott Trudeau, then a civil-rights activist and teacher, but a force to be reckoned with, I suggested, should he ever enter federal politics. (I had no idea he would turn to the Liberal party.) I covered John Turner at the Montreal Forum, Brian Mulroney at Laval (offering hints about each of their futures which make me look smarter in hindsight than I was), Réal Caouette in the boondocks, and Pauline Julien at the *boîtes à chanson*. I hit on the roots of the separatist movement and stage-managed the first sociological survey of its support – thirteen per cent of the voting public, as we announced on the cover of both magazines.

In discovering these stories, I was luckier than I was clever. For one thing, I went to work every day in an office near Peel and Ste. Catherine that was filled by French-speaking journalists, the editors and writers of *Le Magazine*. Though they were not by any means all separatists, a lot of them were sympathetic. The copy editor, in fact, was an early and active member of the old

RIN - the Rassemblement pour l'Indépendance Nationale - and a frequent lunch companion of Pierre Bourgault, that organization's president, whom he would bring back to the office afterward for an informal chat. The editor was Pierre de Bellefeuille, and while it would be unfair to say that Pierre was even a closet *indépendantiste* in those days - as far as I was able to detect his feelings over negronis and blue *steak au poivre* at the Pied de Cochon - it came as no surprise to me when, in his more recent role as a Member of the National Assembly, he left the Parti Québécois over his disagreement with René Lévesque's moderation.

I *liked* most of the nationalists I met, and understood their sense of injustice. Still struggling with my own sense of identity, perhaps not yet having absorbed the lessons of Saskatchewan or my first years at *Maclean's*, I may even have envied them the simplicity of their cause. Though I argued with them all the time - and even suggested in a piece I wrote for *Le Magazine* that the new climate in Quebec was making it possible for them to right those injustices without having to break up Canada-I sometimes wondered whether, if I had been Québécois myself, I wouldn't have signed up with them.

The other advantage I had in breaking original stories was the quality of the opposition. The tradition of English-language journalism in Quebec leading up to the Quiet Revolution had not been a vital one; even after I arrived, there were still a few reporters who, at the end of a political meeting, looked around for an envelope with some money in it-a tip, I suppose, for having got things right. Peter Desbarats, at the *Star*, was by far the best of the English newspaper writers in Montreal, but even Peter, despite his name, spoke awkward French. The two best bilingual reporters writing in English were Thomas Sloan of the *Globe and Mail*, and Robert Mackenzie, who had left the Montreal *Gazette* to join the *Toronto Star*. (Mackenzie's own Scottish nationalist background, I always felt, gave him special insights into what was happening in Quebec, and a sympathy for Québécois causes -he hated the English long before he got here, as someone said.) Both Sloan and Mackenzie, however, were stuck in the legislature in Quebec City, and, as a result, nearly all the major non-political stories in Montreal and elsewhere in the province hung like apples, waiting for a reporter with the interest, the time, and the backing of his editors to come along and pluck them.

I plucked.

It ill behooves me, by the way, to be condescending about Peter Desbarats's unilingualism—or anyone else's. In the summer I had worked on the railroad to Labrador iron, I had added a few phrases of what I learned in Montreal to call *joual* to my Ontario high-school French. I could growl a guttural "*d'accord*", for example, when I wanted to indicate I'd got the point, shortening the vowel and bouncing it off the back of my throat, or ask a colleague (whom I boldly addressed as *tu*) how it went in general rather than, as Torchy Dulmage had taught us at the Galt Collegiate, how they themselves were going *aujourd'hui*. I savoured these little touches, and trotted them out, along with some accompanying vulgarities, to the degree, I'm sure, that I embarrassed and annoyed the francophones who heard them; it was as if someone from Montreal had moved to Toronto and insisted on larding his halting English with the clumsiest examples of regional Canajanisms—"howdafuckarya, eh?" But after the pleasantries, during which my caricature of an accent would send out false signals of familiarity, I might as well have been conversing in Urdu. I faked it a lot, and it would not surprise me now to learn that there are old politicians in Quebec with memories of a young reporter from Toronto who, when they told him his fly was open, had nodded sagely, growled "*d'accord*", and, apparently, made note of the fact in his *cahier*.

I had tried, at first, to do something about my linguistic shortcomings. Through *Visites interprovinciales*, whose name I remembered from university, I arranged to spend my first two weeks in my new territory with a francophone family in Quebec City. Away from the temptations of cosmopolitan Montreal, I would speak only French—self-inflicted total immersion before anyone had invented the phrase.

On the eve of my departure, Jenny, who would be stuck with the children in our duplex while I was gone, and who was concerned, she said, that I would be seduced by the charms of *haute cuisine*, cooked me a glorious *canard à l'orange*. She needn't have bothered. The family with whom I checked in the next day in a walk-up apartment in Lower Town put a chicken in the oven after breakfast – *du toast*, usually, *avec du café instant* – took it out once when Papa returned from his morning shift at the print shop, carved some, served it up for the noon *dîner*, put it back, and took it out again for the evening meal at six, by which time, needless to say, it was cooked well enough to make *sabots*. For dessert, on a big night, Papa would bring home *des donuts*, which we would munch in front of the TV.

Food aside, my sojourn in *la ville en bas* did little to improve my biculturalism. However graciously Maman and Papa worked to include me in their lives, most of the time I just felt stupid. I missed the jokes and garbled the simplest conversations. In a family whose intellectual pretensions stopped somewhere around the *Heure des Quilles* on television (the bowling hour, in case you're as culturally deprived as I am), I was the dullard, my contributions to their social gatherings limited to a recitation of my children's ages – "*et le p'tit* Peter (we will not discuss the translation of the verb *peter*) *a trois ans*" – or to a description of what I did as *écrivain*. Frustrated, I quickly began to cheat, sloping off to subtitled movies in the afternoons and, in the evenings, smuggling copies of *The New Yorker* into my *chambre*. Before the two weeks was up, I went home to Montreal.

Even in my short time in Quebec City, though, I had had a revealing glimpse behind the curtain of the province's *realpolitik* – a far cry from the lofty discussions in the pages of *Le Devoir*. After *L'Heure des Quilles*, for example, Maman and Papa had sat spellbound before the televised charms of Réal Caouette, who had booked air time for his Ralliement des Créditistes and filled it with the zeal of an evangelist. Their interest sent me on his trail in the surrounding countryside, where I saw a fervour whose intensity matched what I had seen on the prairie, and when I returned to Montreal I was able to pick up a few dollars in bets and an enhanced reputation as a prophet by predicting some election results in 1962. (I said on a Montreal television program that Caouette would win fifteen seats, and was dismissed by my co-panelists as an outsider from Toronto; he won twenty-six.) Long before the days of detailed opinion-polling, it was an ineradicable lesson in the difference between what journalists perceive from their isolated vantage points near the seats of power, and how the real world makes up its mind.

So, no, my French did not significantly improve. My *joual*

accent, in fact, may have been reinforced. Not long after I got back to Montreal, Jacques Hébert, who is now a senator best known for his diet but was then a bustling and important publisher, suggested to me at a book launch at Le Cercle Universitaire that, in deference to my hosts' sensibilities, I switch to English. But I had learned something more about politics. And, more important, I had absorbed forever the reality of living in a second language. If I believe now–if it shows through on *Morningside* that I believe–that all people who live in a country that calls itself bilingual should have the right to express themselves in the Canadian language they grew up in, and to deal at least with their government in that language, it has a lot to do with the experiences of a young father of three, sitting at a dinner table in *la ville en bas* in 1961, chewing his dry, overdone chicken, feeling tongue-tied and inadequate and so much less than himself.

Monday, August 24, the cottage: Fulford has been named to the Barker Fairley chair of Canadian studies at University College at the University of Toronto. Not bad for a high-school dropout. Though the appointment is for one term only–he'll take it up as soon as he and Geraldine return from the Orient–and will pay him, he says, only twelve thousand dollars, I'm delighted for him.

He's also going to write his memoirs. I don't suppose it's a *terrific* idea that, if I finish this, we'll be on the shelves at the same time, but I, for one, can't wait to read his recollections of the places our paths have crossed.

The editor of *Saturday Night*, by the way, will be John Fraser, formerly of the *Globe* –the man whose father stuck his tongue out at Gill at Janet Turnbull's wedding. I hope John, whom I scarcely know, is as independently minded.

It occurs to me as I record this that now, in 1987, nearly all of us who broke in at the old *Maclean's*, from Berton to Peter Newman to all of us who left together in 1964, are out of magazines. Barbara Moon is still doing some editing at *Saturday Night*. But, other than that, it's a new age.

With Max Ferguson and Alan McFee at a celebration of
Alan's first fifty years on the air. I should have known that
as soon as I put the balloons behind my hero's head
someone would take a picture.

CHAPTER EIGHT

*Warming up for the new season . . . A case
for the jury . . . Opening-night jitters . . .
Homage to McFee . . . Secrets of a pre-dawn
television-viewer . . . Why I couldn't be a
foreign correspondent . . . "Is Pierre Berton
a Canadian?" . . . And now, here's
Craig . . . My non-working smoke place . . .
Summer's end*

Tuesday, September 1, the Morningside *office, Jarvis Street, Toronto,
10 a.m.:* Not counting the August meeting, this is my second
day of duty for the new season, but yesterday, the first day of
school, was so casual that it feels as if things are only starting
now. We always begin slowly, like a baseball team loosening up
its muscles, and being careful not to strain them while they're
still stiff. Spring training, Morningside style. Still a week till we're
on the air. Plenty of time for pressure later on.

Gloria's not here. Her mother has died, at last, in Montreal.
I'm sad for her; the long illness has hit her hard, and being unable
to help the pain must have been terrible.

The office feels comfortable and relaxed, even though there's
some sickness going round – Talin is seeing a doctor about her
feeling of exhaustion, and Nancy, Susan, and Carole Warren all
have illnesses in their families.

Hal is in fine fettle, looking forward to the new literary season
and still not swamped by its demands. The veterans have all
taken advantage of the staff changes to improve their seating

arrangements (not that it makes much difference in this impossibly crowded room), and Hal has grabbed Jim Handman's old private corner, walled off by bookcases. He'll soon spill over, as the autumn torrent of books starts to roar. He's as messy as I am, without a Lynda to give him the semblance of organization. He and Jennifer are expecting a baby this winter, about the time he and I are supposed to go the Olympics. His trip to Calgary is part of the deal Gloria and I worked out with the television people. Hal will help with my daily reports on TV, and produce a piece I'll do each day for *Morningside*.

John Spalding, who's in charge of the CBC's Olympic television, called today to talk money. "The most anybody's getting is $5,000," he said. "I don't know how much to offer you. Let's start at six."

"Okay," I said.

"And you'll get a *great* coat," he said.

12 o'clock: My first piece – I can't call it an interview – of the new season. Being able to package stuff, to tape it in advance, is one of the advantages of coming into the office for a week before we go on the air. We can build up a reserve for the days (I don't know why there aren't more of them) when guests don't show up or the technology breaks down. Particularly now, when there's some time, it allows us to do some items whose complexity makes them risky to do live. Today's first effort certainly qualifies. It's what we call a "jury". We worked out the format a couple of years ago, for a trial of Louis Riel, except, rather than re-trying the case as it had originally been heard, we set the scene in the present, and entertained arguments about whether Riel should now be pardoned. In the studio in Toronto, we put two opposing lawyers, and, after hearing their opening statements, we let them each call two expert witnesses from here or from other cities, and we linked the whole process elecronically. I was, ahem, the judge. We assigned twelve listeners, whom we picked from the mail – our "jury" – to listen as closely as they could, and that afternoon we taped their votes, announcing the result, which was a draw, when we finished. Exciting. But, as you can see, complicated.

Today, we're hearing the case of Baby Andrew, the Toronto child whose parents disagreed with the treatment the doctors wanted to give him, which has been ringing through the news-papers. The way Talin and Susan, who've been working hard on the story, have phrased the question we'll try is, "Should parents have the final say over medical treatment surrounding their children?" After much thought, they've dispensed with lawyers and expert witnesses for today's package, and they've added to the dramatic possibilities by persuading both Andrew's mother, Agnes Gordon, and one of the physicians most closely involved, Dr. Alvin Zipursky of Sick Kids, to present the two sides. In another way, though, they've made the process more complicated. They've arranged to have the jurors listen in live–or live on tape–from the studios in their various home towns. When the arguments have been presented, the jury will be asked to talk over what they've heard, and we'll all eavesdrop on their deliberations.

One of the reasons I like doing this sort of thing is that it's such unadulterated *radio*. I can't see how any other medium could match radio's ability to bring so many disparate elements to-gether from so many different places, or (since I'm really think-ing about television) be willing to give them the time they need to explore the ideas the story raises. It's still not real, of course –Talin and Susan have had to ask the principals to simplify their arguments to the bone–and a real jury would hear a lot more questions and have a lot more time to think. But it's involving, and, if it works, it forces the listener to join in the deliberations. I can't remember who said that if he wanted to conquer a nation's minds he'd do it on the radio, but I agree with him; radio is the best of all media for the consideration of ideas.

When it works, that is. The trouble with technology is that it breaks down, and right now we're having trouble. Susan and Talin have lined up five jurors, in Toronto, Edmonton, Halifax, St. John's, and Thompson, Manitoba. But while Mrs. Gordon and Dr. Zipursky sit patiently by–Mrs. Gordon, somewhat intim-idated but determined, has asked to sit in a separate studio in Toronto, so she can concentrate on her script–we can't make contact with Thompson.

This is why we pre-tape things, I guess.

We twiddle our thumbs for twenty minutes, while Mrs. Gordon gets more and more nervous. It's a tough situation for Susan and Talin. Not only does Thompson give us an odd number, to preclude another tie vote, but the juror we've lined up there is an especially interesting person, Eunadie Johnson, a West Indian woman who now does police work in Northern Manitoba. Now, as the technician fusses with the board, she can hear us but we can't hear her.

We give up. We'll go with four, and if necessary I'll break the tie.

Talin nods a cue to roll the tape, points her finger at me to begin the first part of my sixth season at *Morningside*, and . . . . . . to my own amazement and dismay, I break out in a fit of nerves. My stomach flutters, my hands seize. As I read the opening lines of the script Susan and Talin have written and I've worked over, my voice quavers. I can't believe it. Five years, on *Morningside* alone . . . a thousand programs . . . somewhere over ten thousand interviews . . . and I am as nervous as a rookie.

I stop the tape, take a deep breath, and start again. It's all right now, I think, we're rolling. I plunge again into the script.

2 o'clock: Opening-night jitters affect the best of us. With the jury behind me (they found for the doctor's side, after much thoughtful discussion, and everyone left in good spirits – except Eunadie Johnson, I guess, who heard the whole thing from Thompson but couldn't add a word), I turn to the subject of the day's second pre-tape, the incomparable Alan McFee. McFee is here to celebrate his fifty years at the CBC and is, I discover in the office, as skittish as a butterfly.

McFee is very special to me. He was the sidekick on the old *Gerussi* show, and when I sat in for Bruno, in 1969, for my first shot at morning radio, I inherited him. At the time, he scared the wits out of me. I knew his reputation as a cranky and outspoken rebel around the CBC, and, indeed, I saw his often savage sense of humour at work. One day, when a pretentious young producer, complete with MA and stopwatch, both new, pointed his finger at Alan for a network cue, McFee, smiling guilelessly, inserted a curse word between "This is the . . ." and "CBC radio network." Unseen from the control room, of course, he had played the switches of his on-air microphone and his talk-back so adroitly that, while the producer heard the dreaded interjection clearly, and thought it had gone on air, all the listener heard was the network cue with a barely perceptible pause in the middle. In miniature, this was a modern version of one of McFee's most storied pranks, in which, on the old *Hohner Harmonica Hour*, he and Tommy Tweed arrived surreptitiously early at the studio and set all the clocks ahead two minutes and then, on *that* producer's cue, and triggered by Alan's apparent stumble on "Hohner Harmonica" ("This is the Horror Hormonical Hour . . ."), had launched a tirade of mutual and obscene abuse, only to revert to their usual polished perfection when the true air-time arrived. And, in spirit, it was a sign of the McFee I had heard so much about.

But with me, he has never been anything but supportive. While I was still feeling my way as Gerussi's substitute, he brought into the program one day a tape of his attempts at the narration of an episode of the television series *Five Years in the Life*. The family portrayed in the episode was Inuit, and Alan, who was (and is, for my money) the world's greatest announcer, had stumbled mercilessly on its members' polysyllabic names. After many of the stumbles, he had let fly an oath or two at his own incompetence. But before bringing the tape to me he had had someone clean it up; the result was unadulterated bungling – and very funny. "Here," he had said, "use this if you want," and his willingness to make a fool of himself in public had added greatly to the program I was hosting.

It's hard to let him know how much you like him. He is agonizingly shy, and responds to compliments with either dismissive self-deprecation or the mock pomposity he displays so effectively on *Eclectic Circus*, the hourly program of music – it's actually a satire of some very real announcers–the CBC still lets him host. For the same reasons, he's a very difficult interview; it's almost impossible to tell when he's serious.

Today, as I say, he's all aflutter. He has brought with him the script of the audition he performed to get a job at the CBC half a century ago. In the studio, he spills his coffee on it, and absentmindedly wipes it up. Carelessness is unlike him. He is impeccable, a gentleman. Today, typically, he is dressed in a dark blue suit, striped shirt, and regimental tie. He knows I will ask him to read from his old audition script, and when I do, he clears his throat, flexes his shoulders, and flings himself into it with gusto, even inserting a word or two to help the prose.

As we finish, I ask him about his sense of audience, and

whether he believes, as I do, there is only one person listening. Not quite, he says, and offers instead a moving description of the country where he knows he's heard. On *Eclectic Circus*, of course, he broadcasts to what he calls "vacuum land", and takes the mickey out of all things sentimental. But as I sit today, listening to him ruminate about his years on the air, I see what I am sure is deep emotion in his eyes.

I could be wrong. Who knows? God bless him anyway; I hope he lasts another fifty years.

Wednesday, September 2, the office: If I had to choose one moment to epitomize my discomfort on *90 Minutes Live*, I could scarcely do better than the night Craig Russell, the female impersonator, was on in Toronto. Men in dresses were not my cup of tea in the first place, and I was, shall we say, distressed by the number of his fans in the studio audience who underlined every naughty remark with squeals of delight. Still, he *is* clever, and his own spot was at least amusing. Afterward, though, we kept him on the panel while I tried to do a serious piece with Laura Sabia, the feminist and author. Russell, who may or may not have been chemically accelerated, mugged, kvetched, and mimicked all through Ms. Sabia's spot. His fans squealed, Ms. Sabia boiled, and I wished either he or I would evaporate. The more I squirmed, naturally, the worse things became. I was still a long, long way from learning – or, if I had figured it out, still too achingly self-conscious to apply – the lesson Johnny Carson absorbed so long ago: that when disaster happens you just roll with it; the audience is probably having a wonderful time.

And now, here it is the fall of 1987. I am complaining at a story meeting that the line-up for Monday – opening day – looks too solemn. We need some bite, I say, some sparkle. Maybe Evelyn Hart, the effervescent Winnipeg ballerina, if we can come up with a topical reason. Then someone says Craig Russell is available, flogging his new movie, *Too Outrageous*.

"Book him," I say. "We can tape him tomorrow."

Word is out, of course, that he has settled down – stopped his drinking and his other self-destructive habits. But I wonder who has changed more, Craig or I. Let him do his worst; it should be fun.

5 p.m.: Donna Logan calls. I won't be presenting CBC radio's case to the CRTC after all. André Bureau, the chairman, has rejected the idea of *Morningside*'s broadcasting from the hearing floor. It's a reasonable decision, I suppose, but I am frustrated at not being able to make my case.

Maybe we can work something out, Donna says.

Thursday, September 3, the apartment, 4:30 a.m.: A test run of getting up early.

When the season is under way, this will be late. For my first few years at *Morningside*, I set my alarm at 4:44. After the first *Morningside Papers*, though, when the mail grew even heavier, I found 4:44 didn't give me enough time to read the previous day's letters and still do all my other pre-broadcast chores. I tried 4:14 – I like *some* symmetry to greet my sleepy eye. But toward the end of last season, I often stirred even earlier. Don't know why. Goodness knows I was tired enough.

I like these morning hours, though. After some negotiation, Lynda persuaded the *Globe and Mail* man who delivers in this part of town to do our building at the begining of his route. As a result, unless I'm really thrown by insomnia, when I mute the alarm so as not to disturb Gill and pad down to the apartment door, the paper's waiting for me.

Know the really weird thing about living in one of these trendy condos? There's no sense of weather–no sound of wind, no pelt of rain, no tires singing on the ground. Unless I go and lean against the plate-glass window that overlooks the courtyard five floors below, I don't know whether to wear a T-shirt or pack my parka. Since I'm hesitant to do that–I like to prowl in my birth-day suit until I'm ready to go, and am unprepared to display my aging body to the denizens of pre-dawn Toronto–I usually flick on the TV instead, and try to infer the local forecasts from the continental surveys on CNN (who says we don't need a Canadian all-news channel?) or from the wriggling isobars on channel 38.

I am an expert on television of the wee hours. I know Larry King in replay–"Don't call now please: recorded earlier"–and the solemn young man with two-tone shirts who burns the mid-night oil for CBS. I know more about TV evangelists than Jessica Hahn, where to buy a zircon elephant by calling in my Visa number, and how, I think, to lose weight, grow hair, and make money on real estate all at the same time. I am familiar with all the prejudices of Tom Braden and Robert Novak, who present opposing views on *Cross-Fire*, Braden for the left, as he says (in Canada he'd be right-wing Liberal), and Novak, the most loathsome regular opinion-monger on TV, for the right. In my restless early mornings, I have seen spicy scenes on the movie channel (you can look at heads being cleaved on prime time on television but breasts being bared, apparently only at four in the morning) and, on the sports network, the taped endings of hockey games whose beginnings I've watched live before I went to bed.

This morning I just peruse the *Globe and Mail*, searching for stories we can pick up on for the radio, and attempting the cryptic crossword to kick-start my mind.

11:30, the office: The pace is picking up now, as Monday grows closer. We take advantage of the presence in Toronto of Bryan Johnson, the *Globe*'s Asian correspondent, to record some background on the Philippines, which we'll run next week, as part of our now annual fall series on parts of the world that have been in the news over the summer. Bryan, a likeable young man who is one of the *Globe*'s battalion of skilled and energetic reporters – my feeling is that it's the place to work today as clearly as *Maclean's* was when I was his age – has recently had a scare at his base in New Delhi. All he'll say about it now is that a man on a motorcycle, whom he recognized from a story he'd been working on, pulled up beside him and said, "We don't have to warn you, but this is a warning." I don't ask him any more. It occurs to me that when all of Bryan Johnson's friends went to Moose Jaw (or wherever) and he went to the Orient, he stepped into a life I'll never know. Though I am his senior in journalism by a good many years, he has mastered a part of the business that is as exotic to me as nuclear medicine. Plunked down in one of the locales he covers as familiarly as I do interviews on Cape Breton, I would be as helpless as a tadpole.

On *Morningside*, at least, all Bryan has to worry about is keeping his tenses right, so it won't be too evident next week that he's commenting on events that may have changed before he's heard, and I can help him with that.

12:30: More pre-packaging, this time a panel to add to a one-hour special – a "cover story", as we like to say – on housework. Susan and Nancy have combined forces for this project. "A Puff and Pain Production" they've labelled it, since Nancy (Puff) is known around the office for her abilities with frivolous stories, and Susan (Pain) for digging into tough ones. Their self-caricatures are unjust – or at least exaggerated. But it's good to have them working together, and to have them able to put in the extra care the pre-season pace allows. Today, for instance, they've enlivened their housework package by inserting old radio commercials – "Rinso white", and "It's so easy when you use Lestoil."

Wish we could do more of that through the year.

1:15: Pierre Berton, to talk about his new book. Pierre's presence means I've won this season's fight with Gloria – and, to be fair, with a lot of the other producers as well. We have the same squabble, or so it seems, every fall. Pierre brings out a book – always in September, since he believes in getting a jump ahead in the race for the best-seller lists. I say let's do it; he's one of the great talkers, always interesting. They say let's not; he's over-exposed. So far, I've won most of the battles, though sometimes at a price. One year, at least in part as over-reaction to the office feeling, I was uncharacteristically aggressive with him. It was over his book-length essay, *Why we think like Canadians*. I lit into him, saying, for example, that his thesis about our having made peaceful settlements with the aboriginal Canadians didn't take into account the slaughter of the Beothuks, and that he hadn't done justice to Quebec. He defended himself well enough, to be sure – he thrives on that sort of challenge – but a lot of people, including Elsa Franklin, who looks after his book promotion, were taken aback by my belligerence.

People, probably including my colleagues, assume Pierre and I are friends. Not so. In the nearly thirty years since we overlapped at *Maclean's*, I've run into him dozens and dozens of times. I've read him, interviewed him, been down the bench from him at *Front Page Challenge* (a game he takes more seriously, by the way, than Nancy Howard takes horse-racing), and occasionally sought his counsel. But I've never spent more than a few minutes alone with him that I can recall, or dined with him when he was not on display. I think, for what it's worth, that he is an absolutely stunning genius of the craft we both practise, an eloquent writer, an insatiable reporter, a compelling anecdotalist. Whatever the academics make of his works of history–and surely at least a few of them have been a *tiny* bit jealous–I also think we have been blessed that he has turned his eye to our past, and that for generations to come we will be grateful to him. It bothers me no end that, in our curious Canadian way, we have elected him to prominence and then, from time to time, criticized him for the very stature we have awarded him–or, as even my own producers do, begrudged him his prolific output. (I once asked Wayne Gretzky if, having been so celebrated so early, he feared a later reaction – the same thing that happened to Berton. Wayne, bless his heart, said, "Is Pierre Berton a Canadian?")

At the same time, I am bothered by Pierre's lack of self-questioning, his insistence on being right all the time. It is almost impossible to tell him anything he doesn't already know–or need to top. It is as if his expertise in a lot of fields (and he really does know a lot about a lot of things) has convinced him he knows everything about everything, which he doesn't.

If I can take just one inconsequential but, I think, telling example: We were at a baseball game together last spring, among a whole gang of McClelland and Stewart authors Avie Bennett had invited to a private box. Berton, who knows about as much about baseball as I know about placer mining, decided to take over the commentary. "Here comes the big left-hander," he announced as a Baltimore pitcher strode to the mound. "Amazing," muttered Harold Town, who does know baseball. "The guy warmed up *right*-handed." Later, when a Baltimore player popped up to the outfield with two out and two on and the runners came automatically jogging round the base paths, Pierre leapt to his feet to alert the Blue Jays, the rest of the crowd, and us. "Run coming in," he cried. "Run coming in."

Well, he is a hell of a writer, and I'm happy to have him here. This year's book is the first volume of his autobiography. He tells a few stories, some old, some new, at least to me. Good radio. Perhaps because I've spent so much of the summer working on this journal and gazing into my own belly button, I ask him as we finish whether it ever seems to him wrong that he has become so famous himself largely by writing about the famous.

"But I always give interviews to everyone who asks," he says. "I remember what it was like trying to get there."

Maybe I mis-phrased the question.

2:15: And now, here's Craig. Reading the research – the producers have given me the usual massive file – has reminded me how naughty he can be. "If Karen Carpenter and Mama Cass had shared a sandwich," he told one reporter, "they'd *both* be alive today." But when he shows up, he is bright-eyed (and clearly sober), funny, and surprisingly warm to me. He remembers the evening on *90 Minutes Live* –"Oh, yes," he says, "with old Sore Labia" (which we take out of the tape) – and recalls another instance of his misbehaviour from another program. He was a guest on Alan Thicke's talk show in the U.S., he remembers, on the same edition as Margaret Trudeau. Before she came out – she was married to the Prime Minister then – he called her "Canada's worst lady", and said, "You can see the light in her eyes; it comes through the back of her head."

It's hard to tell whether he's repentant now. After the huge success of his first movie, *Outrageous*, he got caught up in the fast lane. He had a breakdown in Vancouver in 1981, appearing on stage in white make-up and with his head shaved, and changing costumes in front of the world. People walked out, and his tour was cancelled. He's obviously over that sort of thing now, but the most attractive quality about him is his honesty about it, without any of the embarrassing *mea culpa* other reformed sinners have exhibited.

Maybe he's not totally reformed, anyway. When the interview is over, he gives me a hug–which, somewhat to my own surprise, I happily return. I like him. But when he offers a back rub, I flinch. According to the research, he sometimes offers the same therapy to his friends. When they accept, he cracks their necks.

Friday, September 4, the office, mid-morning: I have been wrestling all week with this season's first write-in, and today, the last of spring training, I am determined to finish at least the first part.

I'm having trouble.

I started this annual rite in 1982, when I had just come back from my years in Rockwood, where I lived after *90 Minutes Live.* That season, I wrote a series of five essays about having moved back to the city from the country. I read them on the air, and asked people who had made similar transitions to write to me about their experiences. There was a rich and varied response, an instant reminder to me of how many literate people listen to CBC radio and are willing to contribute to it. Each year since then, I've tried to do the same thing with other subjects–private passions last year, for example (my own for playing Ms. Pac-Man and buying Canadian paintings), or on why people lived where they lived, which I launched after I had spent a summer on the road for television, looking enviously at places where I'd happily nest if my work didn't keep me in Toronto. Every time, the results have been heart-warming and rewarding. We've made a lot of free radio out of them, reading the best letters on the air, and, later, I published many of them in the *Morningside Papers*.

That may be at the heart of the trouble I'm having now. When I came back to radio, I was bursting with my observations about the differences between being a city mouse and being a country mouse–I *needed* to write what I'd figured out. Or, when I finished my summer on the road, I *wanted* to talk about the beach I'd found on Prince Edward Island, or the nook in the Ottawa Valley where Wayne Rostad has built a house. But now I've started to question my motives. Am I, I wonder, just writing these pieces to get free radio–and to solicit stuff for my profitable books? If I am, is that legitimate? People do, obviously, enjoy taking part in these exchanges. As their replies to my requests for permission show, they delight in seeing what they've written in print. But the pleasure, surely, lies in the spontaneity–I'll tell you mine if you'll tell me yours. What if it loses that? At what point does it become pure exploitation? Even though I had put together a book from my three years at *This Country*, it didn't occur to me until well into the first couple of seasons that I could make one out of the *Morningside* mail. It just happened. But after the first *Papers* came out (and when I was already pretty sure there'd be a second one), I could tell that some people were writing with an eye to seeing their work appear in a book. That's wrong; the books have to come from the radio, and not the other way around. If I work too hard to contrive one of these write-ins, if it looks as if I'm starting on *The Morningside Papers III* before the second one is even out, I'm dead.

Hell of a time to get conscience-stricken, eh? The producers expect a script by Monday. I'll work on something over the weekend.

12:30, still at the office: Everyone but Sue Kilburn, our receptionist and den-mother, is at lunch, saying good-bye to Paul Kennedy, who's been sitting in the host's chair all summer. The producers' phones—at least the phones of those who have figured out our new communications system—are on call-forward to Sue's desk.

We haven't had a great record with receptionists. It's an unglamorous task: answering the phones for our continually changing cast of producers (and trying to figure out who's handling what *this* week), opening the mail, looking after tapes, sorting out the loonies from the people who have legitimate story suggestions, running interference between the tender egos in the office and the people who pay our salaries. Sue Kilburn is the best we've ever had. She's a two-time divorcée, not far from my age, who's worked in TV, done public relations, helped out at art galleries, and raised a terrific kid on her own. A couple of years ago, when the last in a long succession of candidates showed a tendency to hyperventilate during crank calls, Gloria, who's known Sue for a long time, talked her into holding the fort for a while. She's been holding it ever since.

Now she smiles as I light a cigarette. She pretends not to notice as I carry it into the main body of the office while I look something up in the files.

Over the summer, the CBC radio building became officially non-smoking. With the exception of a few areas like the corner of *Morningside* just outside my office, there are signs everywhere. Gloria warned me about it by phone, and asked what I intended to do.

"I don't know," I said.

"The non-smoking areas will include the studios," she pointed out.

"Right," I said.

"And . . . ?"

"And I'll cross that bridge when I get back."

So far, I haven't had to. In the pre-tapes, I've just lit up, right under the sign that says "Welcome to our non-smoking work place". (I'm tempted to change it to "non-working smoke place".) No one's said anything. I think the assumption is that if someone lays down the law, I'll quit – my job, that is, not the weed. They think I'll say they're making a choice between a non-smoking policy and me, and I guess they don't want to risk that. They might be right, too, though even I have qualms when I think about newspaper stories that say I've left the best job in Canadian broadcasting because they won't let me smoke.

It's weird. I hate smoking and am ashamed of myself for being hooked on it. My teeth are yellow and my fingers brown. My clothes stink and so, I'm sure, does my breath. I have holes in my rugs and scars on my furniture. (Once, last year, trying to hold a live cigarette out of the wind, I set fire to the pocket of my windbreaker, and more than once, talking on the phone, while I cradle my chin with my smoking hand, I have smelled smouldering hair.) Nearly all my smoking friends – Lefolii, de Pencier, Dave Amer, who used to help me pollute the atmosphere in here – have quit, and some of them have turned into well-intentioned nags. Lefolii, when he's in Toronto, won't even let me smoke in his apartment. Gill is on me all the time, and, privately, I am much more concerned than I let on about my morning cough and shortness of breath.

But I *am* hooked. I'm an addict. I smoke, long after I've lost the pleasure of it, because it's easier than not smoking, and trying to stop it would be a full-time job. When people say that if you want to cut down you should begin changing the activities you associate with smoking, I don't know where I'd start. I smoke on the john, in the car, on the phone, after sex, before breakfast, while I read, when I write (I'm smoking now), and, most of all, on *Morningside*. I can't *imagine* trying to do radio without a cigarette in my hand. Some day, I know, I'll quit – if I live long enough. But right now, I haven't got time.

Furthermore, I am just stubborn enough to dig in my heels at all the pressure; I don't want to be legislated into health or nagged into clean living.

Stupid, isn't it? Think I'll take off for the cottage, for my last weekend before the rush.

How do you call-forward these newfangled phones anyway?

Sunday evening, September 6, late afternoon, en route from Lake Simcoe to Toronto: I've squeezed every drop the last two days: golf, bridge, visitors, food. Did some work, too, reading for next week's author-interviews, and a first draft–I'll finish it tomorrow morning, when I go in–of a piece to prime our fall exchange of letters. It *is* contrived a bit, but it's the best I can do, and Gloria thinks it will be fun. I've stolen the old "lists" idea, as in *The Book of Lists*, which was an American best-seller in the 1970s, or *The Canadian Book of Lists*, which–inevitably, I guess (says a guy who's lifting it a decade later)–followed it. (My favourite passage in the Canadian book is the list of the ten greatest Canadian novels. The authority for that list, a splendid choice, was Beth Appeldorn, the eminent Toronto bookseller. Like a lot of the other authorities cited, Beth dictated her entries over the phone. Trouble is, even after all the years she has lived in Canada and run her remarkable Longhouse Books, Beth still has a Dutch accent. As a result, her list of choices, at least in the first edition, included a book called *Divorce* by Timothy Findley. For readers who didn't realize that "divorce" was Appeldornian for *The Wars*, it was a puzzling selection.)

On Monday, I'll start with my own list of the ten best things in the world–strawberry ice cream, gas barbecues . . . just things I like a lot (I'll leave out the naughty one I sometimes shock my kids with when we play this game)–and see where it goes from there. On the first day, I should do a list of things I *don't* like as well–maybe the toughest interviews I've done on *Morningside*. The success of these write-ins is often a function of how well we seed them; you have to give guidelines, but you also have to leave room for the *Morningside* authors to take off in their own directions.

On Saturday, we watched *I've Heard the Mermaids Singing* on the VCR, the interviewer's friend. Ostensibly, that was work, too, since I'll be interviewing its director, Pat Rozema, soon. But it didn't feel like it. Sometimes, when the season gets going, I resent having to watch even the films I like, just because it's hard to enjoy something you *have* to do, and I have learned how to use the fast-forward button of the VCR to watch as quickly as I read. But *Mermaids* was a pleasure. I enjoyed it in spite of (oh, maybe a bit because of) Peter Sibbald-Brown's tongue-in-cheek (I think) running religious analysis of what seemed to me to be a pretty simple film–"Don't you see? Sheila McCarthy's parents are even called Mary and Joseph?"

Over lunch today: a meeting of the Hedge Road Press. Lucinda, just back from Italy, needed catching up on the Ridley book and some other projects we're thinking about. Gill, forgetting where Lucinda has been all summer, served a pasta salad. My contribution was my gazpacho, which is at least Spanish. I hope the publishing plans of our little company are more astute than our choice of menu.

Now, as I turn south from the last of the country roads and onto the slick blacktop of the superhighway to the city, I'm in two moods at once. I'm happy to be starting up again–it *is* a new beginning – but I have left the cottage with deep regret. After the Hedge Road meeting, Gill took off to visit her nephews and I was alone for a while. I sat at the butternut table where I have spent so many hours since the end of May, staring out at the light on the golf course. Then I went out to the cedar deck for a last check of the red honeysuckle, where I saw the hummingbird, and worked on the cryptic-crossword puzzles while the mists rose from the fairway. Next year, the vine will fill in. There'll be more birds, more flowers, more breakfasts in the sun. Maybe we'll see an ivory-billed woodpecker. Maybe I'll break 90–or, as Gill said when I told her I still hoped for an ivory-bill, 70, which is about the same probability.

Where did it go? The summer that stretched out so endlessly when I watched the midnight rain last May has vanished. Summers always do, don't they? But I wasn't *finished* with this one; there was–is–so much more I want to think about, and write.

When I started this journal, still feeling the exhaustion of the last season, I wasn't sure how much longer I could do *Morningside*. Now, with a summer of rest and reflection behind me, I still don't know. I'll see how the fall goes. All things considered, though, if I had to make the decision now, the season that begins tomorrow would be my last.

Gloria, probably taking some of my stumbles off a tape.

*What I face when I come to work: the Morningside office
in the pre-dawn.*

CHAPTER NINE

*Off and running . . . The man who won't go
to meetings . . . The sweet professor of
Manitoba . . . Struggling with the mysteries
of pop culture . . . Mordecai and the Anne
Murray fan club . . . The reflexes of
Vladislav Tretiak . . . Much depends on
Visser . . . Tricks of the trade . . . Immoral
porpoises*

Monday, September 7, 5:30 a.m., Morningside: Opening day at last.

I am just touching up the examples of lists I want to offer when Gary Katz, our studio director, comes into the office. This won't happen much through the season. Compared to Gary, I sleep like Rip van Winkle, and usually by the time I arrive he will have a pot of coffee on and will be sitting at his desk, perusing his copy of the greens, as we call the notes and research for each day's program, twisting a tuft of his Old Testament beard while he checks for errors of fact or perception, and tries to anticipate the difficulties of the day.

It's good to see him. Gary, a graduate lawyer who, instead of practising, joined the CBC back in the days of *This Country in the Morning*, has built a career for himself by running radio programs from their control rooms. At *Morningside*, after his dawn arrival, he works with intense concentration until we wrap up our broadcast at eleven. While he's there, he supervises the line-links, checks all the scripts – including mine – for grammatical niceties and factual detail, serves as a jury of fairness for my restless pre-program doubts (he combines an uncommon sense of human decency with an exquisite faculty of logic), conducts our three hours of live broadcasting like Andrew Davis at the podium, and generally makes things work. But the instant our closing theme comes to its conclusion, he gets on the streetcar and goes home to his chess computer and his collection of *Life* magazines. He has not yet been seen at a meeting – he wouldn't have dreamed, for example, of going to my cottage for our August session – and only those of us who patrol the mornings know how valuable he is.

We're a good team, Katzie and I. The precision of his mind makes up for my occasional wanderings, and my willingness to try new things keeps him, I think, happily amused. (Among his eccentricities is a refusal to direct the program when I take a week off, which flatters me but drives Gloria to distraction.) About the only complaint I have with him is that, although he's better at cryptic crosswords than I am, he won't help me on the mornings when I've been stuck. He gets the *Star* at his place, reads it in his taxi on the way to work, then clips the puzzle from an office *Globe* to do on the streetcar home. I am not allowed to discuss the *Globe* puzzle with him until the following day.

This morning, his reading of a different newspaper has another effect.

"Are we going to do anything about Paul Hiebert?" he says.

My heart sinks. Somehow, and without having to ask, I know that Gary's question means Dr. Hiebert has died. He would be – what? – ninety-five? – and though I have not kept in touch with him much for the past few years, I have been aware his health has been failing.

He was a lovely man. I didn't meet him until I came to radio, when Alex Frame, who was a committed fan of the poet Dr. Hiebert had invented – Sarah Binks, the Sweet Songstress of Saskatchewan – introduced him to *This Country in the Morning*. He became a kind of patriarch of those years, a much-loved occasional guest. As part of the last program we ever did, we flew him from his home in Carman, Manitoba, so he could join us in the party we threw on air. I can see him now, a twinkling elf, flirting outrageously in the studio with Edith Butler, who was young enough to be his granddaughter, and charming Edith and us all.

He was very wise. He was a chemist first, and a teacher (W. O. Mitchell was among his students at the University of Manitoba), who started to compose Sarah's awful verses as a reaction to academic pretension – it amused him always that one publisher had turned down his manuscript because Sarah wasn't "significant". Later, he published two reflective books on religion and the scriptures. We talked about them on the radio, too. When I put together my own book about *This Country*, the first words I wrote were, "When I grow up I want to be Paul Hiebert."

This morning, Katz, with typical foresight, has brought his copy of *Sarah Binks* from home. In the morning quiet, we read some verses, chuckling. Gary points out the sonnet that appears on the inscription page of *Sarah*, and I decide, in the place where Patsy Pehlman's line-up has indicated I should read my lists, to read it on the air instead:

> When I have turned life's last descriptive page,
> And written *finis* to a somewhat unplanned tale,
> With here its moments of poetic rage,
> And there long prose of dubious avail,
> My friends will come and say, "He was a sage,
> Lo, count the leaves, in truth, 'tis noble, look!
> All this acomplished in his single age!" –
> And sigh, and reverently close the book:
>
> But from the multitude will come a few,
> Sweet sprightly souls who read not to enlarge
> Each chapter to heroic tome, nor view
> The title page as bright emblazoned targe –
> But lovingly, to thumb each page anew,
> And chuckle at the doodles on the marge.

In the billboards, the paragraph I write each morning to begin the program, I dedicate today's edition to the memory of Paul Hiebert, 1892-1987, and my sixth season as host of *Morningside* is under way.

Thursday, September 10, the apartment, 3 p.m.: On the fourth day, we have finally hit our stride. I don't know what's been wrong up to now. It hasn't been *bad* radio; it just hasn't cooked. What a relief that it's working now!

Lynda has bought me a thick, heavy journal, about the size of a clipboard, bound in green linen, with a ruled page for every day. I've been scribbling in it regularly and now, as I catch my breath in the afternoon's solitude, I leaf through my first few entries, looking for clues.

Stuart McLean gave us a pleasant start on Monday with one of the finely crafted combinations of reportage and whimsy he has developed for us, like oral versions of *The New Yorker*'s Talk of the Town–this week on spruce beer, which he remembers from his childhood, and has found again somewhere in Quebec. After Stuart, we had a panel of four senators on a possible showdown with the Commons over the drug-patent bill, the Craig Russell tape (*sans* "Sore Labia"), and some phone calls around the country. But, somehow, the program failed to take off.

John Turner was on on Tuesday, struggling to prove he's not in as much trouble as everyone has been saying (the worst thing that could happen to him, I have noted in the diary, is that people start to feel sorry for him), and Daniel Richler made his debut as our pop-culture columnist. But, again, as they say at the racetrack, we just didn't fire.

I wish Daniel had been stronger, though it's not his fault. *Morningside* has been trying to find a way to cover the music, films, fashion, and trends young people are talking about almost as long as I've been here. It came up again–and eyes rolled–at our meeting at the cottage last month. The trouble has always been that the people who know about it and take it seriously have always presumed so much knowledge on my part that they lose me before they get rolling; they want to *comment* on what I need *explained*. Daniel was to be the solution. To keep his expectations of my prior knowledge low, I told him to try to think of talking to me on the air as making things clear to his father. (*90 Minutes Live* once flew Mordecai to Halifax, along with Daniel's youngest brother, Jacob, so Mordecai could read *Jacob Two-Two and the Hooded Fang* on television. We kept them around when their segment was finished, and brought out the evening's featured singer, Bruce Murray. "He's Anne Murray's brother," I said. "Who's Anne Murray?" Mordecai asked, raising eyebrows–and hackles–all over the Maritimes.) On *Morningside*, Daniel is trying valiantly. But it's hard. Like me attempting in the sixties to write about Canada for *The New Yorker*, he doesn't know how much to leave out. On Tuesday he talked about the magazine *Rolling Stone*, which is now twenty years old. I looked at the clock when I thought he'd told me everything I needed to know. There were nearly eight minutes left.

Wednesday wasn't much better, though it did feature a man I've wanted to meet for some time, Vladislav Tretiak, the Soviet goalie, who's in Canada to promote his new book. Hal Wake, with typical imagination, took advantage of his presence to set up something of a reunion. Along with Tretiak, he booked Paul Henderson, who scored the most famous goal in hockey history on Tretiak, fifteen years ago this month, and Yvon Cournoyer, who, as we sometimes forget, had scored on Tretiak just seven minutes earlier, tying the game Canada had appeared to be losing, and setting the stage for Henderson's heroics. Preparing for the program, I looked up the famous photograph of Henderson's moment of immortality–the one by Frank Lennon of the *Toronto Star* that has become the basis of so many memories–and, sure enough, there were all three of my morning guests: Henderson leaping in the air with his arms upraised and his stick brandished in triumph, Cournoyer, hugging him and helping to hold him aloft, and, in the background, Tretiak, sprawled on his back, his right hand still flailing the empty air. As I looked at the photograph, I became excited all over again. Jim Summerfield, the technician, who has been part of the *Morningside* unit long enough, you would think, to become inured to celebrity, was so exhilarated at the thought of meeting Tretiak in person that he called home to make sure his wife tuned in. ("All she said was, 'Who's Tretiak?'" Jim reported, with the same dismay Anne Murray's fans must have felt at Mordecai Richler.)

Tretiak turned out to be much bigger than I would have thought–he is only a little shorter than Ken Dryden–but every bit as affable as I'd been told. Like everyone who had watched him in the series of 1972, I had been amazed by his reflexes, and yesterday afternoon, when Hal brought him back for an interview on his own, he cheerfully agreed to take part in a highly unscientific experiment. While the tape rolled, I smoothed out a dollar bill and, pinching it from the top, suspended it vertically over the studio table. Following my directions, Tretiak held out his hand, heel down, thumb and forefinger about an inch apart. "You musn't touch the bill while I'm holding it," I told him through his interpreter. "But when I release it, you have to try to catch it as it falls." He missed, for what it's worth – he's human, after all. He kept the dollar bill, too.

On Wednesday as well, we played both the Berton tape we made last week and, for a whole hour, the jury–pretty solid pieces of radio–so the discontent I was feeling about the first few days of the season may well not have been shared by the listener. Still, as I say, things weren't clicking for me; the melancholy of the end of summer lingered on.

Today, though, everything came alive. I'm not sure I know why. Last night, the unit gathered at Bev Reed's house in Cabbagetown to say goodbye to last year's departed, Handler, Handman, and Puxley. I wrote a silly little verse for Jim and Richard and Peter (you had to be there) and read it aloud. There were some recycled inside jokes and some clever presentations. Afterwards, Handler made a gracious speech, about working with people who, he said, "cared". I think he's right. There are tensions in our unit and always will be–there have to be, in a place that demands as much as *Morningside*. But they're a good lot. When I got home after the party, I wrote in the diary, "I realize how much I like these people." That thought, coupled with the fact that the valediction marked the end of an era and reminded the survivors of the tradition we're a part of, may have a lot to do with my reinvigorated spirits today.

NEARLY EVERYTHING we did this morning was live. That makes a difference, too, at least for me. Tape is safer; you can take out the off-colour remarks and the stumblings and redundancies. But what you gain in concision, you lose in energy. On tape, knowing your mistakes can be rectified, you never quite give everything you have; you hold a bit back for the second try. Live, knowing what you say is what the listener will get, the adrenaline flows. Through a live morning, such as today, the energy builds. If a piece goes well, you get momentum; if it goes badly, you work harder on the next one. Nearly all television is pre-taped now, and more radio than most people know. As It Happens, for instance, records most of its interviews in the afternoon; before they go to air, the producers tighten them up and write new introductions. *Sunday Morning*, excellent as it is—it's really a television show without pictures—is *all* tape. But *Morningside*, characteristically, is live, warts (bless 'em) and all, and that's one of the things I like best about it.

This morning we launched our panel of three attorneys general. Brian Smith got up in time to be in our studio in Victoria at 5 a.m., coughing and spluttering as we set up the lines (he smokes a pipe, though he doesn't want anyone to say so on the radio); Roland Penner was in Winnipeg, and from Quebec City we had Herbert Marx. We looked at a very Canadian subject: the legislation of morality—the number of laws that seem aimed at making us a more decent people. Susan Rogers, who has taken control of the panel, did a green that used the federal government's proposed ban on advertising tobacco as a take-off point, and it worked. Our AGs weren't Camp, Kierans, and Lewis perhaps, but the conversation was lively and enlightened. A promising start.

After our political panel this morning: Margaret Visser. Margaret, as I probably say too often when I'm promoting one of her visits, is our most popular occasional regular, and the person about whom I'm most frequently asked when I travel—even by people who can't remember her name, and think of her only as "that English lady who talks about food and things". She's a classics professor at York University in Toronto with a voracious appetite for information and a delightfully animated manner of communicating it. The rich, fruity accent that catches people's ears, full of rolled r's and a classicist's careful enunciations (which she ornaments with her infectious laugh), is in fact from Africa. She grew up in what she still calls Rhodesia, but lived and studied around much of the world before settling in Toronto. She's in her forties, I would guess (I wouldn't dream of asking her), tall and big-boned, handsome as opposed to pretty, but not unattractive. She dresses with academic nonchalance, and her long auburn hair could often do with an extra brush stroke or two when she comes to the studio. Her pieces for us make up what Richard Handler, who worked closely with her, called "the anthropology of everyday life" – conversational essays that explore the history, lore, symbolism, and often politics of everything from soup to Christmas. Foodstuffs are her specialty (she put together a book called *Much Depends on Dinner* last year, based on some of her *Morningside* material), but recently she has broadened her base. This morning she talked about gloves.

I'm not nearly as comfortable with Margaret as (I hope) I sound. The best interviews – the best of the sort I do, anyway – seem to me to follow their own logic. They achieve the flow I couldn't generate with, for instance, Northrop Frye, because each question arises from the previous answer. There are exceptions, of course (sometimes the most effective questions are the ones that *interrupt* the flow and catch the interviewee by surprise), and all kinds of little tricks you use along the way – the throwaway, informal first question designed to put your subject at ease, the "I don't quite understand" that is really an attempt to go back over a confusing or disputatious area, the "Oh, surely not!" that is a signal to the listener to pay close attention, and a hundred other devices that are part of the repertoire of the craft – but internal logic is the basis on which all the good pieces are built. It's what the producers try to put into the greens, and what I look for when I think my way through each piece in advance. But it is also the reason that the craft of interviewing is so much more complicated (and interesting) than following a list of questions, and it is why so many of the most memorable interviews on *Morningside* (or on any good interview program) do what we call "leave the green" – take off in directions no one could have anticipated, and follow instead the logic that is offered by what happens on the air.

All this is why the only two useful pieces of advice I can offer any aspiring interviewer are: (1) do your homework and plan every moment in advance, and (2 – and most important) listen to what is being said to you and be prepared to abandon your plan – never be caught trying to find a way to get to the next question on your list when the man you had planned to talk to about flower-arranging admits to robbing the taxi driver on the way to the studio. It is also why the most rewarding compliment I can receive about my work is to be told I have asked exactly the question the listener would have asked if he were in my place.

With Margaret Visser, though, the energy that keeps the piece moving is simply the pattern of her own peripatetic curiosity, or her own urge to impart a piece of information she's uncovered in her library research. Like Bob Fulford, she is a compulsive communicator, and the language that gave us "to fulford" could well include "to visser"–meaning to embroider ordinary knowledge with fascinating insights. But what comes after any particular point in her presentation does not necessarily follow *from* that point. It makes sense to Margaret, mind you. It's part of the elaborate structure she has worked on in advance. But it's not self-evident. What she does, delightful as it is, is really more illustrated lecture than interview, and it often leaves the interviewer–me–flailing the air like Tretiak's glove. "Oh, really?" I say, instead of proceeding to the next question.

Still, she is a performer at heart, so enthusiastic about her discoveries and such a compelling talker, that the occasional "Oh, really!" is all she needs. I should just relax and enjoy her as much as the listener does.

After Margaret, and still in today's first hour, we had our first Quebec report of the season. After all the August talk, we've settled on Eric Maldoff, a lawyer and past-president of Alliance Québec (the organization that's assumed an important role as a rallying-point for anglophones without being tarred as anti-French), and Daniel Latouche, a political scientist who now teaches at McGill but has a history of involvement with the Parti Québécois, as well as a quick and ready wit. There's a healthy energy between them, and they showed it in their debut today. So far at least, we seem to have a solution.

In between live conversations, we did play the McFee tape this morning, while the control room set up a complex link to Winnipeg. The Winnipeg item was a reprise of a panel we were particularly proud of last spring. I had been invited to speak at the University of Winnipeg on what turned out to be the day after the federal government announced some new–and inadequate –aid for prairie farmers. Leaping on the coincidence, the producers, on very short notice (Bev Reed was particularly heroic), rounded up a number of farm families to come into the studio. We recorded them the afternoon I arrived and played the tape the next morning. It was an adventure in radio for us – eight voices we realized the listener would be unable to tell apart but giving, in their overall effect, a powerful picture of how farmers were feeling. (I can still remember one young man, the fourth generation of his family to work the same piece of land, saying how he hoped his newborn son would know a different way of life.) This morning, we brought five of them together again, to talk about their summer and their prospects for the fall. Once again, I think, it worked.

And on yet another bright note – I wonder how long this euphoria will last–we brought on a new correspondent from the north this morning. Her name is Joanna Awa. She's an Inuit, a reporter for CBC radio in what I still have to remind myself to call Iqaluit, and a natural on radio, with a good story sense and a lilting laugh. This morning, she talked about the season's first blizzard in Resolute Bay, the manufacture of seal and walrus salami in Igloolik, an upcoming election in Iqaluit, and some people who are hunting for narwhals to take to a zoo in the U.S.

When she was finished, Katz said into my earphone that "you can hunt narwhals for anything you want, but you can't export them for immoral porpoises." In the mood of the the day, I just smiled.

The raw material: This is how I looked at This Country in the Morning.

The finished product: The cartoon Terry Mosher handed me on 90 Minutes Live.

CHAPTER TEN

*A long way from the crunchy granola: the
story of 90 Minutes Live . . . From the
singer with the curious allergy to the man
who hit his son with a whip . . . Berton's
finger, Atwood's triumph, Aislin's
cartoon . . . What it feels like when the
critics mow you down . . . Even the
moments (rare as they were) when everything
seemed to work*

Saturday, September 12, the cottage, early morning: The light
breaks a little later over the golf course every day now, and
there's a bite to the air today. Starlings flock. A squirrel and a
crow, autumnally crabby, are squabbling in an oak tree on the
lawn.

My spirits remain buoyant. Thursday's momentum carried into
Friday, and I'm still cashing in on the homework I did before we
hit the air: Pat Rozema on her film (to my surprise she agreed
with some of Peter Sibbald-Brown's comments), an excerpt of a
play I saw at the Edmonton Fringe, Harold Horwood's thoughtful book on the Annapolis Basin, which I read in galleys last
weekend. The publishing season will hit its stride in a couple of
weeks, and I'll be swamped. But right now I'm in control. La-
di-da.

It's easy to forget, when life is going sweetly, how bad things
were before they turned around, and now, in the September
morning, I turn my mind back to the darkest days of all.

I wince now even typing those words. My leap to stardom and my downfall. My Waterloo.

How innocently it all began.

In the last season of *This Country in the Morning*, Alex Frame and I had occasionally talked of taking some of the techniques that had worked so well on radio to television. Our conversations were mainly casual. If there was one moment when the idea was born, it would be on a lunch hour in Montreal, in our last season. We had just done a stimulating edition of the program, and, as we walked down Dorchester Boulevard, we were still high on it. High, and at the same time dissatisfied. In the radio studio, Pauline Julien, her chestnut hair tousled, groping for the English to express her passion about what had happened to her and her husband during the October crisis of 1970, had reached across the table and seized my hands while her eyes blazed with eloquent frustration. Walking down the street, Frame and I had begun to speculate on what it might have been like for the audience to have *seen* that moment. The thought was intoxicating.

There were other times, too, when we felt limited by radio. We wondered if we could have shown pictures of the Arctic games we saw in the Mackenzie delta, or enhanced the drama of John Diefenbaker telling stories in the court-house in Prince Albert, or the warmth of W. O. Mitchell being surprised by old friends in High River – we had done a kind of *This is Your Life, Bill Mitchell* there – or the plaintive magic of Winnie Chafe and her Nova Scotia fiddle. Visions of video danced in our heads.

Now, in restrospect, I realize how naive we were. Much of what had worked for us on radio had worked *because* it was radio. We had moved our wires and our microphones into the school gym in Aklavik or the library in High River and, without further fuss, simply broadcast what went on. Television, as we were to learn, was infinitely more complex. To put the Arctic games on television live – to cite one ambition we fulfilled – would require shipping the athletes from Tuktoyaktuk to Vancouver, where there was a studio large enough to accommodate their activities, recruiting enough Vancouver firemen to help them with a blanket toss, seeing them go shyly inarticulate before a gaping studio audience, then staring fearfully as the firemen, for all their good intentions, hurled them from their blanket to within inches of the hot white overhead lights. Pauline Julien, who, like the Inuit athletes, also made it to *90 Minutes*, appeared in evening gown and make-up, her tresses coiffed to perfection. She sang unforgettably – a moment we could match on radio only by playing her records – but the conversation that followed, surrounded, as we were, by blaring lights and a studio audience waiting for one-liners, was about as intimate as a post-game interview at the Forum. Winnie Chafe, as I recall, a soft-spoken Cape Bretoner who had made my heart sob with "Dark Island" when we broadcast from Sydney – she will play at my funeral, I resolved – never did make it to our travelling TV show. Not sexy enough, I guess, or too lacking in schtick.

But in 1974, still giddy with the success of *This Country*, and wondering what we could do for an encore, Frame and I thought television was just radio with pictures.

At the same time, Peter Herrndorf, recently appointed head of public affairs at CBC television and a rising star in the bureaucracy, was wondering about developing a late-night talk show. While Alex's and my thoughts were still vague, he called us to have lunch.

Herrndorf had been impressed with *This Country*, he said, and he, too, had wondered if we could translate its appeal to television. But, unlike Frame and me, he understood the complexity of making the change – and, more important, the machinations of the CBC establishment. He was – and is – a complex man himself: smart, ambitious, gregarious but private, outwardly imperturbable, engagingly knowledgeable about everything from U.S. politics to baseball, deceptively casual, compulsively hard-working. In 1974 he was thirty-three, already handsomely bald, with a moustache he twiddled when he thought, the only sign, except for the Rothmans he smoked incessantly, of the nervous energy that drove him. He was a Winnipegger, the son of immigrant parents; he had graduated in law from Dalhousie, and, after a brief career in newspapers, had joined the CBC.

As a current-affairs producer in Edmonton, he was principally remembered for two things. One was that, as a novice, he had not realized he had to tell the cameramen not only to start dollying backwards but to stop, and on the first day in a studio he had been staring intently at the control-room monitors while two of his crew backed cheerily off the set and out a door – fade to black. The other was that he had hired, as a tyro TV host, Joe Clark.

He had found his niche in management, accelerating his rise by taking a year off and, with the CBC's enouragement, picking up an MBA from Harvard. For all his bureaucratic style, which was to study every decision with the care of a military invasion, he was a visionary; he believed in Canadian programming and in the necessary excellence of the CBC. The determination with which he moved his late-night idea toward reality was later to be a part of more successful innovations at the network, *The Journal*, for instance (for which he also raided radio, taking Mark Starowicz and Barbara Frum from *As It Happens*), and some of the most far-reaching of the current-affairs specials. Though there were people within the corporation who later grew impatient with his plodding, methodical decisions, he was, once behind a project, a producer's – and a host's – dream: protective, supportive, enthusiastically encouraging.

For the idea that became *90 Minutes Live*, he needed all his management skills. From the outset, he faced opposition from almost every quarter in the CBC, and the closer his idea came to getting on the air, the more vitriolic the opposition became. The sales department foresaw the loss of millions of dollars of revenue. The variety department resented the idea of a "current affairs" show that would include comics and song-and-dance men. The local stations and affiliates wanted the late-night time to run profitable old movies, and fought Peter's idea of truncating the local news so we could get a head start on Johnny Carson. In Toronto, my old mentor Ross McLean (as I have learned this fall from a memoir published by Knowlton Nash), then program director of CBLT, trotted out his inimitable prose style for a memo to the brass. The idea of a national late-night show, he said – "a blend of gaucherie and dangling hostmanship" – would "confirm my bleakest view of this company's infinite capacity for self and public torment." And every other producer or department head with an idea of his own resented the money and resources the late-night experiment would suck from an already beleaguered budget.

At the time, of course, all this was beyond my ken. Our exploratory lunch in the spring of 1974 was the launching-pad for a number of increasingly larger and more excited meetings. Frame and I, with *This Country* behind us, moved into an office at 1255 Bay Street. Herrndorf's department picked up all of Frame's contract and most of mine, the remainder, in my case, being charged to a short-lived afternoon radio program called *Gzowski on FM*, which replaced two hours of wall-to-wall classical music and alienated more listeners than it attracted.

At 1255, where I spent my mornings, we talked and dreamed. We made lists of what we had done well on the radio and what we thought we could do on TV. We signed up for the CBC's training-courses and tried to learn the difference between a two-shot and chromo-key. We met with audience researchers and directors and set designers. We played with titles and formats, and, in defiance of the practice of the executive offices around us, we watched TV. When we didn't have enough to talk about, we filled the days in our small executive office by playing five-letter word, the pencil-and-paper game we had discovered on our flights around the country for radio, or walked the Toronto streets, seeking pin-ball parlours and a place to think.

After a few months, Herrndorf found us a tall and comely cohort named Nancy Oliver, who had worked at CITY-TV in its formative years and knew the vocabulary of CBC television as well. The three of us set off in various combinations for Los Angeles, London, and New York to pick up what we could from other people's experiments, and we studied the success of a Radio-Canada venture called *Appelez-moi Lise*, which starred Lise Payette, who was, like me, a radio graduate.

By the following spring, I had written—and, under Herrndorf's patient guidance, rewritten three or four times—a forty-five-page proposal, replete with charts and diagrams, and bursting, as Knowlton Nash recalls with some accuracy in his book, with "hype and sociological jargon". Our program would be, I said, a "public affairs show like no one has ever seen before" (I was right there, wasn't I?), and, in unspoken acknowledgment of the opposition we faced from so many quarters, I went on to make ambitious claims about the scores of thousands – nay, hundreds of thousands – of "sophisticated, educated" viewers we would draw, "sophisticated" and "educated" being words that make the salesmen of television advertising salivate.

We presented our brief to the brass at a memorable meeting, for which Herrndorf had prepared us meticulously, right up to role-playing rehearsals. With some misgivings–I can still remember Don MacPherson, a vice-president, making paper airplanes while we talked–and in spite of the fact that our slide projector wouldn't work, the decision-makers gave us a tentative go-ahead. Alex and Nancy expanded the nucleus of our unit by hiring some young producers with radio experience or backgrounds in television, and, in the winter of 1975, we took our act to Halifax for a try-out on the road, one of our premises being that one week out of three we would originate our program outside Toronto.

Even in Halifax, an experiment shown only in Nova Scotia and Prince Edward Island, I should have seen the danger signals. Perhaps I did see them–though hindsight gives me a perspicacity I didn't have at the time – and was, like everyone else in the group that was now headed on a collision course, too preoccupied to notice. But, buoyed by a positive review in the *Globe and Mail* ("Gzowski Show Has Big League Aura") and by the fact that more Maritimers had watched us than had normally watched the late-night movie (though 155 of them phoned in to complain about missing the advertised science-fiction epic *Space 1999*), we marched inexorably on.

One of the danger signals, I know now, was that very *Globe* review–not in its opinion, which was to change in subsequent months, but in the fact that Canada's national newspaper had sent its television critic chasing after us to the farthest reaches of the country. The anticipation our own hype had created around the CBC, we were to learn–our hype and the seething internecine animosity, which was known thoughout the business – meant that every television reviewer in the country had his sights trained on our every move.

A second signal that I should have heeded involved the way I dressed on camera–and what we did about it. In my radio days, I had developed a considerable reputation as a slovenly dresser, much of it, as Ian Sclanders might have said, well earned. Contrary to some published opinions at the time–few magazine stories on the program avoided the phrase "unmade bed" – my rakishly informal attire was not a studied effect. I didn't *strive* for fame on *Chatelaine*'s list of bad dressers, I achieved it through natural talent. Never a clothes-horse even when I was editing *Maclean's* or mixing in circles that called for a jacket and tie–I have, by and large, had less interest in fashion than I have in Albanian politics–I had fallen happily into the CBC radio uniform of jeans and sweaters. As the years of *This Country* rolled on, I grew more and more carefree about how I looked, often forgetting to wash or comb my long 1960s hair–the sixties lasted well into the 1970s in Canada–and usually, in the morning dark, just climbing into whatever clothes were lying about the bedroom floor, and slipping a pair of running shoes onto my feet.

Even when Frame and I had first begun to talk about television, I had realized I'd have to pay more attention to my attire, but on the program I saw in my head, though I might have had my coiffure trimmed, and exchanged my drooping jeans for tailored slacks, I wore a sweater, and felt at ease. By the time we arrived in Halifax, that vision had been amended, and I checked into the Dresden Court hotel with a wardrobe of blazers and jackets and three-piece suits.

My last, if half-hearted, hold-out –I still didn't think it mattered very much–was against a necktie, the symbol of everything I had hoped the program wouldn't be. Frame, by now an expert on the conventions of television, and determined to lead us into the land of the large numbers, urged me to wear one. We compromised. For half the shows in Halifax I would wear ties; for the other half, my shirt-collar could remain open. A demi-victory.

But I had underestimated the importance of the number-crunchers. Into Halifax, on the heels of our producers and technicians, the CBC had sent a platoon of audience researchers to measure our success with questionnaires. What the other lessons of their surveys were, I never learned. But on the matter of my neckwear, they were adamant: beyond a doubt, the research proved, the audience preferred me with a tie; otherwise, they said, I looked impolite. From then on, I wore ties.

I dwell on this petty detail now because, as I look back, it seems to sum up much of why *90 Minutes Live* went wrong. Between the dream and the broadcast, as the way I agreed to dress symbolized, we lost the essence of what we had set out to do. I don't know where this happened, or precisely when. Certainly there was no moment at which Frame or I–or anyone else–said, "Let's throw out everything we know from *This Country* and everything we have believed in and try to become something we're not."

Nor, in any of our countless meetings, did the CBC brass – even those who were cynical about our chances from the start – urge us to give up on our ideals. We did it on our own. Little by little, as we sat in our cramped office at 1255 Bay, doodling on pads of paper between games of five-letter word and excursions into the world of television as it already was, we bought the message. The need for large numbers, and our own promises to achieve them, transfixed us. Whatever *This Country in the Morning* had been, television was show-business, and if we were going to succeed in it we had to do it in show-business terms. We would have a band, a studio audience, bright lights, and big names, and if the biggest names we could come up with were American, well, so be it; that's what was required to get the numbers. Guests, if they sang or danced or told jokes, would perform in front of the audience and then retreat to a "talk area". I would sit behind a desk and beside a couch, and, one by one, the guests would parade out, do their turn, and line up beside me, just like the big time. I would be not so much the interviewer as the star. Carson with a Canadian accent. Carson with maple syrup. Ugh.

In all this, I hasten to add – the "ugh" is highly retrospective – I was a willing victim, not so much raped by television as seduced. My last-ditch stand against a necktie notwithstanding, I, too, had fallen under the spell of the charts, the research, and, to be honest, the glamour. Frame, talking me into the formality of a cravat, was only my guide.

For our first night in Halifax, we had an impressive line-up of guests, which ranged from the former Vietnamese army colonel Nguyen Cao Ky, whom we had flown in from his refuge in the U.S. (what a charmer he was), to the incomparable Max Ferguson, who called in good wishes in his best Pierre Trudeau voice and then emerged from behind a curtain. Knowlton Nash, may the gods forgive him, remembers a guest named Cherry Vanilla, the world's most unreserved groupie, who cheerfully told me the characteristic pastime of her colleagues in the groupie world was "going to bed with rock stars".

But the vignette I recall most vividly from that first program is of an American singer who had the number-one record on the disco charts. Though I had not heard of this particular superstar before our planning meetings (I needed a Daniel Richler even then), I agreed to the assessment that she would draw the younger viewers we were hoping for. She arrived in Halifax by herself, bearing a gown for her performance and charts of her hit song for our band. I watched her rehearsal in the afternoon, admiring the professionalism with which the Halifax musicians we had hired picked up her arrangements – many of them, including the bass player, Skip Beckwith, and the clarinetist, Donny Palmer, had a long history of playing with the biggest names in the business – but wondering what on earth I would talk to her about when she moved onto the couch that evening.

After rehearsal, she retired to her dressing-room. By the time her live performance rolled around, late in the program, I had forgotten my concerns. She sang into a microphone we had, at her request, painted white, and though she performed well (so far as I could tell), tears streamed down her cheeks as she belted out her lyrics, and her nose was running so dramatically that, I learned later, the people in the control room were afraid to take a close-up.

She put the microphone down and moved to the talk area.

"Did the lyrics really get to you," I asked ingenuously, "or do you have a cold?"

"Oh no," she said. "I guess I'm just allergic to white paint."

"I'm sorry," I said, concerned.

Just out of camera range, the musicians, who had noted the time she spent in her dressing-room getting ready to perform, broke into uncontrollable laughter.

I had, as they knew, come a long way from the blue jeans and crunchy granola of *This Country in the Morning*.

4 p.m.: There is a flash of grey and yellow feathers over the deck, just above the pentagonal corner box Gill has filled with pink impatiens. I haven't realized how long I've been sitting here, lost in memories of television. For a moment, the bird flaps against the sweep of windows, as startled as I. I leap for the Roger Tory Peterson, fourth edition. But before I can find my prey, he – perhaps she – is gone. The best I can do is narrow it down to page 249: Confusing fall warblers.

Right.

90 MINUTES LIVE WASN'T ALL BAD. My favourite program of all, I think, was broadcast from Vancouver, when we were still in the experimental stage. We had brought in, from New York, the food writer Craig Claiborne and the social critic Gail Sheehy, both of whom made intelligent chat in the talk area. But the star of the evening, and the person whose performance leaves me with a pleasant afterglow still, was the Quebec monologist Yvon Deschamps.

Getting Deschamps at all had been a coup. He was a personification of the solitude of Quebec, part of the torrent of indigenous talent unleashed by the political and social revolution of the early 1960s. His one-man shows, in which a nameless character wrought wry, bittersweet essays about his anglophone *"boss"*, who was kind enough to allow him to keep *"un bon job"*, filled the Place des Arts for thirteen weeks at a time. But in the rest of the country – or, as he would have said, in Canada – he was virtually unknown. He had, however, been an occasional and happy guest on *This Country in the Morning*, and it was one of the proudest boasts of our *90 Minutes Live* proposal that we would deliver him to an English TV audience. That had been, it turned out, more easily bragged about than achieved. Yvon was – and is – comfortable in English, and, indeed, was (and is) married to an anglophone. But even on *This Country*, he had never performed the monologues that had made him famous, which depended, as he pointed out, on nuances of language; he had simply appeared for informal and often rambling conversations, sprinkled with his outrageous views and irresistible laugh. It had taken persuasive powers that I had never mustered in my days of selling ads in Timmins, and all the chips of the friendship we had developed during his appearances on *This Country* to persuade him to try his hand at performance in translation.

I don't think, that night in Vancouver, I introduced him very well. I think I made the mistake of building him up too much. I may even have said he was funny, which can be, as I ought to have known, the kiss of death, so that when he walked into the thin spotlight and took his position on a high stool, the studio audience, conditioned as they were to the patter of American TV comedians, kept waiting for a punch-line that never came. Instead, Yvon talked – in English (I have the manuscipt of his scribbled self-translation still) – of his *grand-père*, and became a child again, and laughed his cackling laugh at age and death. In Vancouver, the audience seemed bewildered, and though I rose from behind my desk to hug him when he finished, I wasn't certain he had brought it off.

Later that evening, I knew. Because of the time zones–*90 Minutes Live* really was live – we did our Vancouver shows early in the evening, when they could be beamed into the Atlantic night, and afterwards there was time to go to dinner. After Yvon's debut, he and I and Gail Sheehy and Craig Claiborne went to the Three Greenhorns. Just after Claiborne had done the ordering, the headwaiter, looking puzzled, asked if there was a "Mr. Duchamps" with our party; he was wanted on the telephone. Yvon, equally puzzled, left the table. A few minutes later, he returned, beaming.

"My mother-in-law," he said. "She just saw the show in Toronto and she called every restaurant in Vancouver until she found me."

"And . . . ?" we said.

"And she loved it. She said I'd been married to her daughter for ten years and she had never, until tonight, known why everyone thought I was such a star."

"I didn't know your mother-in-law lived in Toronto," I said.

"Oh sure," said Yvon Deschamps. "She's an actress. You may have heard of her. Billie May Richards. She used to play children. For years and years she was the kid on something called *Jake and the Kid.*"

THERE WERE OTHER GOOD MOMENTS, TOO. Some, inevitably, were provided by our imports. Our producers spotted Robin Williams long before anyone thought of *Mork and Mindy*. He appeared on a program with the then-prodigy René Simard, and, picking up the record Simard had been flogging and turning it into, at various times, a frisbee, a pizza, and an animate object, put on the most brilliant demonstration of spontaneous comedy I have ever seen. Chuck Berry came to Vancouver and, in spite of–or maybe because of–having taken a post-rehearsal break in his hotel room with the girlfriend of one of the cameramen, set the whole studio rocking with live recreations of some of his timeless hits. Joan Rivers, to my astonishment (for even then she seemed to me to embody everything I disliked about television), flew in from the coast, and gave our tiny audience the kind of all-out performance only a consummate professional could have offered.

But the evenings that linger most pleasantly for me involved Canadians, many of them in contexts they had not been seen in before. In Toronto, Margaret Atwood received the longest ovation I have ever heard from a studio audience, and showed the disarming humour that lies behind her often intimidating façade by revealing that she was also the cartoonist Bart Gerrard in *This Magazine*. In Montreal, Maurice Richard received one almost as long, dwarfing the reception Ken Dryden had been given just before him and erasing the sadness I had felt in the green room earlier, when the Rocket had given me his business card, an ad for Grecian Formula. In Ottawa, Patrick Watson appeared in a turtleneck and turned into a sit-down comic. In Vancouver, Jack Webster sang "I Belong to Glasgow". In Halifax, John Candy, still otherwise undiscovered, played town-crier, and, during a Christmas week, helped us stage a live panorama of the twelve nights, with gold rings, laying geese, leaping lords and all. (The partridge was the easy part.)

In Calgary, Terry Mosher–the cartoonist Aislin–responded to a question the producers had ordered me to ask ("Do you ever put your editors on the spot by giving them a controversial cartoon right at deadline?") by reaching behind his chair and pulling out a drawing he had done of me, sitting suited behind a desk and saying to the camera, "Our next guest, an extremely talented lady, has a fine voice, and nice tits."

That night in Calgary, I kept my poise. Enjoying the moment as much as Mosher, I held the cartoon up to the audience. But on too many other occasions, what happened in front of the cameras threw me for a loop. Some of these arose through the program's frantic efforts to draw attention to itself, as when Irving Layton presented his poem "The Farting Jesus" (which drew fire in the House of Commons the next day and an embarrassing apology from Al Johnson, the president of the CBC), or when Don Arioli, an imp from the National Film Board, came on with his animated cartoon about Jimmy Penis and Victoria Vagina.

But some were just guests I didn't get along with or couldn't understand: the Duke of Ook, who tinkled incomprehensibly on the piano one night in St. John's; two giddy imports from *Monty Python's Flying Circus* (they had arrived in Newfoundland hoping, they told the producer who greeted them, they could meet a "nice, hairless young Eskimo boy"); Thor, who blew up hot-water bottles with his mouth; Benny the Bomb, who blew *himself* up for our cameras in Toronto; or a guy whose name I have forgotten who we flew in from, I think, Transylvania, to talk about vampirism, and who sported fangs and an accent that would have made Bela Lugosi sound like Mr. Rogers.

Even the two editions of the program that people still most frequently remind me about had overtones of discomfort.

In one, the discomfort was public. We had arranged a demonstration of the 1970s' trendiest kitchen gadget, the food processor, and, following the convention of television, I invited all the guests in the talk area to take part. In spite of all the producers' pre-show warnings, Pierre Berton, who had been on talking about one of his books, opened the lid while the machine was still spinning and stuck in his finger to slow it down. Before our eyes, and our cameras, the whirling, razor-sharp slicer-blade opened his finger to the bone. Without blanching, Berton put his hand behind his back, and, gesturing left-handed, continued to take part in the discussion. But, as I craned around behind him while the camera took another shot, I could see dollops of blood dripping to the floor, leaving stains the size of quarters. As quickly as I could, I went to commercial. Fortunately for us – and for the stoic Berton – the guest slotted for just after the food-processor demo was John Tyson, a doctor from Winnipeg. During the commercial break, while Frame and his backstage colleagues hurriedly rescheduled the remainder of the show, Tyson clamped his fingers over the pulse in Berton's wrist, called for the producers to summon a taxi, and rushed him off to an emergency ward downtown. Berton, to his credit, insisted on returning the next night to allay everyone's concerns, but the moment of his near dedigitization remained in all our memories. When I finally called it quits for *90 Minutes Live* a year or so later, the staff presented me with a plastic artificial finger, autographed by Pierre, and a food processor of my own, which I have treated, as you may imagine, with deferential caution.

The other evening most frequently mentioned to me was, publicly, a much happier event. It was a Friday in Toronto, and, Friday being the biggest night of the week for wee-hours television, we had stacked our panel with celebrities. From the U.S. we had brought the author Kurt Vonnegut, Jr., the (then) frazzled guru Timothy Leary, and the singer and songwriter Jimmy Webb. For good measure (and Canadian content), we added David Suzuki. As it all too frequently did not, the mix worked, and the first seventy-five minutes or so of the program (minus commercials) flew by on wings of words, television talk as it almost never is, real and stimulating conversation.

Friday was also, however, the night we had chosen – younger viewers, remember? – to present the regular spot we called, internally, "Tiny Talent Time". Frame and I had stolen this idea from *The Gong Show*, an American program in which hopeless amateurs sang, danced, told jokes, or otherwise made fools of themselves for a panel of TV celebrities. We talked John Candy into hosting our weekly segment – presenting the talent, as it were, to me – and began casting about for people who, whether they knew it or not, would be bad enough to be good. Occasionally, we scored. In Calgary, a group of law students who called themselves a "gastro-intestinal band" belched the score of *The Sound of Music* without cracking up, and there were other hits as well, precursors, I suppose, of some of the zanier moments David Letterman now enjoys on NBC. But more usually, it was hard to separate the guests Candy presented from the Duke of Ook or Benny the Bomb or other acts we expected the audience to take seriously, and the night of Vonnegut, Suzuki, *et al.* was one.

As the five of us sat in the darkened talk area, our conversation truncated, Candy brought out his first performers, a father and son. The father had a great snake of a whip in his hand, with which, to warm up, he snuffed out a couple of candles. Then the son, aged perhaps twelve, put an unlit cigarette in his mouth, and took up a position at one side of the performing area, profile to his dad. Drums rolled. The father reared, brandished his arm, cocked his wrist. The whip curled out behind him. The son stood steady, hands clasped behind his back, the cigarette jutting from his lips. And then – *crack!* – the cigarette was gone. The audience oohed. The father bowed. The boy smiled wanly. I led the applause.

From his seat at the end of the couch, Kurt Vonnegut, Jr., leaned over my desk.

"He hit him," he said.

"Oh, I don't think so. Mr. Vonnegut," I whispered. "He just flicked the end of the . . ."

"On the nose," said Kurt Vonnegut. "The whip hit the boy's nose."

"Oh, surely not," I said behind my hand, as Candy began to introduce the next act.

"Oh, yes," said Vonnegut. "He hit him."

The next day, in a darkened screening-room, I viewed the tape. He hit him.

And so it went.

WE NEVER DID GET THE NUMBERS our proposal had promised. Although the initial response was encouraging – more than seventy per cent of the sets in use were tuned to us in Halifax, and we lit up the switchboard in Vancouver when we made our national debut the next spring – the viewers quickly turned us off, choosing instead of our ninety minutes the easy pleasures of Johnny Carson, a movie or, presumably, sleep.

In the corridors of the CBC, there was mounting pressure to end our misery. Frame and Herrndorf did their best to shield me from the pressures they were feeling. But what they couldn't protect me from was assault by print. The critics were merciless. The *Globe and Mail*'s supportive notice from Halifax and an even more enthusiastic reception of our first show from Vancouver by Bill Musselwhite in the *Calgary Herald* ("90 MINUTES LIVE, YAHOO!"), had soon been drowned by a torrent of vitriol, much of it directed at me. In the *Toronto Sun*, Bob Blackburn said I was "gauche, erratic, inattentive, irrelevant, often rude, often sycophantic, coy and dull". Dennis Braithwaite, in the *Star*, said I suffered from "incurable infantilism". *Maclean's* found me, and the program, "an embarrassing mix of awkwardness and incoherence". Both inside and out of the television business, *90 Minutes Live* – or *Dead*, as some of our less imaginative analysts labelled us – became a synonym for disaster. On CBC radio, Dave Broadfoot of the *Royal Canadian Air Farce* said the similarity between *90 Minutes Live* and Otto Lang, the agriculture minister who was involved in a squabble over the international poultry trade, was that "they both believe in importing American turkeys," which was, come to think of it, both telling and funny, except that at the time it cut me to the core.

It all hurt. The lesson I had absorbed at Ralph Allen's *Maclean's* – that criticism of my work was not necessarily criticism of me – did not seem to apply. The critics *weren't* writing about my "work"; they were writing about *me*. "How is it possible," Dennis Braithwaite asked the readers of the *Star*, "that for the permanent host of a talk show, the CBC Brass picked a man who can't talk with any facility, who is manifestly insecure, who won't face his audience or the camera, who has no show business background, doesn't project, and who lacks wit, grace and any kind of TV personality?"

Well, gee, Dennis–I can say now–nobody's perfect. But at the time I was devastated. I grew to dread opening the entertainment section of a newspaper.

The worst part was that I halfway agreed with the critics. I resented their rush to judgment and would often wonder what might have happened to their own careers if they had had to stand or fall by the first few columns they had ever published. I was (and remain) convinced that nearly all the people who write about television in this country really don't like television. But in my heart, I knew they were more right than wrong; I was terrible–ill at ease, tense, twitchy. And the more savage the critical battering grew, the worse I became. The attacks fulfilled themselves. The CBC decked me in tailored suits, shirts too expensive to have breast pockets, and colour-coordinated ties, one of which, each night, the director would pick out for me. They gave me socks that rose up my shinbone, and put weights in my pant-cuffs to combat static electricity. They smeared an anti-glare coating on my glasses (I drew the line at contact lenses), and, every evening, they blow-dried my hair and covered the lifemarks of my weathered face with layers of allergy-tested, fragrance-free, honey-beige Clinique. They told me to act naturally, to relax. I couldn't.

Acting naturally, it seemed to me, was the most *unnatural* of acts in the circumstances of my job. In the blaze of the lights, with a studio audience gaping at my every move, with producers holding cards in the air to suggest questions, a make-up lady standing by to pat powder on my glowing nose or straighten a vagrant lock of blow-dried hair, with a floor director counting down on her fingers and the band counting in to the next commercial–commercial *break*, I guess, since we didn't sell many ads –and aware, always, that every critic in the country had his rifle trained between my eyes, I developed, if I had not had it before, a terminal case of self-consciousness.

My personal habits didn't help. Here, too, cause was tangled with effect. Jenny and I broke up in the fall of the program's first season. I moved into Yorkville, then to a furnished apartment in Mayfair Mansions, the heartbreak hotel, as someone called it, of Toronto's upper middle class, with a doorman in the lobby and, in every refrigerator, a petrified lemon, half a bottle of flat tonic water, and a rock-hard orange wafer of green-tinged cheese. I was lonely. I saw the kids on weekends–when the program was originating from Toronto–but missed them daily. One night at the end of the show, I did what I thought was a light little essay to camera about being newly separated. "I thought when you ran out of toilet paper you just yelled 'We're out of toilet paper,' " I said, and wondered where all the liberated women were who, when I was married, I thought would like to take me to dinner. To my surprise (for I had not intended to elicit dates), I had some calls, including one, which I returned, from a cellist who worked the same hours as I did, but who turned out not to like tobacco smoke or self-pity.

Mostly, when the show was over, I would walk back to Mayfair Mansions, turn on Carson, whose poise grew ever more impressive in contrast to my own (I could not bear to watch myself), and drink Scotch whisky. On more evenings than I like to admit, I drank more than I should have, and began taking tranquillizers to ease my morning nerves. I was a long way short of being a candidate for the Betty Ford clinic (if there was such a thing at the time)–I couldn't even do that as well as the Americans–but as the program wore on I needed increasingly heavier applications of Clinique to cover the bags under my eyes.

In the summer that followed the first season, I slunk onto a plane to Edmonton, where I moved in with Jan Walter, a serene and gentle woman who had been the editor at Hurtig's for my book about *This Country in the Morning*, and whose own marriage, to a man she had owned a bookstore with, had broken up not long before. That fall, Jan took a job at the Macmillan Company of Canada, in Toronto, and we rented an apartment together on Bernard Avenue, in the Annex. Peter Herrndorf had left for Ottawa, to become vice-president of planning at the CBC's head office, and the internecine warfare over the program's future carried on.

We made some cosmetic changes. Somewhat over my objections, Frame brought in from Winnipeg an interviewer named John Harvard, who had won an ACTRA award for his aggressive style on the local supper-hour show. The rationale made some sense; I had had a hard time switching from the easy banter of the show's entertainment elements to the brisker style required for current affairs and politics. But Harvard, an exemplar of the hard-nosed style of questioning, was the wrong solution. He pulled his chair up to his subjects and leaned into them until his breath fogged their glasses, and he badgered them until, no matter what their villainy, the hearts of the audience went out to them. The contrast served only to highlight my often-bumbling niceness. Furthermore, both on and off the air, Harvard and I didn't get along. I found him humourless, and he, I'm sure, must have thought me soft-headed and (with some justice) jealous. The tension spread through the unit. Frame got rid of Harvard, but we never did figure out how to mix tough journalism and light entertainment. Entertainment won. We killed the desk, as they say, moved couches, and played with other accessories.

But the show continued to be a bad imitation of a foreign format, and to flounder. By the middle of our second year, the audience had dwindled to as low as 150,000, and though the critical pressure eased – there were few epithets left to hurl – we knew we were beaten. Before I could be pushed, I jumped. I wrote a memo of resignation to Frame. "The program needs an entertainer," I said, "which I am not. I need journalism, which the show does not."

That decision made, I began – to the surprise of even myself – to get better on the tube. I was still no Alistair Cooke. I still stammered and felt lost in the lights, and I never did grow accustomed to an audience in the studio, watching me talk. But I was better. The inevitable mess-ups of live TV no longer seemed to reflect on me. I learned to relax and enjoy them. (Well, to enjoy them.) Part of my new-found comfort, I'm sure, was due to an improvement in my private life. After a bad scare with some stomach pains, I had cut myself off both booze and tranquillizers and, with Jan's quiet and patient support, was attempting to eat regularly and sleep through the night. But part of it too, I'm also sure, was that I was finally free. The ordeal was over. There was nothing else anyone could do to me. I had – almost – a good time on television and it showed. On the last night, after we'd played some clips, I took off my tie, lit a cigarette on camera, and said goodbye to whatever viewers remained.

Know what, though? I still think we could have done it. If Frame and I had just kept walking down Dorchester Boulevard that afternoon in Montreal, and resolved that whatever happened, we would not lose sight of what had made *This Country in the Morning* work . . . if we had stuck to our guns about desks and lights, and studio audiences and the band . . . if we had never met a consultant or a researcher or watched another program . . . if I had just stuck to *sweaters* . . .

Well, we'll never know now, will we?

Bonnie Buxton (LEFT) and Keitha McLean, two contributors, with the promotion poster the Star Weekly's publishers put together in 1966.

CHAPTER ELEVEN

*The best things in the world . . . The most
difficult interviews . . . A Canadian
haircut . . . What if they gave a press launch
and nobody . . . ? . . . Why we don't love
"the CBC" . . . Business business . . .
A golfing breakthrough (not mine) . . .
Lunch with Flora . . . One magazine dies;
another rises*

Tuesday, September 15, the office, early morning: My list of the "ten best things in the world", which was postponed in favour of Paul Hiebert's poem, was:

Home-made strawberry ice cream (Gill and I have a Donvier ice-cream maker, which I swear by; the secret is to use all whipping cream);

Sable Island (I was there in the summer of 1986, filming a television program that was never shown);

Roger Angell writing about baseball in *The New Yorker*;

Gas barbecues (I scarcely cook with anything else at the cottage);

Handknit socks;

September (a reflection of my own good mood these days, I'm sure, and the golden days at Lake Simcoe);

Shirtwaist dresses (I had to call Patsy Pehlman at home to see what "those simple dresses with collars" were really called);

Evelyn Hart (whom I had met and been enchanted by, both on and off the stage, on another television shoot of 1986 – that program was shown);

Newly talcumed babies (ah, Stephanie, my perfect grand-daughter, whom I saw briefly at the end of the summer when Maria and her husband, Scott, brought her to the cottage); and **"Somewhere Over the Rainbow"**, which I substituted at the last minute for Ian and Sylvia's original version of "Four Strong Winds", and which Dave Amer played on the radio, by Judy Garland, when I finished reading.

I noodled around a bit on the air as well, saying I'd considered but not included Wayne Gretzky, Northern Dancer, and Ontario corn, among other contenders, and then, as I'd been planning, added the eight most difficult interviews I had ever done on *Morningside*, to help promote a more varied response. They were: **Martin Short**, whose wife, living in Toronto, was a fan of the program and urged him to accept our invitation when he was in town, but who turned out to be as pedestrian in conversation as he can be hilarious on television; **Betty Friedan**, who, from our Ottawa studio one day, assumed I was an enemy of her cause and shouted hostility at me no matter what I said (I was later told she was hard of hearing); **Mordecai Richler**, who in spite of–or perhaps because of–our friendship refuses always to respond to any question to which he knows I know the answer, and inevitably turns the tables on me with unbridled glee ("I have your picture over my bed," he said once after an embarrassing poster had been released by the CBC, "right next to Boy George"); **Northrop Frye**, for reasons I've already explained in this journal; **Ray Hnatyshyn**, who, as minister of justice, replied to my questions on the Tories' censorship bill in impenetrable political circumlocution; **Mavis Gallant**, who, while good, if superstitious, company at the race-track, where I took her one day when she was writer-in-residence at the University of Toronto, in public conversation intimidates me almost as much as Northrop Frye; **Shirley MacLaine**, who is as solemnly wacky in person as in her books, and not much fun; and a woman named **Elvira Lount**, who came in one day, dressed like a Queen Secret gypsy, to promote a film about her great-uncle, Samuel Lount, and turned out to know somewhat less about him than I know about how to hit a golf ball straight.

But it's not working. The lists that are arriving in response to my solicitations are too serious. My guess is, two out of three of them just try to outdo me on the ten best things in the world, and at least half of *them* start, or finish, with the smell of home-made bread. That's okay; I might have included bread myself. But the wit and imagination that have made earlier contests work is, for some reason, missing.

I've done something wrong, I'm sure. But maybe I won't have to worry about *The Morningside Papers III*, after all. Maybe there won't be any.

2:30 p.m., the Ivan barber shop (formerly Mr. Ivan's), downtown Toronto: Carmen, the star of the Ivan, is one of the constants in my kaleidoscopic life. He has been cutting my hair for ten years, ever since CBC television stopped paying for it. He has seen me through four books, a lot of hangovers, love, separation, the birth of my granddaughter—of all my friends, he understood the pleasure best – and the evolution of my beard, which he refused to scoff at in its youth ("Looks nice, Mr. Peter"), and which he came into *Morningside* to shave off, live, on the radio, when the Edmonton Oilers won their first Stanley Cup. He is a stocky, smiling man, unfailingly good-natured, but respectful of his clients' private moods. If you want to admire the multi-hued parade of beauty that passes by his window on summer mornings, a symbol of the changing face of the city, he joins in your appre-ciation. But if you don't want to talk, he works silently. He wears a shirt and tie, uses steaming towels and pungent lotions, trims your beard with a straight razor, and rubs your shoulders with a vibrator. Every couple of weeks, I make an appointment with him. Ritualistically, I inquire after the progress of his daughters through school, deplore the state of the Maple Leafs or the Blue Jays, celebrate the triumphs of Italian soccer and Stephanie's latest achievements, and fall asleep under his ministrations. My hour with him–he will not be rushed–is an hour of peace.

Today, he has become a citizen. The customer before me, he says, has told him he'll have to cheer for Canada in the World Cup, and drink Canadian wine. He is beaming. "When you get home, tonigh', Mr. Peter," he says, "ask you girlfriend if you look any differen'. Tell her you hair-a cut by a Canadian."

4:30, 1255 Bay Street, sixth floor: I have made my way, as bidden by the brass, to CBC radio's annual reception for the press, where they will unveil our new plans and old tribulations. The problem today: no press. There is Pamela Young of *Maclean's*, the faithful Bill Musselwhite of the *Calgary Herald* (who, in a draw for the door-prize, wins a radio embedded in the model of a human head), someone from the CBC's own *Radio Guide*, and, so far as I can see, no one else. A heap of unclaimed name-tags fills a table by the door.

To one degree or another, this happens every year. The CBC brings in entertainment writers and critics from all over the country. Public relations people play them excerpts from the new television season, line up interviews with the stars, and generally show them a good time. Since the reporters are in town anyway, radio is allowed to throw its own affair, replete with wine and cheese, and, as today, nobody comes.

The bureaucrats, however, are here in force–about six for every reporter, by my count – and nearly all of them make speeches. Michael McEwen, vice-president of English radio, says our budget is fifteen per cent below last year's. Ron Solloway, head of FM, talks about new plans for music and entertainment. Harold Redekopp, the director of operations, talks about how important the CRTC hearings are. Alan Clark, head of sports (and the man who rode down the elevator with me last year, smiling coolly after I had suggested we get rid of his department), unveils plans for the Olympics, complete with a sales pitch from Mark Lee, the capable and earnest young host of *The Inside Track*, who will be going to Calgary. Arthur Black, the Saturday-morning man, does a very funny stand-up routine. Donna Logan welcomes all the new hosts–Enright of *As It Happens*, Danny Finkleman and Mary Ambrose of *Dayshift*, Linden MacIntyre of *Sunday Morning* –and, as she says, "one old one", me.

From under my fresh Carmen coiffure, I smile forlornly at my colleagues.

I THINK I UNDERSTAND what's happening here (or not happening), why there's so little response from the press to our plight and why programs such as *Morningside* are suffering without much public outcry.

My theory begins with the suggestion that Canadians don't love CBC television. We may love individual programs on it: *Hockey Night*, *The Journal*, *Beachcombers*, *The National*, *Anne of*

Green Gables–who knows, maybe *Reach for the Top*. We may even feel benign about it: a Gallup poll this spring said 59 per cent of us think the CBC is getting about the right amount of money and only 23 per cent think it gets too much. But for most of us, in an age when you can flick your way from channel to channel with a press of your thumb, the network, as an entity – even though some 85 per cent of us watch at least some of it every week–doesn't matter very much. It's just there, plugging along, and if the politicians want to trim some of the fat from its budget, well . . . just so long as they don't cut *Hockey Night*.

Radio is a different story. CBC radio doesn't reach nearly as many people as television does–about three million out of eighteen million anglophones, compared to television's remarkable 85 per cent. And not everyone who listens loves everything we do. *Morningside*, with a score of 81 per cent on what the bean-counters call their qualitative approval index, does very well (an area, as Christine Wilson pointed out in August, where we came second to the *Air Farce*). But others – *Prime Time*, if you must know–score as low as 50 per cent. Still, our listeners stay with us. Many of their radios, as the surveys make clear, seem welded to our frequencies. To a large extent, to be sure, this is just a function of the way people use the two media: they watch a television *program*; they tune to a radio *station* – or, in our case, a network. But it's also a reflection of the way they feel about this particular institution. We matter to them–in a way, I would argue, that the television network does not.

So why don't they scream when the cuts come down? Because, I am convinced, they know only in the vaguest way that we are *being* cut. In the minds of most Canadians, "CBC" means CBC television. CBC radio is a thing apart. At the corporation's head office, however, where the decisions about money are made, TV and radio are pieces of one body. When the flow of money slows down, the supply to all parts of that body is decreased proportionately. When it was evident near the end of a fiscal year a few seasons ago that television would fall ten million dollars short of its projected advertising revenue, radio, which carries no commercials, was forced to trim one million from its budget. And now, when the crunch is on, and regardless of where it is aimed, radio is getting caught.

What's the solution? Other than giving the whole corporation back the money that has been siphoned off by recent governments–or, as I'd be prepared to do, going back to first principles and redesigning the whole thing – I'm not sure. Maybe radio should be an independent corporation, independently funded. Maybe we should sell T-shirts.

I'm sorry, when I think about it, that I won't be talking to the CRTC this fall.

Wednesday, September 16, the studio, 8:20 a.m.: Our newly configurated business column still has a way to go. David Levi, an NDP activist who is also a successful investment broker in Vancouver, and Bruce Little, an assistant managing editor at the *Globe and Mail*, are both well-informed and responsible. But it's not the same as it used to be. Even Diane Francis, with no one to play off, is less than her usual self.

Like our national-affairs trio, the old column–Diane, Richard Osler, and Christopher Waddell–took a long time to form. When I came back to *Morningside* and wanted to get business on the air, I called my old cohort Sandy Ross, the former editor of *Canadian Business*. Sandy suggested Richard, who had been a newspaperman before he went into the securities business, to be his partner on the air. Richard was an instant hit: smart, a market insider, given to sprightly word-play and outbreaks of a delightful cackle. When Sandy left us for other pursuits, we kept his protégé. After several experiments, Chris Waddell, who has a PhD in political science and was then writing for *The Financial Post*, replaced Sandy. From time to time, we added Diane, whose work was appearing in the *Toronto Star*. She was too good not to make a regular. She is a self-made journalist, a tough and worldly ex-American who grew tired of being a housewife and flung herself into the world of business writing. She has a gift for radio, where she acts as a one-woman wrecking crew of pretence and skulduggery.

For more than three full seasons, that threesome was my Wednesday treat. They *liked* each other, and the chemistry made them greater than the sum of their parts. Over the years, the four of us developed a number of familial patterns – Richard explaining the stock market to me in terms of a hypothetical hockey-stick business, Chris, who has an appealing, Jimmy Stewart hesitancy on the air, solemnly bringing Diane's outspokenness down to earth. Richard remarried and took a brief hiatus in New-foundland, trying to write a book about the history of sealing. Diane and Chris both changed jobs, Chris going to the *Globe* and Diane, a rising star (and much in demand from other broad-casting outlets), accepting a lucrative offer to write for all three of *Maclean's*, *The Financial Post*, and the *Toronto Sun*. But every week, even when Richard was in Newfoundland or Diane was out peddling the splendid book she wrote on corporate concen-tration, they would check in with us. It was fun, and it almost always lifted me for the remainder of the day's program.

This morning, I had to work. Looking across at Diane, I could tell she missed her friends. So did I. Chris, at least, will be here on Friday, part of our new Ottawa column. I wonder if Richard, busy as he is, was listening.

4:30 p.m., the apartment: I cannot shake the emotion from a panel we taped earlier this afternoon.

The panel was composed of refugees. We assembled it in the light of the bill now before the House of Commons, which, among other things, would restrict the people we admit to Can-ada to those fleeing regimes we have formally defined as "repres-sive". In Toronto, and in some other studios, I talked to a widowed mother from Lebanon who had escaped to Greece, to a man from Chile who had been arrested by the state police, to a woman from Argentina, and to a beautiful twenty-two-year-old Somali who had been raped by Ethiopian soldiers before making her way to Canada, where, like the others I met this afternoon, she had arrived without a passport. As I understand the proposed new law, all of them would be turfed out of Canada.

I am troubled. I look up a history of my own great-great-grand-father to check some specifics, and, to make sure of my thesis, call an immigration lawyer at his office. Casimir Stanislaus Gzowski, I tell him, took part in an armed uprising in Poland in 1830. The insurrection was crushed, and, as one of the books I've checked puts it, "Poland sank into a worse state of subjection than before." Young Gzowski and his fellow rebels were incar-cerated in Austria. After two years of being shipped from prison camp to prison camp, they were sent to the new world. In Can-ada, before he helped to found the Queen's Plate, Gzowski built the first bridge across the Niagara River, paved Yonge Street, laid out much of the Grand Trunk Railway, and, for those and other contributions to his adopted land, was knighted by Queen Victoria. I ask the lawyer whether, in his opinion, if the proposed law of the 1980s had been in effect a century and a half ago, my ancestor would have been allowed in here.

No, he says, almost certainly not. Even if we had recognized that Poland was a repressive regime, we wouldn't have thought so of Austria–the "third country" (as Greece, for example, would have been the third country for the Lebanese woman I talked to this afternoon)–"and we would have sent him back there."

I write a brief essay on the point, and resolve to read it on the radio in the morning, when we play the tapes we made this afternoon.

Thursday, September 17: After passing a cross-examination by Gary Katz on the legal niceties of my argument, and calling Gloria at home to check it out with her ("Why not?" she says), I do.

Friday, September 18, the Briars, 2:30: Martin O'Malley arrives for golf. I still don't know anyone who loves the game and its ambience more than he does. His bag, and the pull-cart he totes it on, look like a floating golf boutique, festooned with gimmicks people have given him for Christmas or on birthdays: an umbrella, a telescopic ball-retriever to fish the ponds with, towels with funny sayings, and, his latest pride, a tube of plastic that dispenses tees. He has everything, I sometimes think, but a good swing.

Today, though, he is playing like Arnold Palmer. With rain threatening, Derek Halfyard, the Briars' appropriately named pro, has let us leapfrog the players who started earlier and start on the eleventh hole. O'Malley can do nothing wrong. His drives arc to the centre of the fairways and his irons burrow into the greens. Even his normally erratic putts seem to have eyes for the hole. By the time we have circled back to the clubhouse and are halfway through the first nine holes–our second–he has won six dollars from me, but his joy is so contagious I can only root him on. He is having, as they say, a career round. When the rain finally hits, he has only to keep up the pace to break, not 100, which is his usual target, but 90, for the first time in his life. He hoists his umbrella and trudges on.

I, on the other hand, am drenched. My shoes squish, my glasses are fogged, and the wheels of my pull-cart throw rooster-tails of spray. I suggest a detour to the cottage, where we can get outside a glass of Scotch while we wait for Gill and Karen to arrive for dinner and bridge.

He will have none of it. The course is empty now, except for us, but we plough on, two sodden figures in the grey September rain.

We finish the ninth, the seventeenth hole we have played, and, peeling the waterlogged glove from my hand and tucking my useless glasses into my shirt pocket, I head shivering for the shelter of the pro shop.

O'Malley will not hear of stopping. Borrowing an electric cart from Derek, he heads out by himself down the tenth fairway.

He needs a five to break 90.

Miraculously, he keeps his drive in play, and climbs onto his cart, squinting into the downpour. Derek and I peer after him through the rain that now washes the pro-shop windows in an unending stream.

He chooses an iron, takes a leisurely practice swing, addresses the ball, swings, and . . .

We cannot see where he has hit it.

He drives to the edge of the green, and dismounts.

"By God, I think he's on there," Derek says.

We watch as he lines up his putt. We see him make a stroke with his putter. Then he walks to the flag, pulls it out, and hunches again.

Moments later, he has replaced the flag and is roaring back down the fairway, the cart cutting a swath down the wet fairway like *Miss Supertest III* on the Detroit River.

"Par," he says, as he sloshes into the pro shop. "Eighty-eight. The best round of my life."

If it can happen to him, I think as I we head at last for the Scotch, some day it can happen to me.

Sunday, September 20, the Harbour Castle Hilton, Toronto, 12 o'clock: I have shown up too early for a lunch with Flora MacDonald, the minister of communications. Flora – I actually call her this – is in town for the Canadian film awards. Her office has called me and asked me to come down today for an off-the-record session. I didn't write down the time, and here I am, wandering the lobby.

I'm no fan of off-the-record talks. I think if someone in public office is going to tell a reporter something, he should be willing to put his name to it. I've never had to work in Ottawa, of course, where the off-the-record briefing has become an accepted part of life, and where, presumably, there are sources who'd lose their jobs if they let you put their names to what they told you. And, working as I now do, on the radio, I don't have to worry; what's said on the air is said. But I still think it would be a neater world if both reporters and their sources abolished the principle, and people had to stand by what they spread around.

The reason I'm here today, in any case, has more to do with what I want to say than with anything I might pick up. I am seeking the minister's ear. Since I won't be talking to the CRTC this fall, maybe I can say something useful over their heads.

I don't know what to make of Flora. When Marcel Masse, who turned out to be much better in his support of English cultural institutions than anyone had dared to hope, moved on last year, I had wished his portfolio would be given to David Crombie, or, failing that, to Barbara McDougall. Their coming from Toronto, I would like to think, had nothing to do with my support for them; in a cabinet that has far more than its share of yahoos and culture-bashers, they at least know what the CBC is, and understand its importance to the country. Even the bitter speech McDougall made last year about some of the CBC's transgressions showed she took it seriously.

Flora was a lukewarm alternative. She is familiar with the corporation, I know, and, I suspect, is sympathetic to it. The reason I feel free to call her by her first name is that on one of *90 Minutes Live*'s better nights she came back to her native Cape Breton to appear with the miners' chorus called Men of the Deeps, and, after her lively guest appearance, she was the life of the post-show party. In her heart, she's a nationalist. But I have reservations about her determination and doubts about her clout. She's still dilly-dallying over a new broadcast act, and it's hard to figure out why. Though she obviously agreed with many of the points in the Caplan-Sauvageau report of last spring, she doesn't seem to be willing to do anything about it.

I don't think there's any doubt that in these perilous times the

CBC suffers from having as its president a former Liberal cabinet minister who, I'm sure, does not have the Prime Minister's ear, who can't phone and say, "Hey, Brian, what are you guys *doing*?" Last year (and speaking of off the record), a delegation from the well-meaning group called Friends of Public Broadcasting suggested to Mr. Juneau that he resign. But he's stubborn. He seems to think stepping aside would be an admission of defeat. In the Prime Minister's Office, I assume, we are well represented by Dalton Camp, himself a Friend of Public Broadcasting as well, of course, as being a *Morningside* alumnus. But we need more. And, in cabinet, I have visions of Flora's colleagues listening impatiently to what she has to say, and then, with understanding smiles, getting on with the real business of the club.

Still, she's all we have. In the suite where the lunch is to be held, I find Malcolm Lester, the publisher, as confused about the time as I am. We locate some coffee and chat while other invitees drift in. A table is set for about thirty, but by the time the minister enters, trailing her public relations officer, fewer than a dozen of us have showed up: Denis Harvey and Knowlton Nash from CBC-TV, Mimi Fullerton from TV Ontario (Ms. Fullerton is also a member of the Caplan-Sauvageau committee who has this week, surprisingly, written to the *Globe and Mail* in defence of Flora's delay with the broadcast act), Gerry Caplan himself, the book publishers Jack Stoddart and Anna Porter, the film producer Peter O'Brian, and one or two others. We are almost, if not quite, outnumbered by Flora's functionaries, including one – "Hi, I'm Jeremy" – who turns out to be her deputy minister, Jeremy Kinsman, smart and articulate, who has arrived in a corduroy jacket and parked his tennis racquet by the door.

While Harbour Castle waiters unobtrusively pack away the unneeded chairs and assemble the remainder in a more intimate circle, Flora works the room. During my audience, and after the customary small talk, I bring the conversation around to the possibility of making radio an independent corporation. The minister seems intrigued, though it's hard to tell what's genuine interest and what's just normal politician's style. "I could fill your ear about what radio needs," I say. Before I can, she is whisked away to another supplicant.

We sit for lunch. The conversation bounces all over the lot. Led by Kinsman, there is some talk about whether the best way to get more Canadian content onto private television is "regulation or incentive". Unasked, but hoping I can turn the talk back to the CBC, I say, "Those bandits have already figured out a way to fulfil the regulations in the minimum way, and you can't have incentives for excellence." But no one seems to notice, and we are back to more generalities. Flora, obviously, wants to talk about copyright, which also falls under her jurisdiction, and on which she may bring down legislation in this session. On broadcasting, it's hard to pin her down.

As the lunch draws to a close, we are joined by Moses Znaimer, president of CITY-TV, resplendent in a broad-shouldered white jacket, fashionably too big for him. He hasn't missed much, even on the matter of private broadcasters' obligations. Years ago, when Moses was a rising star at the CBC, a self-possessed interviewer (I remember a piece he did on Gloria Steinem in which they chatted while she ironed) and a promising producer, we ran a piece in the *Star Weekly* suggesting that some day he'd be running the CBC. Instead, he's rich. That's too bad, if not for him. He'd have made an interesting president.

That's off the record, of course.

The apartment, 4 p.m.: I am still thinking of Moses' wealth (before he moved to CBC television, I remember him around the radio building, brand-new stop-watch around his neck), as I contemplate the disheartening developments in my own financial situation this fall. In one – this was just settled Friday, and the documents are before me now – the lawyer I have engaged to help me settle affairs with Jenny has told me that indeed the house belongs to her, lock, stock, and chimney. In the other, the income tax people have laid down the law. I've owed them a whacking amount of money since I filed my return last spring. Now it's time to pay up. The correspondence Gill has spread pointedly on the dining-room table uses the word "seize" in relation to my bank account.

Oh, dear.

There is justice here, of course. The house *is* Jenny's – I haven't lived in it for eleven years – and I've been foolhardy, as my lawyer quickly made clear, to imagine that when she sold it any part of the profits would accrue to me. And the tax *is* due. With television, books, speaking fees, and the occasional film narration on top of my considerable income from *Morningside*, I'm in a bracket I used to think was occupied only by people with roman numerals after their names. The fact that, aside from the cottage, I have so little to show for it (Johnny Canuck *might* have been a good horse) is no one's fault but mine.

Still, as I thumb through the ominous paper before me, it's hard not to think of what might have been.

IN 1967, WHEN I HAD BEEN FREE-LANCING for three years, the owners of the *Star Weekly*, a supplement of the *Toronto Star* which was also sold independently across the country, decided to give their financially ailing publication one last chance. On the advice of an American consultant, they planned to go after the market for "young adults" (the phrase was the consultant's). As editor, they picked me.

For almost exactly a year we had an exciting time. From the nucleus of people at the *Weekly*, from my old coterie at *Maclean's*, and from the pool of free-lance writers I knew from around the country, I put together a staff as capable as any, I think, that's ever run a Canadian magazine: Jack Batten, Harry Bruce, Bill Cameron, Margaret Daly, Sylvia Fraser, David Lewis Stein, and Walter Stewart, to mention some whose names may be familiar (Bill Cameron is a regular host of *The Journal* these days and Marg Daly an important producer at CBC radio, while books written by the other *Weekly* graduates in the years since would fill a fat library shelf). Added to their regular contributions were occasional pieces or columns by such luminaries as Fulford, Callwood, Berton, Richler, and Patrick Watson. In the period when the New Journalism of New York was bringing new life to magazine-writing, we flourished editorially, and on the newsstands. "Gzowski gzwings", said a poster the *Star* distributed around the ad agencies, and our confidence grew.

Then, one afternoon, Beland Honderich, the president of the company, asked me to meet him for a drink at Winston's after work. Honderich ordered a double manhattan, asked me what I wanted, and, when I said a martini, suggested I make mine a double too. Then he told me the *Weekly*'s days were over. The reasons boiled down to the fact that the magazine was still losing money and the *Star* needed capital to put up a new building. I received a year's salary (thirty-five thousand dollars) and a blow to my still-inflated ego – the gzwinging boy wonder was now thirty-four – that sent me reeling.

I reeled to England, on the Soviet ship *Aleksandr Pushkin*, dragging Jenny and the kids along, and walked the streets of London. There, after Jenny and the children had gone home (she left, she told me later, thinking I was so down she might never see me again), I began to think about starting a magazine of my own. In New York, Clay Felker, who had been running a supplement of the *Herald-Tribune* not unlike the *Weekly*, had suffered a similar blow at the hands of his owners. Instead of sulking, as I was, Felker had bought the title, and founded *New York* magazine, which, by the time I went to London, had become the showplace of the New Journalism. I resolved to make a similar try myself.

On my return, I went to see Felker. He received me graciously, warned me not to try to publish a copy of his magazine – "copy our *principle*," he said, "and make it apply to *your* city" – and wished me godspeed.

Meanwhile, Michael de Pencier and another well-born Torontonian, Phillip Greey, were renting a corner of an old warehouse at the corner of Church and Front streets, and looking around for publishing ventures to explore. On the letterhead of their first, a magazine called *Building Management*, Michael, whom I had met once or twice – Honour had been an editorial assistant at *Maclean's* before they were married – scribbled me a note. And that note, my children, was the beginning of Key Publishers, one of the most successful small publishing companies in Canada.

Much, of course, was to transpire before Key took shape. Michael and I pounded the pavements to try to raise enough money to start and never quite made it. In 1969, I went back to *Maclean's*, this time as editor, foundered again (I felt that the changes that needed to be made were profound but that I did not have a commitment from management solid enough to allow me to make them), and, after nine months, left. At the same time, I was beginning to become involved with CBC radio, hosting a weekly phone-out program called *Radio Free Friday*, and talking to Frame about the idea that was to become *This Country in the Morning*. In the meantime, a group of westerners, riding the success of the monthly *Vancouver Life*, moved in on the opportunity I thought I had seen, with the glossy *Toronto Life* –

with Barbara Amiel, I can't help remembering, on their first cover.

But in the fall of 1971, just after *This Country* went on the air, we heard that Michael Sifton, the newspaper heir who had bought *Toronto Life* from its Vancouver-based proprietors, was losing more money than he wanted to. De Pencier offered Sifton a dollar in cash and said we'd take none of the debts – the magazine was losing $750,000 a year – but all of the responsibility. I put up the last five thousand of the *Star*'s money, and called John Macfarlane at *Maclean's* and a good art director named Ken Rodmell. Michael called some other friends, as well as his banker, and we were in business.

Now, sixteen years later, the company Michael heads (it's called Key after a hotel magazine he cagily bought to help finance *Toronto Life* through its adolescence) owns magazines all over the country, with significant pieces of *Canadian Business, Your Money, Quill and Quire*, and a whole newsstand full of similar ventures. The office in the corner of the old warehouse at Front and Church – now one of trendiest addresses in Toronto (this condominium is just across the street, in fact) – fills the whole building and part of its neighbours, and the company, with more than a hundred and fifty employees, turns over about $20 million a year. Michael has made himself much richer than he was born, and a lot of other people are well off too. For the last few years, by coincidence, the publisher of *Toronto Life*, reporting to Michael, has been Peter Herrndorf, who joined Key when his own career at the CBC seemed, for a while at least, to have run out of steam.

Me? I was a sort of editorial godfather in the early years, applying some of the lessons of the other places I'd worked, and sometimes, between full-time editors, writing titles and assigning stories from my kitchen table. I've been a director of the company from the outset as well, and taken part with Michael in some other ventures. But, except perhaps that *Toronto Life* is a fulfilment of Clay Felker's advice to me, and is as much about money and power and sushi bars as *New York* is about survival – "copy our *principles*" – it owes its current prosperity to other minds than mine.

If I'd kept the stock the *Star*'s five thousand dollars bought, and excercised the options that have been available to me over the years I'd have made . . . Oh well, if I sell what I do have left, I can get the tax people off my back.

I wasn't meant to be rich, anyway. And I'd far, far rather be friends with Jenny than squabble over the real estate that is, whatever my wistful fantasies, rightfully hers.

"I recognize Peter, but who's the guy
with the mike?" With a copy in his free
hand, Wayne Gretzky helps to
celebrate the publication of
The Game of Our Lives.

Jack McClelland at my golf tournament, 1987.

CHAPTER TWELVE

Missing the fun of This Country in the
Morning . . . *The trouble with formulae . . .
The Great M & S book launch – without
M . . . Promoting "a stinkerooni" . . .
The column that had no bite . . .
Jack McClelland to the rescue . . .
Wayne Gretzky's book idea . . . Our Hughie
hits the jackpot*

Monday, September 21, the Morningside *office, noon:* Dave Amer calls me aside. "I'm not having any *fun*," he says. "I'm worried about it."

Amer and I, the old guys around *Morningside*, met just after Jenny and I moved back from Montreal. Our families lived near each other, and our first-born sons, then in short pants, played together. When Frame was building the unit for *This Country in the Morning*, I recommended Dave, who had a background in commercial radio and an imaginative and eclectic taste in music, and he has been around the CBC, more or less, ever since.

He is a big, handsome, gentle man, with thick glasses and a soft, deep voice. He is not, as they say, work-oriented. Though he's ventured into production a couple of times, he has preferred to work in the background. When I came back to radio, he had been taking occasional free-lance jobs at the CBC but generally enjoying a kind of Travis McGee existence – the part where McGee takes his retirement in advance, in instalments. I persuaded Nicole to bring bim back, but his contract with *Morn-*

ingside is for part-time service only, and he does not come in to the office until the story meetings are over. For all his casual attitude, though, he has an intense pride in his work, and a keen ear for radio. We are – as our sons remain – friends, and when I want to talk about how things are going, I often seek his counsel.

I know, now, what he means by not having fun.

This Country in the Morning, where I worked from 1971 until 1974, was almost *all* fun – even the serious parts. We decided, the day before, what subjects we would explore the next morning, and which guests we'd interview. The producers would talk whomever they could into coming into the studio, and make appointments with the rest for phone calls. Only occasionally did we try anything as difficult as a line-link with another city; until we started going out on the road ourselves, nearly everyone we talked to, except by phone, was in Toronto. We seldom pre-taped. Often, we would go home at night with holes in the show, and fill them in the morning with phone calls to people we heard about on that day's news.

We pretty well made things up as we went along. There was no such thing as a studio director, the role Gary Katz now fills. At eight o'clock, Frame would stick Amer's stack of records under his arm, I'd pick up a file of letters and scribbled notes, and we'd amble down to the studio. I would ad-lib an introduction to the first guest and off we'd go, loose and relaxed on some days, frantic and excited on others, but always open to whatever might happen.

Now, by contrast, everything is planned. The office is dominated by a big white plastic board, where the week is plotted out like a military campaign, in red grease pencil when an item is being worked on – still in pink, as we say – in black when it's confirmed. A length of time is written beside an item as soon as it's conceived – we have discussions about whether a piece should be twelve minutes or thirteen – and, to a remarkable degree, we stick to it. Intros, extros, billboards, links – everything that can be written in advance is written, and, in the mornings, Janet Russell reads it all over to time it to the second. Amer's music is all slotted in advance as well, two minutes of Mozart here, a clever comment by a folk-song there, and Janet plays that every morning, too, stop-watch in hand, to make sure the times on the record jackets are not a second or two off. On rare occasions, items are still in pink when I go home, but I know that when I arrive in the morning they'll be black, and that the files for them –the greens–will be complete. Gloria, in Frame's old job, hardly ever comes to the studio. She arrives at work just as the program begins, turns on her office monitor, and begins making phone calls, answering memos from the bureaucracy and planning strategy and tactics for the future. *That* day's edition has been taken care of long ago.

Over all, I am convinced, we have a much better program than *This Country* used to be, less self-indulgent, wider-ranging, much more appropriate to the cool 1980s than our old, loose ways would have been. But progress has had its price. With the decline in spontaneity, there is less sense of adventure, and almost none of event. Musicians (who, because of budget, are almost always on record now) seldom break into song together, as Mimi Farina, Sylvia Tyson, and Maureen Forrester once did in response to my challenge (they sang "Amazing Grace"). We don't skin muskrats live on the air any more or surprise Bill Mitchell from behind the library shelves in High River, or send musical groups out on scavenger hunts. (The Canadian Brass, I remember, who were asked for a "live, furry creature", brought in Angelo Mosca.)

As well, with the substitution of studio links for our impromptu phone calls, we have tended to have fewer of what broadcasters call "real people" on the air, talking from their homes, as I remember a lawyer from Skidegate once rambling on about octopuses in the Queen Charlottes, or Elizabeth Webster, the wife of the actor Hugh Webster, describing her life in a converted caboose. We are reluctant now (too much so, in my old-fashioned view) to call people who have been at the heart of a story–"principals", in the jargon–and instead rely on reporters, observers, and, alas, experts, who are willing to come into the studio. (As A. J. Liebling said, a reporter is someone who goes somewhere and tells you what's going on; an observer goes somewhere and tells you what's going on and what he thinks about it; and an expert doesn't go anywhere and tells you what it means. Which is at least more subtle than something I once heard in the north, where, I was told, an expert is "some bastard from the south, with slides".)

Dave Amer knows all this as well as I, and neither of us, for all our nostalgia, would return to the slapdash days of yesteryear.

The trouble we sense–the melancholy Dave is feeling–arises not from the format but from the way it's being applied. The danger in a pattern as useful as the one that has evolved at *Morningside* is that it can become a goal unto itself. Because it works, people defer to it. Instead of following their instincts to their natural conclusion – I remember Frame one February morning saying, "I'm horny," and launching into a telephone search for signs of spring–they bend them to fit what has gone before. "Could this be a jury?" they ask at story meetings now, or "Could we make a *Morningside Drive* out of . . . ?" They are trying to tailor the content to fit the form instead of, as it should be, the other way around.

With so many new producers struggling to learn the ropes this fall, we are particularly susceptible to this syndrome. The new kids–forgivably–are too tense. They're like students transferred to a new school trying to memorize the rules. At the story meeting that just ended, during which we tried to put something together on the last days of the baseball season, and were tossing out names, someone said we needed "a woman from the west".

They should relax. If I had two rules to offer aspiring journalists, the first would be: follow your own curiosity – it's the greatest guide you have. The second would be: have fun. But I don't think that would be necessary if you obeyed the first one to the fullest.

6:30, The Art Gallery of Ontario: The season's authors from McClelland and Stewart, the critics, columnists, and reporters who will discuss them, the factotums from M & S, and a variety of other literary figures and hangers-on and traders in gossip have taken over a couple of rooms to launch the company's impressive list of fall books. Lots of drinks, lots of canapés, distributed by uniformed waitresses moving among the Group of Seven, lots of speeches. Especially speeches. Avie Bennett speaks, and introduces Pierre Berton, who, he says "stands head and shoulders above other M & S authors." (In the crowd, Elsa Franklin, who handles Pierre's promotion, winces.) Berton speaks, listing some other people with promising books this year, including, unfortunately, Eddie Greenspan, who is published by Macmillan. Adrienne Clarkson, the president, speaks. Doug Gibson, of Douglas Gibson Books–an imprint he has put together at M & S after years as an editor and publisher at Macmillan–speaks. Roger Abbott of the *Air Farce*, without whose cheerful presence no gathering of the culturati is now complete, performs a lengthy monologue, carefully giving all the season's authors equal time. But it is all flat. In his remarks, Berton has reminisced briefly about Jack McClelland and the early days of Canadian book promotion (to pass the time in empty stores, Pierre said, "Farley and I used to sign each other's books"). But, with that exception, the man who started it all is forgotten.

NOT BY ME.

In 1977, when I was finished with *90 Minutes Live*, I moved, with Jan Walter, the second of my Js, out of Toronto, to Rockwood, Ontario, just east of Guelph and not far from my boyhood turf in Galt. In the next five years, I put four books together, tried my hand at a newspaper column, took part in some publishing experiments with Michael de Pencier, did a few film narrations–God bless Bob Duncan, who called me one day when I was at my lowest and asked me to do the voice-over for his portrait of W. O. Mitchell–and picked up some other odd jobs that kept the mortgage paid and Jenny and the kids looked after. But there were long months when the phone didn't ring, and when I was certain my broadcasting days were over. I felt exiled, and there were more occasions of despair than I am comfortable admitting. If Jack McClelland hadn't been around, I'm not sure I would have survived.

Rockwood was an achingly pretty place to lick my wounds. From the road, a cul-de-sac off Highway 7, the house Jan and I bought appeared to be tiny. But out of sight at the back, it spilled down a hill and into a country kitchen, which had been modernized by two previous owners, two young men who had opened a restaurant in town–Ian and Sylvia as the locals called them–and a dining-room, whose casement window overlooked the rolling garden.

The house had been the quarry-master's cottage for a limestone pit, and its walls were thick, cool grey stone. Beyond the abandoned quarry were six hundred acres of evergreen Ontario wilderness, the Rockwood Conservation Area, through whose gorge ran the Eramosa River, dammed for a now ghostly mill. Across the highway was a property still known by the Dickensian name of its original owner, Squire Strange, and on the crest of the hill there was a cathedral-like stone barn, built for the squire nearly a century earlier by Sir Casimir Gzowski. I set up my typewriter in the casement of the dining-room and settled in.

I wasn't ready to write. I ground out an unsatisfactory piece for *Toronto Life* about my television experiences. But, after that, nothing would come. In the years away from print, my skills had atrophied. I fretted. I missed the kids. I worked on a suntan and, in Ian and Sylvia's old kitchen, cooked meals for Jan, who was commuting to her publishing job at Macmillan's in Toronto. I took up drinking again, and fell into a habit of watching daytime TV, sitting mindlessly for hours in front of *Jeopardy* and *Donahue* and wondering how I'd ever thought I might have made it in their midst.

When at last I began to stir, and with the help of Selena Dack, who'd been a producer on *90 Minutes Live* – help, hell, Selena did the dogwork while I made decisions – I put together an anthology called *Spring Tonic*. I thought I could recapture some of the appeal of my book about *This Country in the Morning*, which, after I left the radio program, gave me, first, an introduction to the joys and rigours of a triumphantly successful book tour and, second, a significant nest-egg for my years away from the air.

Spring Tonic bombed. A stinkerooni. The stores where, only four years earlier, I had been greeted by throngs of Visa-waving fans were empty. I passed long hours behind tall stacks of my unwanted work, trying to figure out who was more embarrassed, the booksellers for me or I for them. "I can't understand it," they would say. "I guess the weather's too nice for people to come to bookstores." Or, in other cities: "Sorry it's raining; it's keeping everyone at home." Out of sympathy, the storekeepers would bring me what were transparently copies for their own families, and ask me to sign them, while I, from the motivation that had made me the owner of a homburg hat in Timmins twenty-four years earlier, would buy the works of other authors from their stock. In the end, Mel Hurtig, my publisher (as he had been of the *This Country* book), sold eight thousand of the twenty-five thousand copies he had printed, the bookstores had an instant remainder, and I had an indelible lesson in the perils of trying to capitalize on vanished fame.

When the news of my departure from television had hit the

papers, Martin Goodman had called from the *Star* to say I could have there "any job you want – except mine". After the first summer in Rockwood, I was ready, and though Marty had moved from the editorship into the president's office – he is dead now, of pancreatic cancer, which he fought with terrible gallantry – he kept his word. I started a column that fall.

At first, the stiffness of my writing muscles showed; I would sit for hours staring at blank paper, and, when I finally typed something, it was hesitant and demure, too cute by half. When my muscles did limber up, I had trouble finding the energy to dig up zingy stories of my own or the confidence to take strong positions on other people's. Never an opinion-monger at the best of times, I was, with the sting of what had been said about *me* still ringing in my ears, too timid to issue proclamations, or to be nasty when nastiness was called for. I wrote, instead, little features – profiles, essays, odds and ends. Some were fine, but as an *oeuvre* they had no bite.

I looked up once again what Pierre Berton had done with a similar opportunity in the same paper twenty years earlier and, rather than being inspired by his prodigious output and creative leaps, felt overawed. I knew that even if I had the ability to rise to Berton's standards (which I didn't), I didn't have the heart. The *Star* had put me at the top of their columnists' pay scale, and given me a private office and the services of a researcher. But the salary was half what I'd been making on television, and, though I had no desire to return to that world, I missed its perks. I had chosen the wrong time in my life, and the wrong medium, to start again. After six months – a hundred columns – I packed it in. No one at the *Star* seemed to mind.

Not long after that, I heard from Jack, whom I had been acquainted with since my days at *Maclean's*. Like everyone else who knew him – surely all the writing world – I revelled in his company. I had never approached him with a book idea, though, at least partly because everyone else I knew had, and, indeed, I had taken some pride in having my two anthologies published by someone else – especially someone outside Toronto. But the *Spring Tonic* debacle had cooled Mel Hurtig's ardour for my sale-ability (in the book business, as they say, you are only as hot as your last work), and, after the *Star*, I was a free agent. Jack offered me a chance to write the story of two young people – a brother-and sister-in-law – from Estevan, Saskatchewan, who had been in a plane crash in the mountains of Idaho, and, to survive, had eaten the flesh of the girl's father. I had seen the story in the newspapers, and had thought little of it, except, perhaps, that it would make a book some day. But Jack, who had been approached by the couple's lawyer, dangled visions of best-seller lists and movie rights. I signed up, and took off for the prairie.

In spite of the detailed diaries the couple had kept on the mountain and the help of an excellent researcher, I had a hard time getting going. I holed up in a house in Estevan and, between game shows on the television and trips to the liquor store, paced the floor. I drove a young reporter from the Regina *Leader-Post* over to Oxbow to visit the museum they have made there for Ralph Allen in his father's old railway station, and grew depressed when she didn't know why I was so moved. But the visit stirred me from my lethargy. I went back to Ontario, and, at last, began to write.

When I finished, I drove the manuscript to Jack's house in Toronto. I found him shirtless in the living-room, watching a football game and nursing one of his ubiquitous vodkas on the rocks. But that night, the phone woke me from exhausted sleep in Rockwood, and Jack, who had picked the manuscript up when the football game was over and read right through, told me I had written "a hell of a book".

Other people, who know him better, have other stories of Jack McClelland, of his drinking exploits, his literary enthusiasms, his daring promotions, his headstrong business ways. And, I suppose, if I searched my own memory, I'd have others, too. But that's the one that sums him up for me. His business was struggling then, as it had been for years, and he could never shake the financial pressure. When I'd been hunkered down in Estevan, he had flown out to complete the details of the deal, by scheduled airline to Regina, and then, with typical panache, by charter. As I drove him back to Regina, he sat in the front seat, a bottle of vodka open in his lap, and said, among other things, that each day he went to work he faced the prospect of making three thousand dollars just to service the company's debt. He was down.

Yet after all the literary titans he had published over the years, many of whom would not have achieved their reputations without his gambler's instincts or his cheerleader's support, he would still take a minor manuscript by a difficult author up to bed with him and, when he was finished, call to say what the author needed to hear.

The Sacrament, as we called it (the young couple had seen religious significance in being sustained by the flesh of the girl's dead father), staked me – emotionally as well as financially – to a book on hockey. I had thought for a long time that the kind of serious writing Americans had enjoyed on baseball might be matched on our national sport, and, having loved playing hockey as a kid and written about its heroes for magazines, I thought I might give it a try. I went to Moscow with a team of pros, and hung around various hockey arenas, looking for an angle. The breakthrough came when I called Wayne Gretzky, whom I had interviewed as a thirteen-year-old phenom on *This Country* and made a short film about for *90 Minutes Live*. We played golf, these being still the days when Wayne could go out in public without being mobbed, and he suggested I follow his team, the Edmonton Oilers. For much of the next year, I did. When, in the spring of 1981, they unexpectedly caught fire in the playoffs and many of them superstitiously allowed their beards to grow, so did I, and, with the exception of the spring a couple of years later when my friend Carmen helped me fulfil a pledge to them on the occasion of their first Stanley Cup – and I had to accept my first honorary degree with bare jowls – I have not shaved it since.

I drove the first draft of the book that came out of those adventures into Toronto too. That night, however, I waited in vain for the phone to ring. Two days later, when Jack finally did call, it was to say he had reservations: though he couldn't quite put his finger on the reasons, the book just wasn't working for him – *some good material*, I couldn't help thinking, *much of it well handled*. He asked me to name my own editor. I chose Gary Ross, who had worked on an excerpt I published in *Saturday Night*. With Gary's help, I set out to do a repair job, and the result of that work, *The Game of Our Lives*, became by far the most successful of my writings, a critical hit, albeit mostly on the sports pages, and a healthy best-seller – though, to be fair, seven thousand of its twenty-five thousand copies were snapped up by Peter Pocklington as trinkets for his season's-ticket subscribers. While there are passages in it I would rewrite now if I could – I wish, for instance, I had probed more deeply into the boyhood of the three Finnish players on the team – for what success it achieved,

I am grateful, again, to Jack. Though no one, I'm sure, has meant to slight him in the speeches they have made, I wish he were here.

Tuesday, September 22, Morningside, *6 a.m.:* Katz looks up from his paper. "Did you see who's won the lottery?"

"No," I say. "The *Globe* doesn't stoop to such inconsequential stories."

"Someone named Hugh Garber," Katz says. "Three point two million dollars. Do you suppose that's *our* Hughie?" I say I have no idea, but it's possible. Our Hughie is a restaurateur, a gregarious and clever bachelor who sometimes takes part in panels when we need a touch of downtown Toronto. Most recently, he's talked about diets. He was good. If he's won the lottery, maybe we can get some insights into how that feels.

7 a.m.: Katz calls Hughie's number. It's been disconnected.

"It's him," he says.

7:05: We call Patsy Pehlman at home for permission to change the line-up, and start waking up producers until we can find someone willing to go and knock on Hughie's door.

"I'd go myself if there was time," Patsy says. "He isn't married, is he?"

9:30: Hughie Garber arrives for an interview, still rubbing the sleep from his eyes.

"I worked late," he says. "I have no plans to quit my job."

While he was on his way, I have rummaged around my office and found a sweatshirt he once presented me, advertising his restaurant.

He doesn't seem to notice I am wearing it.

Thursday, September 24, Morningside: The listeners' lists are getting better: less fresh bread, more fresh ideas. I ought to know better by now than to underestimate the brains of this audience. Maybe there will be a *Morningside Papers III* after all.

If I stay long enough on the air, that is.

My daughter the radio producer: Alison in Newfoundland.

CHAPTER THIRTEEN

*Sleeping in in Newfoundland . . . The
critical-mass theory of regional culture . . .
Alison the CFA . . . The diplomatic Charles
Ritchie . . . The long road back to radio . . .
Don Harron's special genius . . . Krista: a
tragedy . . . A casual encounter with
Barbara Frum . . . The Speech – not bad,
eh? . . . A review: lousy*

*Friday, September 25, the CBC radio offices, St. John's. 8:30 a.m.
– and still, since we're on Newfoundland time – more than an hour
before we go on the air:* Last night was my first speech of the
season, and today, therefore, is the first road show. We started
doing this a few years ago, when I was invited to Halifax to speak
at a money-raising dinner for the Nova Scotia College of Art.
That one cost me a few dollars, as it turned out. I took no fee
for the dinner, and, indeed, bought a painting in the auction
that followed. But my expenses were paid, and we did *Morningside*
the next day from the CBC's Halifax studio. Now I do get a fee
– an outrageous one. I have an agent in Vancouver who fields
all the requests (I get about three a week) and, when I agree to
accept one, does the talking about money. I think the fee now,
on top of my expenses, is $3,500 (they've just raised it again),
of which the agency takes twenty-five per cent. But the real
benefit for me and the program – though I don't turn the money
down – is that with our hundred-dollar-a-week travel budget, the

expense money makes it possible to move the program – or my part of it – outside Toronto.

It's a long way from the old travelling circus of *This Country in the Morning*, when we settled into, for instance, Newfoundland for a week, or took off for the arctic with Angèle Arsenault, Bob Ruzicka, and all three of Ryan's Fancy, chartering buses and filling gym floors with our sleeping-bags. Now, it's just me, Gary, and, sometimes, one other person – today, Nancy Watson, who studied at Memorial University.

As always on these trips, we have arrived the night before, and, while I made my speech, Gary checked out the studio with the local technicians. This morning, on the air, we'll carry on with our regular national features. The Ottawa column (which is shaping up strongly, by the way, with Deborah McGregor, Chris Waddell, and Mike Duffy) will lead off, and, from Edmonton, we have the last in a series we've been running from *The Illustrated History of Canada*. But the rest of the program will have a regional flavour. As well as a chat with Father Des McGrath, who helped Richard Cashin found the fishermen's union, Nancy has lined up a panel on St. John's theatre and a reunion in the studio of the remarkable family of film-makers, actors, and writers, Michael, Andy, Michael Jr., and Cathy Jones.

It's no coincidence that there's so much of the performing arts in our choice of guests today. Theatre is strong in Newfoundland. A couple of years ago, when I was making a television film on Edythe Goodridge, who's now head of visual arts for the Canada Council, I attended a performance that began in the old union hall off Duckworth Street, and then took to the streets, with actors popping out of doorways and shouting from rooftops, a mock fire in an abandoned building, a fight in a parking lot, and an intermission in a pub, where the TV, miraculously, carried a newscast on videotape that was integral to the plot. Stratford, eat your heart out.

As well, of course, there are Codco, Rising Tide, amateur companies, the university, and even the Newfoundland region of the CBC, which has produced some remarkable television drama, not to mention the brilliant radio series *Oil in the Family*, which was killed by that other quaint Newfoundland custom, religious intolerance (they dared to deal with abortion).

Theatre here, in fact, is like writing in Saskatchewan or painting in Nova Scotia–a hotbed of excellence. I'm not always sure
how these things arise. There's the Newfoundland tradition of
story-telling, of course, and on the Saskatchewan prairie, as Bill
Mitchell has reflected, kids grow up lonely and develop writerly
imaginations. But why then the visual arts in Nova Scotia–or,
for that matter, the strength of the theatre I saw at the Edmonton
Fringe this summer?

Who cares? The point is that, sometimes through tradition,
sometimes through the inspiration of one person or one group,
and often through carefully nurtured subsidy, in each of these
cases and in some others that would also bear study–I can't help
thinking of the environment that created the Winnipeg Folk
Festival, for example–a regional arts community has achieved a
vibrant critical mass. In their sum, these regional cultures are at
least as important as what we strive for so ardently on a national
scale–may even *be* what we're not sure we yet have. Whether
they are or not, reflecting them is part of *Morningside*'s job, and
one of the benefits of trips such as this; the theatrical richness
of St. John's will come through more clearly with me in a studio
surrounded by the people who make it than it could by satellite
link.

I don't mind sleeping in, either. The alarm didn't have to go
off this morning until nearly six. When we originate from Vancouver, I have to get up at a quarter past one. It's like going to
the police desk for the *Tely* used to be, except in B.C., when I
finish – it's 8 a.m. there when it's 12:30 in Newfoundland – I
could have the whole day to play golf.

IT'S AN UNCUSTOMARY DELIGHT to have Alison around while I
work in the morning. Her job keeps her glued to the phone in
the office next door, but from time to time she sticks her head
in to see how we're doing. She seems to be fitting in okay here,
even though, she tells me, a lot of people still ask, "Are you
related to . . . ?" She's having a hard time meeting Newfound-
landers, she says. For all their warmth (she's still not used to
being called "my dear" when she shops), they're reserved about
asking her into their homes. Her best friends in St. John's, in
fact, are all also CFAs–Come-From-Aways–including someone

I introduced her to by mail, Mark Leier, a young history student who has written to me at *Morningside* from all over the country and is now doing an MA at Memorial.

It's Alison's birthday, by coincidence. She's twenty-eight. I'm very proud of her, and enjoy her ear for the telling line. She told me this morning of a young man from St. John's who had just returned from a trip to Toronto. "There's nothing to do there," he had reported. "Everybody's working."

MY SPEECH last night, by the way, was at Memorial. I did it for less than my full fee, partly because I wanted to see Alison. As always, the people who invited me had wanted a title in advance, so they could advertise the event. Somehow, we settled on "Is Canada worth saving?" I said it was, and managed to stretch the reasons why to last an hour.

Sunday, September 27, the cottage: A meeting of Hedge Road Press over lunch. Thanks to Peter Sibbald-Brown, the Ridley book is close to being on schedule, though my introduction still needs work. Some other projects we've been thinking of are falling by the wayside, mostly due to my inattention. Peter and Lucinda are understanding and supportive, but if this company is going to be my retirement facility, I'd better put more work into it.

How I wish there was more time.

Tuesday, September 29, Morningside, *the second hour:* I do one of the season's least satisfactory interviews – so far – with Lefolii, about his book. Friends are always hard for me to do – see Richler, Mordecai, among my list of hardest interviews – and talking about *Claims,* which I've followed from the sidelines since its inception, is particularly difficult. Fortunately, Ken's own professionalism takes over; at the first opportunity he grabs the initiative and shapes the piece himself, as I've been known to do on the book tour myself when I run into an interviewer who doesn't know his stuff. This morning, the listener is served, but I feel like a dope.

2 p.m., Eastern Sound, a recording studio on Yorkville Avenue: I am to record the narration for a film on back injuries. The producers are a couple of young free-lancers, and their whole operation, at least as far as I've been concerned, leaves any similar work I've done at the CBC in the shadows. They've sent me a draft of their script and a video of their rough-cut to study at home, and asked me to make any changes in the script that will make me comfortable. When I show up, they pour me a cup of coffee, and sit me in a plush chair in front of a state-of-the-art microphone. Their film runs on a TV screen while we lay down the voice-track. It's all smooth as cream, and when we finish, an hour later, they hand me a cheque for $2,500.

I should get out of the CBC and do this for a living.

Except if I didn't do *Morningside*, who'd want me?

Wednesday, September 30, the Morningside *studio, 1 p.m.:* Charles Ritchie has come by to talk about the latest in the engaging series of diaries and reminiscences he has published of his life before, during, and after his distinguished diplomatic career. He is, as always, charming. It occurs to me, as we finish, that he may still be taking notes, and that, since I too have joined the ranks of the diarists, our encounter today may some day be published in two different versions. The concept amuses me, and as Mr. Ritchie leaves the studio, I decide to explore it.

"Are you still keeping a diary?" I ask.

"Why, yes," he says. "But it won't be published for a long time." (The book we have discussed today contains impressions of his childhood nearly seventy years ago in Nova Scotia.)

"And then I suppose it *might* say you were on *Morningside* with, ahem, Peter Gzowski."

"It would record it as a very pleasant experience."

"Ah, Mr. Ritchie," I say. "Ever the diplomat."

As he exits, smiling, Shelagh Rogers comes in to record some letters. (*State of the Arts*, the radio program she hosts, is jealous of her time, and we often pre-tape our readings from the mail to accommodate its producers.) I comment on Charles Ritchie's tact.

"I know what you mean," Shelagh says. "I taped a piece with him earlier for *State of the Arts*. He told me, 'You have a delightful program. I watch it whenever I get a chance.'"

Later the same afternoon: Step by step, Donna Logan's ambitious plans to put on *Morningside* before a hearing of the CRTC have been whittled down to a short medley of taped excerpts, for which I am to write and record the linking narration. The tapes have been prepared by Tom MacDonnell, a producer who has worked with *Morningside* before. They're fine. But where I once thought I'd have a chance to speak my mind, I now get four and a half minutes of links.

Now, Gloria relays a request from Bay Street that I have my script done by tomorrow.

"I'm not sure what I should say," I tell her.

"They want you to say anything you want."

"In four and a half minutes?"

"Yes, well . . ."

She laughs. She has worked at the CBC a long time.

And still later: Frame, to whom I go to get some bitching off my chest, tells me he's thinking of offering Gloria a job as his deputy. He needs her, he says. He wants to shake up some other programs. He wants strong people around him.

And who would replace Gloria at *Morningside?*

"I have no idea," he says. "But I'll promise you I won't take her away until we have a replacement we're all satisfied with."

Including me?

"Of course."

I'm not as shaken as I might have thought I'd be. My own restlessness this fall has been at least equalled, I have sensed, by Gloria's.

Who could blame her? This is her fourth year as executive producer. She put her own stamp on the unit long ago, and whipped it into the shape she wanted. With the arrival of Patsy Pehlman, last season, she finally found the person she, and Nicole before her, had been seeking for years, a strong editor who could handle day-to-day content. Now, except for the office politics and the routine administrative tasks – and there can be little satisfaction in those for her – the program virtually runs itself, and, indeed, there are days when she seems more interested in her life outside the office than in the contents of *Morningside*. She continues to work back-breaking hours, and the qualities we all admire in her, of openness and fairness and a willingness to face the tough parts of her job, remain constant. But I have been wondering this fall if her heart is still in it. She needs a new challenge.

Right now, however, I can't think of who on earth could replace her. As both Frame and I know well, not all the changes that have occurred at *Morningside* or its predecessors over the years have been easy.

THE FIRST HOST of *This Country in the Morning*, after Frame and I left, and despite our urgent suggestion that the program move in a new direction, was Michael Enright, who had been writing editorials for the *Globe and Mail*. Michael, a first-rate journalist who has a voice not unlike mine as well as a similar background, suffered from unfair comparisons and from producers who lacked Frame's vision. He had an unhappy year, and gave way to Judy LaMarsh, who had acquired a taste for radio by sitting in for me toward the end of my tenure. Judy brought an Oriental rug to the studio and flashes of her potent personality to the air, but fought with her producers and never quite found her niche. She moved to Vancouver and a phone-in show in the private sector, handing the host's chair over to co-hosts, Maxine Crook, who had been a story producer and researcher, and Harry Brown, a staff announcer and long-time second banana on *As It Happens* to Barbara Frum. Maxine and Harry quickly proved one of Frame's favourite adages, that co-hosts, at least on radio, don't work–they talk to each other instead of to the listener. Like their predecessors, Maxine and Harry stepped down after a single season.

Still seeking a solution for its flagship daily program, the CBC turned to Krista Maeots as executive producer, and Krista had a flash of inspiration. As host of the program she named *Morningside*, she hired one of the authentic geniuses of Canadian culture, Don Harron, and the morning hours took on a new and distinct personality.

Krista was the child of Estonian parents. She had grown up in Calgary. She had long flaxen hair, eyes as blue as the Bow, a flawless, pale-cream complexion, a self-effacing smile that showed a flash of pink gum, and a quiet voice that belied a bull-dog's dedication to her work. She had gone to university at Queen's, in Ontario, where she had edited the daily *Journal* (the first woman editor since Charlotte Whitton), and been active in the politics of the time. She was, in no particular order, a Marxist, a nationalist, and a feminist. After graduation, she married the economist James Laxer, and, though she pursued a career in news-papers, she was active in the Waffle, the nationalist splinter group of the NDP.

When Frame hired her in 1971 for *This Country*, I had reser-vations about her political prejudices and her earnestness – "Radio humour is very labour-intensive," I remember her telling me once – but in both cases I was proven wrong. Her political ideas remained steadfast and her principles intractable. Once, when we were unexpectedly called back from Regina, with an urgent need to return to Toronto, she refused to ride in an air-plane while the baggage-handlers were on strike, and instead lum-bered back across the country by train, sitting up all night and thinking of the two small children she had left at home. But she was as fair-minded a producer as I have ever worked with (her political enemies stood, if anything, a better chance than her friends of having her help to get on the air), and an instinctive populist with an ear for the quirky, who brought us everyone from deserving country singers to theoreticians of the obscure. Outside Toronto in particular, she burrowed into the everyday world, and much of *This Country*'s success was due to her dogged pursuit of the unsung.

Her choice of Harron as host, as I say, was inspired. Don is as complex a man as walks the earth, a living proof of the theory that Canadians can express their humour only from behind masks. The corny, frequently naughty, malapropisms of his best-known character, Charlie Farquharson, the double entendres of his waspish Valerie Rosedale, the lightness of his lyrics for *Anne of Green Gables*, all disguise the workings of a restless and reflec-tive mind. Like many great comedians, he can be as melancholy in person as he is mirthful on the stage, but – as someone who worked with us both once pointed out to contrast him with me – he is, if anything, more pleasant away from the microphone than he is on it.

On the air, inevitably, he changed the CBC's morning sound. Though interviews (now more tightly structured) remained the program's core, they were supplemented and often overshadowed by Don's star turns: pun-filled monologues, readings from a diary written for him in the style of Samuel Pepys by the clever Ed Hailwood, a weekly cabaret of song parodies (also written by Hail-wood), skits with other actors. Where I and my successors had talked and questioned, Don performed–often brilliantly. Helped by the addition of affiliate stations to the string of stations the CBC owns and operates, the audience grew. But in my car, or as I procrastinated at my typewriter in Rockwood, I listened (between game shows) with a heavy heart. As much as I admired Don's glittering intelligence and inexhaustible energy, the essence of the program Frame and I had put together, it seemed to me, had been altered. Show business, however clever, was supplanting the kind of radio we had set out to do.

I was also, and rather less nobly, as jealous as a jilted lover. When I had left for television, Bill Armstrong, who was then head of radio (he is now an important vice-president in Ottawa) had warmly assured me there would always be a place for me in the service I was leaving. After the debacle of *90 Minutes Live*, and before I accepted Marty Goodman's offer at the *Star*, I called to take him up on his offer. Reality had chilled the warmth. There was no room; the schedule was full. Some time later, in an unguarded moment, Krista was to tell me that if she had known how unhappy I had been at *90 Minutes*, she might have offered me a chance to come back instead of hiring Don, but when I was free, and he had put his stamp on the program, it was too late.

Krista gave me a weekly spot doing sports, and an opportunity to sit in as host during one of Don's breaks. Neither part of the deal worked out. Clumsy with tape, pressed for time as I tried to fit my radio assignments among my newspaper columns, and in a constant tussle with Don and his puns for control of my fifteen-minute segments, I made an unsatisfactory – and unsatis-fied – commentator. As guest host, I was unable to bring off the performance aspects of the revised program. My part-time par-ticipation in the program was doomed.

Then, in the fall of 1978, a terrible thing happened. Krista Maeots committed suicide. No one knows why. She had been depressed for some time to the point of imbalance, unable to come to work. Her marriage had distintegrated. In a gesture that was typical of her in all but its horrible irrationality, she took a bus to Niagara Falls and jumped off the Rainbow Bridge. Her friends – all of us – were hurt and angry and confused. We held a memorial for her at a Unitarian church and carried on. Later, when Don won the ACTRA award he had long deserved, he raised his trophy in the air and thanked her in a breaking voice. She left her mark on the radio forever, as well as on all of us who knew her.

For me, her death had an extra dimension: she was my last link with the program I had helped to found.

IN THE SPRING OF 1981, with hopes of ending my exile from the radio now remote, I was beginning to turn my attention to a book on the race-track when I met Barbara Frum at a restaurant opening in Toronto.

I had known and admired Barbara since the 1960s, when June Callwood introduced us, but we were – and remain – more acquaintances than friends. When she saw me at the restaurant opening, though, her first question was, "How come I never hear you on the radio any more?"

"Nobody asks me."

"You're kidding," she said with the concerned expression the whole country now knows.

"I wish I were," I said.

"Would you sit in for me?"

"*Would* I?"

A few days later, just before she took off for her annual summer leave from radio–*The Journal* was still in the future–I had a call from Bob Campbell, the executive producer of *As It Happens*, with an offer of six weeks' work. I was back in the door.

About the same time, Nicole Bélanger took over as executive producer of what was now formally called *Don Harron's Morningside*. I had known Nicole before, too, though only slightly, a tough, bilingual former film and television producer from Ottawa. After my stint on *As It Happens*, she asked me to sit in for Don. I told her that I had tried before with unhappy results.

"Who cares?" she said. "The listeners still like you."

Later that season, when Don, exhausted, announced his retirement from the radio, Paul Kells, then head of current affairs, offered me a contract for two years. That the offer came from Kells, I knew, was protocol; I was Nicole's choice. I accepted almost before Kells finished spelling out the terms, and now, six years later, thanks to Nicole's determination–and, I am still convinced, thanks to a chance meeting with Barbara Frum–here I am.

Thursday, October 1, Morningside, *8:05 a.m.:* Our opening guests are three rollicking, gutsy singers, Taborah Johnson, Rickie York, and Diane Heatherington, all of whom, as they say, have paid their dues. They are currently the stars of *Bar Girls*, now running at the Bathurst Street Theatre, and in spite of being up late last night for a performance, they have arrived this morning–by stretch limo, if you please–in high spirits. I finished writing my billboards early and went to meet them at the door. Their presence has lifted my heart. I wish we could start every morning with such energy.

As the theme ends and Katz points his finger, I can't resist.

"Hello, my baby," I say. "Hello, my honey. Hello, my rag-time doll."

Tabby and Rickie and Diane, bless their hearts, applaud.

Friday, October 2, the apartment, 2:40 a.m.: Awake.

Insomnia.

Damn.

I don't know where this starts. I went to bed as early as I could last night – around 9:30, I think, with my usual allotment of books: a weighty tome on the Vancouver Stock Exchange for today, for next week Farley Mowat's biography of Dian Fossey, Scott Young's of Gordon Sinclair, Jack Hodgins' new novel, Marq de Villiers' study of his own Afrikaner background, a cookbook, the skiing autobiographies of *both* Ken Read and Steve Podborski (we'll do them together). Nibbled at a few of them before I drifted off, and there they are now, spread-eagled on the night-table, spines up, like butterflies collapsed around the glowing numerals of my radio-alarm.

2:44: Light a cigarette.

Ugh.

I get spells of this: Wake too late to go comfortably back to sleep and too early to go to work. It's one of the reasons for my constant tiredness. It's self-perpetuating, too. I'm so wiped when I finish at the office that I collapse into an unsatisfactory nap when I get home. Then, when Gill arrives for dinner, I'm grumpy and unwilling to go to bed on time.

No nap this afternoon, though. As soon as the program ends,

I'm off to Windsor for a speech. The sponsors are the members of the Essex County Conservation Authority. They're paying my full fee, and, with *The New Morningside Papers* hot off the press, I can take advantage of the trip to sign some copies at a bookstore tomorrow. But the real reason I'm doing the speech, I think – I agreed to it a long time ago – is tangled up with the honorary degree I was given in June. It wasn't quite a trade-off, but when I was invited to the convocation it was politely suggested that I might also address the conservation group in October. I agreed.

Hope there's some time to work on my speech notes when I get there.

LYNDA'S BEEN SICK. Nothing serious, but she's missed a couple of days and isn't expected in this morning, and her absence reminds me how much I rely on her. Today, on the way to the airport, I'll even have to do my own banking. As Gill would say, poor diddums.

I managed to keep the flattering passage I wrote about Lynda in the introduction to the new *Papers* away from her until the book arrived this week, and when she read it she came close to tears.

I still haven't done anything about finding her replacement.

The same day, the Holiday Inn, Windsor, Ontario, 3:30 p.m.: What the heck do the members of the Essex County Conservation Authority want to hear from me, anyway?

Thank goodness for The Speech. I say I don't do this – have one set script that I read from for various audiences–and, in fact, I work up something fresh each time, laboriously writing it out with a felt pen on legal-sized notepaper. But the truth is I have so many set pieces now that much of what I do for any audience consists of what Bill Mitchell used to call "recycling old tapes".

My collection of "I'm sorry's", which I entered in this journal after Martin O'Malley came to play golf in June, is the basis of one routine. I've been doing it for some time now, though the Frye variation is a fairly recent addition. Another standard is a replay of an old occasion on *This Country in the Morning* (I used it, in fact, in my introduction to that book) when someone – I can't remember who–used the phrase "the whole fucking thing" while we were going live to the Atlantic provinces. Attempting to shield the rest of the country's ears, we tried to fix the tape, but bleeped "thing" instead of "fucking", and, in The Speech, I now imagine someone hearing the result in his car and (a) saying to himself , "Did the CBC really say 'fucking'?–I guess they must have since they *underlined* it," and (b) wondering (you pause here as you tell this in public, and, of course, use a synonym for the word itself), "if they left the 'fucking' in . . . *what did they take out?*"

My most popular hit, I think–some day I may just travel the country taking requests–is one I call "not bad, eh?". I'm writing it out once again by hand now, hunched over a cup of room-service coffee before a window overlooking the Detroit River. It goes, as they say at the folk concerts, something like this:

Canadians don't brag. (I usually work up to this with a little aw-shucks patter about my latest undeserved honour–the story, for instance, of how the day after I received the Order of Canada in Ottawa and was trying to take it home, an airport security guard mistook the X-ray image of my medal for a deadly Ninja throwing star.) When Lester Pearson won the Nobel Peace Prize in 1957 for preventing World War III, he said, "Gee thanks." (A Pearsonian lisp embellishes this accurate story, but I am unable to master it.) When Paul Henderson scored his famous goal, he thanked his team-mates and, a few years later, joined the Christian ministry, at least partly out of gratitude. When, on *Morningside*, I told Robertson Davies that a few days earlier in an interview with me Anthony Burgess had suggested he, Davies, be given the Nobel prize for literature, he said, "Goodness gracious, I'm sure I don't deserve it."

A Canadian invented the telephone (I go on), though the Americans have claimed him, as they have claimed Lorne Greene, the Shakespearian actor, voice of doom, cowboy patriarch, and dog-food salesman. Two Canadians discovered insulin. Other Canadians invented Pablum, the variable-pitch propeller, the vacuum radio tube, the photo-finish camera, the snowmobile, five-pin bowling, basketball (though they are not tall enough to beat the people who stole it), Marquis wheat, Social Credit, the co-op movement, the slap-shot, the bloody Caesar, and Trivial Pursuit. While I was not present at any of their moments of triumph, I am reasonably certain that where a Greek would have said "Eureka!" or an American "Hot damn!", a Canadian would say only, "Not bad, eh?"

"Not bad, eh?" could well be our national motto. Instead, of course, it is *A mari usque ad mare*–from sea unto sea. But even that, surely, is an understatement. Even a cursory survey of the map of this lovely land shows that it reaches not two but three oceans–from sea unto sea unto sea . . . *A mari usque ad mare et cetera*. Still (I conclude this routine), two out of three is . . . (pause for effect) . . . not bad, eh?

On a good night, I can get the audience to join me in that final phrase, like Peter, Paul, and Mary doing "Blowin' in the Wind".

Midnight, the Windsor Press Club: I made it. I'm exhausted, but I've come here for a nightcap while I unwind. One of the troubles with ending a long day with a speaking engagement is that I'm still speeding when it's over, and all that awaits me at the hotel is the usual array of dirty movies. (Surely there's something ultimately Canadian, too, about charging six bucks to see a movie whose only appeal is its erotic passages – and then editing the sexy stuff out.)

Sue Prestedge, a rising star in broadcasting–this is one of the few press clubs left where you can still meet actual journalists among the flacks–asks me to give her regards to Peter Downie, whom she's been working with on *Midday*, and who has spent a terrible summer watching a beloved sister die of cancer. I say I will, and that I'm pleased to hear she shares my fondness for Peter.

She asks me how the speech went.

Not bad, I say.

Saturday, October 3, the Holiday Inn restaurant, Windsor, 9 a.m.:   I have read the *Globe* in my room, and to pass the time over a leisurely buffet breakfast while I await my autographing date at eleven, I pick up a fat copy of today's *Toronto Star*. The Blue Jays are playing across the river in Detroit–last night they lost their sixth game in a row and seem inexorably on their way to throwing away the pennant–and there are details to be studied. While I'm still on the sports section, I see Milt Dunnell and Jim Proudfoot of the *Star* come in to breakfast. Looking up from Milt's column, I wave a cheery hello. Idly, I turn to the entertainment section, my own old charge.

Holy cow! On page F3, a young man named Craig MacInnis (he's been writing the *Star*'s radio column this fall) has kicked the living daylights out of my brand-new book – and me. The headline says,

Gzowski toots his own horn
in latest literary knockoff

and the text goes on to lambaste me – "the eminence grise of avuncular radio journalism", as he dubs me – for what he calls "a sense of assurance bordering on the self-reverential".

Who, me?

What's worse, while he acknowledges that some of the letters show what he calls "genuine alacrity" (alacrity?–oh, never mind) "and passion", he damns much of the rest as "the precious purple passages of amateur Thoreaus and would-be Leacocks from sea to shining sea". The whole thing, he says, "may have been good radio, but as reading it is little more than a homely diary, frequently spoiled by the exasperating conceits of its editor (whose grinning puss is plastered on the front cover)."

My goodness!

I have another bite of blueberry muffin.

This hasn't happened before – not to the collections I've put together from the radio. By and large, they've been received as what they are, anthologies of surprisingly literate writing that reflect not only the program that engendered them but the country, and the people, they're from. Critics have celebrated them with, well, alacrity. Now I don't know what to make of Craig MacInnis's frontal assault. Some of his comments, as I examine them closely, are unfair to the point of distortion. He blasts me, for instance, for describing the CBC as "what many people claim . . . is the finest radio service in the world", which I did, but he has changed the tone of my comment by inserting ellipses where I had pointed out that almost no one who made this claim knew anything at all about the competition. He digs in deeply to find, in a light-hearted exchange of verse, an off-hand reference to an honorary degree, and implies I'm crowing about it. Having decided, in other words, that he likes neither *Morningside* nor me, he has worked hard to justify his position – and, I suppose, has succeeded. I ought to be either hurt or furious. To my own surprise, I'm unperturbed. I've been beaten up by bigger men than Craig, for better reasons.

South Shore Books, Windsor, 11 a.m.: If people have been reading the *Toronto Star*, they haven't been deterred. This is the beginning of my book tour, or at least a preface (it doesn't start in earnest until next month), and it augurs well. A steady stream of people comes to the table for a signature and a chat.

Though I sometimes pretend not to like autographings, they can (when they go well, that is, for I still remember the disasters of *Spring Tonic*) be my favourite part of flogging books. I meet people, often, with these *Papers*, my fellow authors, and, if there's time, exchange a word or two about the program. I pick up ideas for future interviews or feedback on things we've already done. Book-buyers bring me things, though I wish they wouldn't, since I never know what to do with them. Today, for instance, I get a clipping about an old labour story in Windsor, a couple of volumes of Dutch poetry, published (in English) by two charming women I'd love to have on the air some time, some home-made jam, and the offer of a pair of hand-knit socks from someone who must have heard my list of the best things in the world. I barter for the socks. The woman who made the offer is an unemployed secretary who says that, though she can't afford the book, she'd like to knit me a pair. I buy her a book on my Visa, and ask for blue and yellow.

The most pleasant surprise of all, though, is a young woman named Shelley Ambrose. She was a classmate of Alison's at Ryerson last year, and has been working as summer relief at the *Windsor Star*. Through the network, she's heard that I'll need a replacement for Lynda, and when I arrived here at the bookstore this morning, she was waiting for me with not only her résumé and a carefully prepared file of her clippings, but a cup of coffee. Without being asked, she has made herself useful at the autographing, ushering the customers to the table, opening books to be signed, and storing the treasures the visitors bring. She's eager, and pleasant to everyone. In an interlude between signings, I tell her how much of Lynda's work is thankless routine and ask her about her typing speed.

"The routine doesn't bother me," she says. "As for the typing, I'm not too fast now, but if I can get the job I'll take a course."

Hmmm.

Who says young people aren't enterprising?

Pearson Airport, Toronto, 4 p.m.: Gill meets me at the plane. I tell her I'm too tired to go to the cottage as we'd planned, and ask her forgiveness. I'll call Peter Sibbald-Brown when we get home, I say, and postpone our meeting on the Ridley book.

"Okay."

We cross to the parking garage. I tell her how impressed I am by Shelley, and review the long Friday, speech and all. She seems distant, as if I've done something wrong. As we get to her car, she can stand it no longer.

"My hair," she says.

"Your hair?"

"I've dyed it. It's red. You didn't even notice."

"Oh, well, I . . . uh . . . the lighting in the terminal . . . I . . . Why, yes, you have, haven't you? It looks . . . uh . . . it looks lovely."

Too little, too late. We go home.

Sunday, October 4, the apartment, 2 p.m.: I call Gloria at home to report on my trip, and, since I had to flee so quickly on Friday, get a rundown on tomorrow's program. She tells me that after much thought she has decided to turn down Frame's offer.

Good. But I still think that, sooner or later, we'll lose her.

Posing with Evelyn Hart for
Gzowski & Co., 1986.

On location for the same series: Two cameras prepare to shoot an
interview with film-director Sandy Wilson on the shores of
Lake Okanagan.

CHAPTER FOURTEEN

*Michael Enright and the league of old
codgers . . . Feeding the monster . . . The
scars of acne . . . A Thanksgiving Day essay
on Americans and Canadians . . . A visit
from Simon Reisman . . . Fighting Words
re-attempted . . . Glenn Sarty & Co. . . .
What you see on the screen is not reality . . .
it's television*

Friday, October 9, the cottage, mid-afternoon: It's cold and grey
outside the plate-glass windows. Golfers wrapped in bulky sweaters blow on their fingers before they swing, then hunt for their
balls among the fallen leaves. I stack my weekend reading on the
butternut table, and hitch up the food processor for cauliflower
soup. (A touch of curry powder is the secret, with thick cream.)
Gill will be here this evening; we'll watch a movie on the VCR
and build a fire.

My notes reflect a draining week. By this time in my career at
Morningside, I would have thought – after five years in any job –
either the rewards would have grown a lot larger, or the demands
would have grown easier. But, as I look back over the days I've
just survived, neither has been the case. This week there were
too many books (I've written that on two separate pages of the
diary Lynda gave me and whimpered about it at at least one story
meeting); too many meetings that last too long; too many pieces
I have to pull and tug at to bring off. The veteran producers are
doing yeoman work, although now that the pace has picked up

there have been no productions to match our cover story on housework or the jury on Baby Andrew. There's never enough time; we feed the monster every day and the next morning it's ravenous again.

The newer producers are trying hard, and Pat Pehlman is working extra hours to build their ideas into stories. But more mornings than not, I find myself rewriting the rookies' intros, reshaping their plans for questions. They still won't loosen up. They're still too earnest.

Michael Enright passed on an observation this week he picked up from Danny Finkleman.

"Earnestness," he said, "is stupidity that went to college."

I LIKE having Enright around. He's blossomed on *As It Happens* the way he never could at *This Country*. He's been through a lot since then, including the demise of *Quest* magazine, which he'd been editing with distinction. There was some grumbling when he took over as host of *As It Happens*. He'd been in the bureaucracy, as head of radio news. He was unhappy there and made no secret of it – I remember him once gleefully reporting that he had received a memo "for your eyes only" with copies to a hundred and four other people – and there was talk last spring that he'd bargained his way onto the air when Denis Trudeau went back to Montreal. But it's all history now. He has a bold radio presence, a nose for the best stories, and an untrammelled directness in his questions. He's Barbara McDougall's brother-in-law, of course (I wonder how that sits with the people who think the CBC is riddled with NDPers), and I happen to know he's fond of her, but that won't influence his editorial judgment; he's too tough. He has the same differences with the energetic young story-chasers of *As It Happens* that I do with the newcomers to *Morningside*, and it helps us both, I think, to compare notes. He's something of a curmudgeon. When I'm finished my morning broadcast and he's waiting to pre-tape his pieces for the evening, we jaw with each other in the hall, two old codgers cackling over the shortcomings of the young.

"I told them," Michael said one day this week, "that I'm not doing any more stories with parts-per-billion in them."

For all our complaints, though, both *As It Happens* and *Morningside* are strong these days where it matters, on the air. A few years ago – about the time Bob Campbell asked me to sit in for Barbara Frum – I was convinced that *As It Happens* was becoming the victim of its own success. Under Mark Starowicz, the brilliant young martinet who had been its executive producer (and whom I had worked with on *Radio Free Friday*), the format had been polished to perfection, and by the time Mark left to launch *The Journal* on television, its producers were almost able to do radio by numbers: a pound of Eritrean Liberation here, a murder trial in New Jersey there, all topped off by a sixty-pound pumpkin or a crusader for the hedgehogs of Reading. Hosts came and went. With rare exceptions – notably Elizabeth Gray – their idiosyncrasies disappeared in the editing along with their mistakes. So, often, did their personalities. Anyone, I used to think, could pick up a script without homework, and bark "What's the situation there?" into the long-distance air, or "How many dead?" Michael's gruff, well-informed professionalism, however, is coming through. He's sure of himself, confident enough to play. For all his grumpiness in the hall, he's having a good time, and *As It Happens* is getting better all the time.

Morningside? We *have* got better, I think, for each of the past five years. We still tinker with the departments and devices that have come to characterize the program since I moved into Harron's chair, and we ring changes in their formulae, but we know how to do them. They work.

And that's what worries me. We're running on momentum. A lot of the innovations of the past five years – not all, but a lot – came from my own renewed vigour when I returned, much of that the result of the mind having lain fallow in Rockwood. Now, I fear, those resources are spent. The producers, thank heavens, are feeding the monster with *specific* new ideas. Ken Wolff, for example, is masterminding a series of what we call "free-trade snapshots" – sector-by-sector examinations of what the massive deal the government is now negotiating will mean in real terms – and we've had other good pieces through the fall. But unless new and adventurous *concepts* come from somewhere, we'll recycle the old ones until we sound stale. Before that comes about, I should move on.

The trouble is, if I left *Morningside* now, I don't know what the hell I'd do instead. For all my whining and self doubts, I'm having the best years of my life. Especially considering the number of jobs and opportunities I've turned my back on or just peed away over the years – not to mention marriages and friendships –I'm a very lucky man to be where I am, doing what I do. Maybe the reason the rewards don't increase from year to year is that they're already as big as anyone could want.

ONE OF THE THINGS that's got me down, I can't help adding, is the ugly eruption on my cheek. It started to bloom about a week and a half ago, and by last Monday it was the size of a quarter, sore to the touch, the colour of a rotten plum.

Let's face it, it's a pimple. For most of my teenage years, I couldn't even bear to say that word and, to tell you the truth, I'm not too comfortable with it now. Pimple. The only good retort I can remember making in my youth – I won't put *this* in the Ridley book, where I'm trying to explain how that worthy school turned my life around–was when a student whose hairline was already receding called me "pus-face", and I said, "Okay, ––––, but when we're twenty my face will be clear and you'll be nearly bald." I was close to right, at least about my complexion. (I haven't kept in touch with ––––.) But in the years before it did clear up, acne–a word I could handle more easily–was the most important factor in my life. I don't think people who haven't had the real thing–I'm not talking a few zits here, I'm talking ugly, festering pustules that bleed through your basketball shirt and reduce your social life to Frank Yerby novels–have any idea what it does to a young person's soul, and if some psychiatrist were to try to explain my sometimes excessive need to be liked on the radio by peering into the history of my epidermis, well, he could have something. But I don't want to think about it. Perhaps the kindest thing ever done for me by J. R. Hamilton, the good man who was headmaster at Ridley in my time (though I won't put this in my celebratory book either), was to call me aside after physics class one day and offer to send me, at his own expense, to a dermatologist he knew in Toronto. But to do that, Hammy had to *mention* them–the pimples–and that, somehow, was the worst part. When no one talked about your skin, you could pretend you looked like everyone else.

Eventually, as I say, it did clear up. I actually had a date for the cadet ball in my graduating year, and by first-year university I was able to risk shaving with a safety razor. Now, thirty-odd years later, you can barely make out the pentimento on my chest and shoulders. But whoever it is who mercifully gives you a new skin every seven years doesn't do the same for your psyche. The thing on my cheek is sore to the touch in more ways than one.

On Monday, when it was at its worst, I went to a doctor. Good guy, about my age. Smiled with some sympathy when I told him how severe my teenage case had been. Looked me up and down with my shirt off. Said I had a "roseate" look–an "adult version of acne vulgaris".

"And what do I do?" I asked.

"Well," he said. "You could cut out coffee, tea, spicy foods, red wine, and cigarettes."

I looked at him.

"Or you could take tetracyclin."

I'm taking the tetracyclin.

It–the thing–is going down. Hope it disappears before I leave for the book tour next month.

Monday, October 12, the Morningside *office, early morning:* Thanksgiving–the real one, as opposed to the date in November when parades in New York and football games from the South fill our television screens.

When I say things like that, I know, I'm often accused of being anti-American. It's an empty charge. With my upbringing, I can't be *anti-*American–I *am* an American, but, of course, an American with a different view of the world and a different set of beliefs. I believe not only that Thanksgiving comes in October and the national news in the evening, but that folding money comes in different colours ("and at eighty cents to the dollar," as someone yelled in Newfoundland when I said that in my speech last month), that there is a "u" in honour, an opposition in Parliament, and three downs in football (even though, I confess, I am no fan of a league that has to put a quota on other people's rejects).

In John Robert Colombo's *Canadian Quotations,* Pierre Berton is quoted saying "a Canadian is someone who knows how to make love in a canoe." Pierre says he didn't say it, or if he did he took it from someone else, but whoever the authority is, if that's the test, I fail. I do know how to gunwhale a canoe (the Colonel taught me, in the river behind Betlyn), portage it, right it without getting out of the water, and sail it home with my hockey sweater tied to a paddle. But make love? You got me.

As a Canadian, though, I do know other things.

I know how to plug a car in at night, and how to pronounce "slough". I know that blueberry grunt comes after dinner, but not when you might expect, and that it's railway not railroad, reserve not reservation, and lieutenant with an "f". I know that hockey is more than Roller Derby on ice. I am convinced crown attorneys – not DAs – should be appointed, not elected, and judges, too, and that police officers should wear ties and call you sir. I drink coffee in the morning, but tea in the afternoon, and eat dinner with my fork in my left hand.

I speak my own bad French and flat English, and say "out" and "about" in a way no American has yet been able to parody successfully (even Robert MacNeil, the star of American public television who was raised in Canada, says in his book on the English language that those words rhyme with "boat", which they do not). One night in the 1960s, when I was in New York to interview Leonard Cohen for a radio documentary, a young woman (her brain, I think, chemically enhanced) came to call for me at my room at the Chelsea hotel and when I said I'd be "out in about a minute" spent much of the next hour asking me to perform a concert of "ou" sounds for her while she stood in the hall chanting "Oh, wow, that's wonderful."

I don't pack a gun, and don't ever want to, but my father went to war in 1939, and, when I think of the price he paid, I am not kindly disposed to people who think the fighting didn't start until two years later.

Though there is much that I admire about American politics, and much I would change about ours, I am convinced that a parliamentary system, with all its flaws, makes for a more responsive government than a presidential and congressional one.

I like the Queen (though not as much as the Queen Mum), and am content to have her representative as a head of state. I like the ceremonies that spring from our royal tradition, too.

I think it's wrong that people should be punished financially for being stricken by illness when they're old or broke (or both). If there is a benchmark of the difference between the American way of doing things and the Canadian way, in fact–and how our political processes have come to reflect that difference – it is, surely, that in the 1980s no major American political party is far enough to what we call the left to stand for a national program of medicare, while in Canada no party would dare stand far enough to the right to oppose it. Our political centre of gravity is different. Our social safety-net – unemployment insurance (including, in this hostile climate, insurance against the perils of seasonal work), family allowances, universal old age pensions, maybe some day (certainly before the U.S.) a national day-care program–is the product of many factors: our history, our heritage, our need to huddle together against the cold. We are a scattered people, thinly spread across a forbidding landscape. There aren't enough of us to entice private capital to establish the institutions that, in other societies, define a nation and tie it together. So, instead, we've used public capital.

We have, by common decision, pooled our resources, used public money to build a railway against the grain of geography, to make an airline, to set up banks–and, of course, to create a broadcasting system that reaches to the farthest corners of the land. Because we have lacked the private fortunes that can, on their own, set up philanthropic foundations, we've made a public one to subsidize our artists, seeding it from the death taxes of two rich old men and continuing to sweeten the pot from the public purse. Sometimes, as with magazines, we have constructed barriers against the forces of the marketplace–in particular against the overflow from the overwhelming culture on our border. But when we've done that, by and large, we've set up rules not so much to give our own institutions an advantage as to militate against the *dis*advantages they suffer in the shadow of the giant.

We are, furthermore, a country of regions, whose right to *remain* as regions we hold dear. (I never did figure out what was wrong with Joe Clark's "community of communities".) If the economy goes sour in one part of the United States, the American belief is that its people can move elsewhere. When a part of Canada dries up, we think it's right to take part of our national pool of resources and pour it in so they can stay there.

That is the way we do things. Not all of it, even on its own terms, works efficiently. Much of it adds to the cost of doing business, as do our clumsy, sometimes arbitrary, efforts to maintain two languages, or, for that matter, the need to heat factories or ship goods over long and lonely distances. But some of it–the

CBC, with all its limitations, would be a case in point – works very well indeed, thank you, and in all of it lies the essence of who we are. It's the society we've worked out for ourselves. It's our culture.

And, yes, we are diffident. "I'm sorry," not bragging, "not bad" – that's all part of it, part of a country that, still not satisfied with the solutions to its own problems, does not see in itself the answer to other people's. Even in trying to describe ourselves we find it necessary to enumerate our faults. "Praise an American," Margaret Atwood has said, "and he will agree with you. Praise a Canadian, and he'll think you're trying to sell him something." But what's wrong with that? If it is not self-contradictory to say so, is it not better to err on the side of modesty than of braggadocio? I do not hold with those who lament what they call our national inferiority complex. I *like* people who aren't sure of themselves, and distrust those with all the answers.

So do most of us, I think. If there are aspects of the United States that we resent – and there are – they are not so much in the popular culture that the American machine, almost unwittingly, spews across our border. We loved those Abbott and Costello movies, after all, and sang the songs of Dylan as our own. But we do take offence, I would argue, at the self-righteousness that accompanies the culture, the idea that the U.S.A. is what someone has described as the "City on the Hill", the model for all the world, and that its God-given role–or, in this hemisphere, Monroe-given (which really means self-imposed) – is to save the rest of us from our mistakes. It's not. The U.S.A. is a model for the U.S.A., and, on this Columbus Day, God bless it. But it is not a model for Viet Nam (as it learned) or Nicaragua (as it does not yet seem able to learn) or, whatever our similarities, Canada. On this Thanksgiving Day, let it–and everyone else–respect the differences.

The studio, 10:25 a.m.: One of the reasons I've been thinking along these lines this morning is the appearance as a *Morningside* guest today of Simon Reisman, the chief Canadian negotiator for free trade.

Like a lot of other outlets in the media, *Morningside* has had what amounted to a standing request in for Reisman for the past several months. Until now, he has ignored us. His unwillingness to appear has been understandable; he's had a tough time, and there's been no reason for him to conduct his negotiations in public. But he's raised a lot of hackles by the tone of his refusals; he's a thorny, abrasive, difficult man, with, apparently, little time for normal civility. I met him once on a fishing trip to the Arctic. Like me, he was a guest of Peter Pocklington, whom I knew through *The Game of Our Lives*. What Reisman's connection was I still don't know, but there he was among the millionaires and hangers-on, watching Peter Puck argue with the Inuit guides over whether he should be allowed to dynamite the char out of the Tree River (he wasn't) and dangling a line in Great Bear Lake. Reisman was as aloof there as he has turned out to be with the press, a loner who stood apart from the card games and the banter. I'm sure the Tories knew what they were doing when they appointed him to handle these negotiations; even the people I know who dislike him personally don't deny the brilliance of his mind, and, in tough bargaining sessions, I suppose I'd rather have him on my side than on my opponent's. But if his style at the table is anything like the manner he showed on the Pocklington fishing trip or the way he has handled the press, it's a wonder the Americans didn't walk out long ago.

My prejudices about free trade aren't as rigid as my musings of this morning might suggest. Instinctively–and for all the reasons that have to do with the importance of our institutions–I'm leery of it. It's hard to believe Simon Reisman or anyone else can negotiate what the Americans love to describe as a level playing-field without flattening some of the programs we've built for ourselves. In one of the few recent cases where the argument has been clear-cut, indeed, the Americans have slapped a healthy tariff on fish from our eastern coast on the grounds that our seasonal unemployment insurance is a subsidy. Furthermore, if there ever was a time when we should tie our fortunes to those of our closest neighbour (and, whatever our reservations, best friend), it is, surely, not now, when even that neighbour's most ardent jingoists admit its economy, power, and morale are in decline.

But in the face of my instinct are a number of modern realities. We need trade not only to grow but to survive. All the world is dividing itself into larger and larger economic alliances, and we're far too small too stand on our own. The Americans, whatever the lethargic state of their own economy – largely because of its lethargic state, in fact – are in a protectionist mood; if we don't strike *some* deal with them now and formalize it – *freer* trade, as the proponents keep reminding us, not a total abandonment of protection – we'll be shut out altogether.

Et cetera, et cetera. In spite of my beliefs about the way we have built some inefficiencies into our system, I am not among those who fear all competition. If we need a trade deal with the Americans to keep our economy growing, and even if there is a price to be paid, then by all means let's get on with it. Just let's be careful. Before we jump in, let's know exactly what what we're getting into, and what the costs really are. Then, in a measured way, we can make up our minds.

What has frustrated me about the debate so far is that we haven't done that. For all the blathering that's been going on – and some of it has been on *Morningside* – we have not had a clear national discussion. We have instead formed two opposing camps, whose style of argument seems in each case to consist of hurling epithets at the other. The people on the pro side call those of us with reservations cowards and whimperers. The people who oppose the deal – women's groups, the cultural nationalists, a lot of organized labour, the arts establishments – accuse those in favour of it of selling out. The truth – doesn't it always? – lies somewhere in between. We've done a lousy job of trying to find it.

Morningside, I'd like to argue, has at least tried to be the exception. We've leaned over backwards, I think, to make up for our own prejudices. We've staged a number of debates, held a number of panels, and, of course, run Ken Wolff's series of snapshots of specific futures, at least half of which have shown a rosy future. But even that's been unsatisfactory. If you listened only to us, I'm sure, your head would still be spinning: on the one hand this, on the other hand that, good for the fashion business, bad for textiles, good for some farmers, bad for others. The cost? It depends on whom you listen to. One person's perceived threat to all that's distinct about our culture – much of it, as is mine, more instinctive than based on specifics – is another's idea of whining. The name-calling clouds the air.

With Reisman's visit today, I'm hoping we can take a step in the right direction. Last week, in Washington, he signed an agreement in principle. There are still a lot of details to be ironed out, and the legislation has to be steered through both governmental systems. But now, with our government's blessing, he's on the road like a book-flogger, making his case. When he agreed to come on *Morningside*, Ken Wolff worked hard to prepare a green that would let him make it, but help me to raise some of the fundamental questions that still trouble me, and if there are answers, hear them.

Alas, it is not to be.

Reisman comes into the studio smiling confidently, but with a copy of the *Toronto Star* tucked under his arm. He's been having a running feud with the *Star* – at one press conference he called their Washington reporter "a hack" – and Ken and I have thought long and hard about whether, in a limited time, we want to address that part of his style. Now, because he has the paper with him, and because there is an editorial in it today that raises some of the points I want to discuss with him, I decide to open it up.

A mistake. Instead of talking about free trade, he launches into a lecture on journalistic ethics. Alhough I have my own reservations about the way the *Star* has let its editorial opposition to free trade come dangerously close to colouring its news coverage (we even had a discussion of *that* on the program), I find myself making the case for its defence.

Another mistake. We are hopelessly ensnarled. I fight to regain control. Reisman bulls ahead, enumerating the *Star*'s editorial points and, one by one, attacking them. The language of our free-trade ambassador is, shall we say, undiplomatic. I glance at the clock, frustration mounting. Too late. We have talked for nearly twenty minutes and the air is murkier than when we began.

Apologetically, I introduce the drama. As the tape rolls, Reisman says he hasn't had enough time, and asks to come back, if we'll give him an hour.

I answer evasively. I'd still like to hear him make his case, but from the facial expressions in the control room, I know I'll never be able to persuade my colleagues to go through the ordeal again.

If that's how the Tories are selling their package, I think, they're going to be in trouble.

Tuesday, October 13, the Morningside *office, 11 a.m.:* I have decided not to do television at the Calgary Olympics. My reasons are complex: I haven't become as interested in the Games as I thought I might have; the CBC's plans for accommodating its personnel look frighteningly rough; and I am still troubled by the producer's plans to emulate *Entertainment Tonight*. Mostly, though, I can use the two weeks in February, if I take them off *Morningside*, to work on the Ridley book and on this journal.

What I am not suffering from–and I don't think I'm protesting this too much–is fear of television itself. I've been back on that horse a couple of times since I was thrown by *90 Minutes Live*.

WHILE I WAS STILL IN ROCKWOOD, two entrepreneurial producers, one of whom had worked with Nathan Cohen on Nathan's old black-and-white CBC program, *Fighting Words*, asked me to host a revival. We shot the new version, in colour and at a round table, at Channel 11 in Hamilton, chauffeuring our guests by limousine from Toronto, and, in the best traditions of syndicated TV, recording as many as four half-hours in a day. (I couldn't help noticing, one day after we'd knocked off four editions, that at a thousand dollars an episode I'd just earned more than I'd made in a year in Timmins.)

I was no Nathan–who ever could be?–but I wasn't bad. Occasionally, as when John Simon, the engrossingly objectionable New York drama critic, and Bob Rae, the leader of the Ontario NDP, almost came to blows, or when Irving Layton, who had been a fixture on the original program, broke into brilliantly egotistical flights of bombast, the program was stimulating and fun to do, and I was–and am–sorry that even with the pauper's budget (by television standards) we made it on, we couldn't sell it to enough stations to pay its way. Aside from the income it generated, it helped to restore my shaken confidence.

Later, after I'd returned to radio, Glenn Sarty approached me with a more ambitious idea. Sarty, a Nova Scotian with a background in big-band music, was one of the original generation of CBC television producers, and over the years he had been the brains behind, among other programs, *Take 30*–the old lunchtime talk show that launched Adrienne Clarkson–and *the fifth estate*. In the 1960s, not long after my adventures with Ross McLean, he had put together the pilot for an hour-long magazine show on the arts, with me as host–he called it *Gzowski!*, in fact –and though no one had risen to that particular lure, he had not lost his conviction that with proper production values I could work on the tube. His proposition in 1985 was that I become the host and on-camera interviewer for a series of half-hour profiles–most of them, once again, of people in the arts–that would be produced and directed by a variety of people all over the country, with him acting as the executive producer in Toronto.

"No," I said.

Sarty looked surprised. It seldom occurs to those who have given their lives to television that the rest of the world is not waiting for a chance to get before the cameras.

"How come?" he said.

I said that, *Fighting Words* aside, I didn't have happy memories of the medium, especially within the CBC, and that *Morningside* and the first *Papers*, which I was just beginning to assemble, were giving me more than enough to do.

"We'll work around your schedule," he said.

"But, Glenn, I don't *like* televi–"

"Why not?"

"It's just not right for me." I made him a speech–we were in the cafeteria, in the radio building – about style and content, about how what I did on radio was a craft that didn't translate to television. I said that especially on location, where his proposed series would be shot, it was impossible to establish a relationship between the interviewer and his subject, since every question had to be asked a second time after the camera had been turned around, and that I couldn't think of anything more stupid–or at which I would be worse–than what the trade calls "cutaways", those pictures of the interviewer nodding vacantly in response to answers he has in fact heard several minutes earlier, when the camera was pointing elsewhere.

"We'll use two cameras," Sarty said.

"No cutaways?"

"No. Real reaction shots. We'll cut back and forth. No re-asks either. When we show you putting a question, you'll really be asking it."

"But I'd still have to wear make-up," I said, "and look like a fool."

"No make-up," said the man who made Adrienne Clarkson a star. "If I wanted a pretty face, I'd hire a pretty face."

The more objections I raised, the more quickly he shot them

down. By the time we left the cafeteria, he had agreed that I would not shave my beard, that I could wear whatever I wanted (including an open shirt), that I would be under no pressure to lose weight, and that I could have editorial control over both the subject matter and the final script. And I, to my own surprise, had agreed to be his host. Some time after that and in spite of my protests–Glenn said he thought my name looked interesting in type – the series was christened *Gzowski & Co.*, and for the next two summers I rode the airlines, from Carcross in the Yukon to Sable Island, off the coast of Nova Scotia–an experience that, as my list of best things in the world this fall makes clear, has stuck in my mind. There, and at points between, we filmed artists, writers, artisans, dancers, film-makers, singers, and, for reasons that are still not clear to me, a chuckwagon driver at the Calgary Stampede.

Sarty kept his word. An extra camera on every shoot made cutaways redundant, and often, as when I was able to talk in the most intimate terms with the gifted young Mohawk conductor John Kim Bell about the murder of his father, a professional wrestler, or when k. d. Lang, the eccentric and thoughtful country singer from Alberta, looked up from the polished surface of a grand piano during an internal monologue and said, "There's somebody cute in there" ("No, there isn't," I replied after peering into the surface myself), the relationship that only two cameras could capture justified the decision.

On the matter of my clothes and make-up, Sarty was liberal to a fault. Though he never once, during the fifty-two episodes we recorded, mentioned my appearance, I would sometimes cringe in embarrassment myself at my wayward hair or crumpled shirts. Towards the end, still unprompted, I began to take a little more care and even, after I saw myself walking a Prince Edward Island beach with Mike Duffy, and feared that the rotund Duffy would disappear behind my ample tummy, went on a diet.

I began also, I think, to understand the medium a little better, both its limitations and its possibilities. Whatever Sarty's extra care, I realized, the mechanics of television would always stand in the way of real spontaneity. Television was not so much recorded as made – created – often by cheating. Sometimes the artifice of *Gzowski & Co.* was amusing. In Ottawa, a mechanical toy we were trying to demonstrate refused to work, and the picture that made it into our film is in fact of the toy being pulled across the floor by a stagehand with a string. From Montreal, the dramatic picture of me in a choir loft, looking down on Charles DuToit and the Montreal Symphony rehearsing while I proclaim the orchestra's glory over the strains of Handel, was in fact shot on a different day; the church I overlooked was as empty as a tomb.

But other times our re-creations were more discomfiting. On a ranch near High River, Alberta, the chuckwagon driver Tom Glass, a big, raw-boned Gary Cooper of a man, cried soft tears while he spoke of his brother's death in a rodeo accident. When we played back the tape that night in Calgary, the sound-track, recorded on remote microphones, crackled with extraneous sounds. The next day we asked Glass to tell the story again. To the producer's disappointment, he did it dry-eyed.

From that same shoot in Alberta, I retain an image which, though it was not photographed, sums up much of my dissatisfaction with television as a conveyance for journalistic truth.

We were on the Sarcee Indian Reserve, on the outskirts of Calgary, the scene that evening of one of the series of chuckwagon races that builds in excitement to the climax of the Stampede. It was a hot, dry prairie afternoon, with the sun crawling across the high sky. Our camera crews had been following Tommy Glass and his entourage through much of that circuit, and I had flown in from Toronto. We had not done any major interviews. The material on his brother, for example, would wait for more tranquil circumstances. Here at Sarcee, all we wanted were some moments of colour and some involvement with me. The process had been a nuisance for Glass, I'm sure. With the two cameramen, a sound technician, the director, a researcher, and me all milling about and bothering his skittish horses, he had pretended to go through his pre-race routine. Inevitably, he had had to repeat simple procedures – "Sorry, Tommy, the light wasn't quite right on that one"; to explain things that must have seemed transparently simple to him, and to do things – "Sorry, Tommy, could you just look at Peter while you're holding that hoof?" – that were unnatural. Nevertheless, he had co-operated patiently, and as the crew sat on the sidelines that afternoon, taking a cigarette break before the real race-preparations began, we felt we'd done a good day's work. In all, we had taken up about four hours of his life to make perhaps two minutes of our film. That evening, when the Sarcee races were run, we would mount one camera and a microphone in his chuckwagon and another on the sidelines and try to make a couple of minutes more.

While we waited, a solitary young woman, in her twenties I'd guess, dressed for the dry heat in shorts and a halter, with a bag over her shoulder, came loping over the rolling horizon. She approached the Glass encampment, set among the wagon people's gypsy village. She asked for Tommy. Someone pointed him out. She moved to introduce herself.

She was, it turned out, a reporter for the *Calgary Herald*, at about the same stage (though working for a much better paper) as I had been at her age, and as I watched her work, taking a notepad and a pencil from her bag and shyly beginning to ask her questions, I couldn't help but reflect on the differences in our circumstances now. Glass – a constitutionally polite man, whose wagon, as it happened, would be sponsored by the *Herald* for the Stampede – was as helpful to her as he could be. But the interview with the young reporter was a distraction for him. For the television, by contrast, he had turned himself over, body and attention. He worked while he talked with her, as he had with us, but the tasks he was performing, unlike the make-work projects he had staged for us, were real and absorbing; he answered her over his shoulder. When she was finished, and our crew, their cigarettes finished, moved in to strap their technology onto his wagon, she drifted into the background, her notepad still at the ready, to see what she could absorb. Once again, we surrounded him. As he wheeled his prancing team off towards the starting-line, I, a microphone pinned inside my T-shirt, stood on the running-board of his wagon for a last-minute exclusive on how he planned to run, while the young *Herald* reporter – me, thirty years earlier – strained from the sidelines for a quote she might squeeze into her story. While the horses and wagons roared around the track, our cameras an intimate part of the action and the fury, she sat on the grassy slope that forms a natural arena at Sarcee, her elbows on her bare knees, her chin cupped in her hands, which is the image I have retained.

And yet, as I think when I replay this tape in my mind, who was getting the truer picture? Was the real Tom Glass the polite, taciturn, preoccupied man who spared her a few minutes while he went about his business, or the one who stopped everything he was doing to explain his actions to the camera? Would he be closer to himself while he chatted casually with his outriders and she hung in the background or when our crew was all over him, with our lights and microphones and cries of "Do that again, please"? From her vantage point on the hillside, did she see the race more clearly–set in a truer context–than our camera inside the wagon?

The answers, of course, are self-evident. The young writer for the *Herald* (I never did read the story she wrote) may not have had the skills to capture the man she was writing about, as I would not have had at her age. But her subject was there for her, unadulterated, as the subject is almost always there for the reporter who is content to watch and take notes. With television, I am convinced, the subject becomes something different; the scientific principle that the presence of an observer changes the condition of the observed may apply to some degree to print journalism, but to television, I would argue, it applies absolutely. What you see on the screen is not reality at all; it is television.

Once I had figured that out, though–and I hope I didn't take myself as seriously as these reflections may suggest–I began, if not to revel in the process, to come to terms with it. In the interviews the two cameras recorded, I remained unable to cure my radio habit of trying to begin at the beginning, find a pace, and ride it to the end–to make a shape. By television's terms, I wasted a lot of tape. In the atrium of his spectacular, airy house near Edmonton, I talked for two hours to the deeply eloquent architect Doug Cardinal about his efforts to impose the poetry of his native heritage on the Museum of Man (as it was still called) in Ottawa. In a living-room in Montreal, I rambled on for almost three with the poet and politician Gérald Godin, about life, women, poetry, revolution, and the brain tumour he had recently had removed.

I continued to be frustrated to know that these conversations would be hacked to bits in the editing. But as I recorded them, and as I joined in the process of trying to bend them to television's needs, I learned to search within the shape for what television people call "moments" – the telling phrase, the unexpected burst of laughter, the downcast eye. I learned to leave pauses so the editor could work around me, and I mastered, or tried to, the hardest and sometimes most powerful trick of all for a television interviewer: silence. (To see this at its most effective, watch the masterful Patrick Watson some time, and note how one skepical lift of an eyebrow can elicit more confessions than all the badgering in the world; what Watson learned long ago is that people in front of television cameras–not interviewers, who might be expected to, but the people they have trained their sights on–abhor dead air, and that when they sense their previous answer has been unsatisfactory they will rush to fill the void.)

As I worked on the post-production, moreover, I realized that the "interview" as I had learned to do it was not at the heart of the program Sarty had envisioned at all. However much I had enjoyed my philosphical chat with Doug Cardinal – and would, if I were king, have put it on the air unedited–the real *television* in the piece occurred when our cameras showed him crawling, exhausted and purged, from the ordeal of the sweat-lodge he had built in a tent beside his spacious home. Three hours with Godin might have pleased *me* (and somewhere, I hope, exist in an archive), but for the purposes of the program we were making they were far less satisfactory than the single exchange – the moment–that occurred when I asked Godin to recreate step by step his middle-of-the-night arrest in the October Crisis of 1970, and the gentle poet turned in a flash into the unforgiving, wronged, revolutionary.

Putting these programs together, in fact, was an education for me. Sarty kept his word on my editorial powers, too, although, while I struggled to learn the vocabulary, he surrounded me with more experienced television people. In time, I came to look on our half-hour profiles as natural extensions of the craft I had studied at the Ralph Allen school of journalism, and, indeed, with *Maclean's* having forsaken the kind of articles I grew up on to become a "newsmagazine", I wondered if, with *Gzowski & Co.*, I wasn't doing on television precisely what I had once done in print. But if that was its function, the CBC didn't cotton to it. We had reasonable numbers, as they say, and reasonably favourable, if not adulatory, reviews. But we were caught in a power squabble between the regions, whose money and resources we were using, and the network, whose time spots we had to compete for. With the budget basket shrinking, the CBC decided to divide its eggs between public affairs and drama, neither of which categories included us. Though they didn't bother to tell me until some weeks after the decision had been made, we were dropped as quietly as we had come on.

Was I sorry?

In one way, very–and, if not angry, disappointed. The embarrassingly named *Gzowski & Co.*, it seemed to me, had been the very definition of the sort of thing a national public television network should be doing: showing Canadians to Canadians and celebrating our own. Furthermore, some of the programs we were turning out toward the end–our Evelyn Hart profile, for instance, or the piece on Tabby Johnson ("hello, my honey") and her sister Molly from Toronto's Queen Street, the portrait of the playwright John Gray that took us from Expo in Vancouver to his old rock-and-roll stomping-grounds in Truro, Nova Scotia–were pretty fair television, and I'd like to have carried on making some more. It felt good, particularly as its success covered the scar tissue of *90 Minutes Live*.

But, on another level, I was just as happy to see it end. The money I earned from all those travels has paid for the cottage at the Briars. Now I want time to enjoy it. Instead of going to the Olympics in February, I'll hunker down there and write. As for television, there may be other chances. If there aren't, then what the hell?

The Morningside Christmas party, 1987. Hal Wake
peers out from behind Carole Warren in the foreground.
Janet Russell is in glasses. Upwards and left to right:
me, Lynda Hanrahan, our technician Carol Ito;
producers Thom Rose, Gail Kotchie, and Patsy Pehlman;
Gloria Bishop and Janet Enright; Dave Amer and
Talin Vartanian, with Susan Rogers and others
in the dark at the top of the stairs.

CHAPTER FIFTEEN

*The perils of cursory reading . . . Could
Eddie Greenspan host* Morningside? *. . .
Missing the mail . . . Portents of trouble in
the office . . . David Crombie (unwittingly)
plants an idea . . . Barbara McDougall,
columnist . . . A call to Ottawa . . . "The
king of the social graces strikes again" . . .
Clearing the air – for now*

Wednesday, October 14, Morningside, *just before the second
hour:* David Suzuki arrives to talk about his autobiographical
Metamorphosis: Stages in Life, and gives me a chance–or so I think
–to clear up a goof I pulled yesterday, when we taped three pieces
with Eddie Greenspan on *his* autobiographical *Greenspan: The
Case for the Defence,* written with the help of his friend George
Jonas (and published, as Pierre Berton apparently forgot, by
Macmillan).

The goof came about because, as usual, I had been reading –
reading *at*, in my interviewer's way–both books at once. In each
case, I had found a wealth of the kind of anecdote I seek, and
the end-papers of both books are filled with my scribbles. Yesterday, I chose a story from Greenspan's college days to begin
part one, to send a signal of my intimate knowledge of his – or
Jonas's–work and to get him spinning some tales. "Tell me," I
said, "about the time when you were a student at Western and
you were afraid of being charged with a crime because you had

deposited a number of coins in a bank just after a robbery and . . ."

"Well, the story's true," said Greenspan, puzzled, "but I didn't go to Western."

Oops. Wrong autobiography.

Now, as we wait for the theme to end before my chat with Suzuki, I tell David how I had confused him with the lawyer.

"But *I* didn't go to Western either," he says.

Oh, dear. He went to *high school* in London, whereas Greenspan went to . . .

Ah, forget it. At least I didn't screw this one up on the air.

Greenspan, by the way, loves radio, and I sometimes think the program he and Jonas do together, *Scales of Justice*, matters as much to him as his brilliant courtroom victories. He would like to sit in some day as host of *Morningside*. I happen to think he'd be good at it, but Gloria disagrees. To duck the question, which he raises every time I see him, I tell him he can do my job for a morning if I can appear in court for him, defending one of his accused murderers.

"Okay," he said once. I still don't know if he was kidding.

Yesterday, to my astonishment (for he appears to have an unshakeable ego), Eddie was still upset by a lukewarm review of *The Case for the Defence* in the *Globe* on Saturday. "I worked hard on the book," he said, "and some guy just picked it up and attacked me."

I mention this to Suzuki when we've finished our on-air chat.

"Me too," he says.

"But you haven't *had* any bad reviews yet, David."

"No," he says. "But I'm worried."

Funny, isn't it? Two of the most accomplished and – justly – celebrated men you could imagine, trembling over the reception of their books. Ego's a strange thing. Thank goodness *I* don't have any, eh, Craig?

Thursday, October 15, Morningside, *early morning:* No mail. Postal strike.

On the one hand, a bare desk when I arrive (Lynda opens the mail every afternoon after I've gone home) means I have more time to work on the day's program–or, as today, to fill in a couple more answers on the cryptic. As well, Lynda will be able to get her answers up to date. (We try to reply to every letter, even if it's just a note Lynda types based on a phrase I've scrawled across the original, or, as when there are several dozen on the same subject, a personalized form letter. Katz laughs at my habit of taking much more care with the critical or argumentative letters –I often get snarly in return, and read my carefully crafted put-downs to him across the empty office–than I do with the people who support us.)

On the other hand, I miss the mail profoundly. As I've written at length in the introductions to both *Papers*, it's invaluable to me. I learn from it every day, am encouraged, enlightened, and often brought into line by it. We get story ideas by the handful, too. Yesterday, for example, Catherine Field, the mother of a hyperactive child, talked to us from Edmonton. Powerful stuff– much more effective, I think, than a hundred pieces with "experts". And we had it only because Catherine had written to us. That happens all the time. With the strike, we'll have a hard time keeping the "real people" on the air. We've come to rely on the mail to turn them up.

Sunday, October 18, the cottage, afternoon: Thank God for this place, with its blue jays and grackles and air like chablis! The butternut table is stacked with books: John Sawatsky on Ottawa lobbyists, Michel Gratton's adventures as the Prime Minister's press secretary, the raising of the *Titanic*, Brian Moore's new novel. I've stayed behind to work on them while Peter and Heather, who came up last night to sample my world-famous cauliflower soup and to beat us at fireside bridge, go with Gill to the race-track. I'm having a hard time getting going. Too relaxed. Slept ten hours last night. Be nice just to stay here, write in the mornings, doze in the afternoons.

I've sent a couple of bets in to the track. On television, I watch the first one, a filly owned by the Aga Khan, romp home. I'm up $27. Then, in the Rothmans, the day's major event, my pick –a colt also owned by the Aga Khan–loses by a nose. I've told Peter to parlay my winnings onto him. He went off at 8-1. I would have been up nearly $400. Instead, I've lost my stake.

At least when I was writing for a living I could *go* to the track to lose my money.

Tuesday, October 20, Morningside, *11 a.m.:* Hal Wake catches me on my way out of the studio. "I don't know whether you've heard," he begins, "but the Association of Canadian Publishers has been looking for an executive director. I've put my name into contention. I'm not sure I'll get it, or even if I'll really want it if they offer it to me. But I wanted you to know what I've done."

My heart sinks. Though I tell him I understand, and offer to put in a word for him at the ACP, I have a hard time imagining *Morningside* without him. In the four years since he joined us, fresh from his own on-air career in Vancouver, he's really taken hold of the book beat, and made himself and the program part of the Canlit scene–which is, of course, why the publishers would be interested in him. If I'm struggling to keep up with the books we handle now, I don't know how I'd do it without his thoughtful, trail-breaking greens.

But, even aside from his literary specialty – and he does a lot of other things as well–this would be an awful time to lose him. We're short of bodies. Bev Reed left yesterday to begin six months' work on a special project on the Pacific. The new producers are still struggling. Hal, Susan, Talin, Nancy, and Ken have been carrying us, with Hal and Susan particular towers of strength. But there's tension between them and Gloria, whose lack of enthusiasm, I'm afraid, is showing. On the air, we're sounding as strong as ever, but I doubt if it can last. As I wrote in my notebook before I took off for the cottage last week, "We're due for a crash."

I can't blame Hal for looking around. My own restlessness must be evident. I bitch too much and don't express enough gratitude for everyone else's back-breaking labours. If I'm just working out the end of my term, it's hard to expect other people to plan a future at *Morningside*, or, as has happened with Hal and the ACP, to ignore other opportunities when they arise.

7 p.m., the apartment: Gill's working late. Flicking through the television dial for something to get my mind off the situation at the office, I come across David Crombie, the Secretary of State, in conversation with Geoff Scott, the back-bench MP who used to be, among other things, Rich Little's comedy partner. Part of the Tories' new political news service, I surmise, and, since that idea has stirred up some controversy this fall – my own feelings are that if TV stations are dumb enough to run the party's tapes without attribution, they can't blame anyone but themselves – decide to watch a few minutes. To my delight, they're talking about literacy, and, somewhat to my surprise, Crombie is full of both information and zeal. He has obviously not only read Peter Calamai's fine series of reports for the Southam newspapers last year, but has digested its importance.

My cause.

My ears prick.

Crombie goes on, citing statistics and outlining some of the things the government–his department–is thinking about doing about them. His plans sound vague, but his concern and his determination are obviously real. I wonder if he knows about my golf tournament? Then he talks about possibly setting up a literacy secretariat, a national body funded by Ottawa, to lead the campaign.

Wheels turn in my mind. If they're going to do that, I think, they'll need someone to head it all up. If they're looking around, what about me? Surely with my exposure on *Morningside*, my background in writing and editing, and my established commitment to the cause, I'd at least be a contender.

Like Hal, with his possible new job in publishing, I'm not sure I want it, and I'm very *unsure* about whether I could be a bureaucrat. But if my time at *Morningside* really is coming to an end – if, indeed, I'm looking for a way out with honour now–this could be the opportunity. Peter Gzowski, czar of literacy. Maybe. Maybe not. But I know that if I were to read in the paper that the feds had set up a secretariat–or anything else–and I hadn't even been considered, I'd be very disappointed.

I've met Crombie, but don't know him well. I remember, though, that Barbara McDougall used to be his campaign manager. I call Janet Enright and, without saying why I want it, manage to pry her sister's home number out of her.

Is this the way things happen?

ALL DURING THE TIME I was researching and writing *The Game of Our Lives*, and as I began looking at the race-track for the book that was to follow, I was also working with Michael de Pencier at Key Publishers.

We had some interesting adventures. At one point, Michael bought control of a weekly publication called the *Bargain-Hunter*

Press, a collection of free classified ads that people bought to shop from. In that format, the *Bargain-Hunter* had made a lot of money for its original owners, but our idea–my idea, really–was that we could make it the nucleus of a new downtown weekly, a sort of Toronto version of the *Village Voice*, but as different from it as the now hugely successful *Toronto Life* was from Clay Felker's *New York*.

Cautiously, we made some changes. I arranged for regular columns from a number of people who have gone on to success in other media or other fields. Arthur Kaptainis, now music critic of the Montreal *Gazette*, reviewed concerts for us; Christopher Hume, now on the entertainment pages of the *Toronto Star*, did art; Marion Kane, who moved on to the *Sun*, wrote about restaurants, and I commissioned a weekly column on the stock market–for $25 a time–from a woman Mel Hurtig had drawn to my attention when, recently divorced, she moved back to Toronto from Edmonton to work on Bay Street: Barbara McDougall.

She wasn't bad. Her copy came in on time, neatly typed and double-spaced (she may have had a secretary, of course), and, there among the ads for baby carriages and used guitars, she made some points that might have been useful to the sort of reader we were after.

If we'd stuck with it, the *Bargain-Hunter* might have worked. But, as it was, with revenues declining while we took less and less interest in the ads and expenses mounting while I kept signing up more writers and commissioning more features, it was a financial haemorrhage for Key. Our choice was to pour perhaps another million dollars into it or take our losses (about $400,000) and bail out. We bailed. A rival classified paper called *The Buy and Sell* picked up the wreckage and, throwing out all my editorial innovations, made a thriving hybrid. A weekly tabloid called *Now*, published by hungrier entrepreneurs than we were, captured the audience we had failed to attract.

Too bad. It was, I realize as I write this, my last fling at periodical publishing, and I'm sorry to enter it on the list with the *South Shore Holiday*, the *Star Weekly*, and my second run at *Maclean's*. Things turned out all right for our financial columnist, though, didn't they?

Wednesday, October 21, Morningside, 12 noon: Barbara's call–

she wasn't home last night, after all–summons me from the story meeting. I tell her what I've been thinking and ask her to look round for me. In a curious reversal of roles, I, the journalist, ask her not to say anything–even to her sister. She chuckles.

"Leave it with me," she says.

Friday, October 23, the Morningside *office, 5:45 a.m.:* The mail is flowing again. Lists are still coming in–there *could* be a third *Papers* if there's anyone around to edit them–and I am happily ensconced in my morning pile when I hear Katzie cursing quietly by the coffee machine.

He has, as he does every day, begun his morning ritual by preparing an industrial-strength brew. Today, however – I do this all the time at home–he has filled the machine with water, inserted a heaping paper cone of the finest grind, pressed the "on" switch, and neglected to replace the glass container under the drip. Coffee as strong as creosote has been spitting onto the bright metal element of the machine and has spilled over the table by the door of Gloria's office, running thickly around the bases of cups bearing the insignia of the CBC's Saskatchewan morning show, *Daybreak* from somewhere else, the seventy-fifth anniversary of Timmins, Ontario ("the only city with a heart of gold"), *Canada AM*, the ACTRA awards, and other souvenirs of places we've been or guests we've had. It has run over the side of the table. A dark pool spreads on the threadbare carpet.

Gary sighs, and turns to go for paper towels.

"I can't make coffee till I've had coffee," he says.

12:30 p.m.: Sticking my head into Gloria's office before I leave for the day, I overhear her talking with Dalton Camp at the Prime Minister's Office in Ottawa. She is trying to negotiate an interview with Dalton's friend Richard Hatfield, whose Conservatives were wiped off the map in New Brunswick a couple of weeks ago, but who has been impossible to book.

Another light goes on in my head. I gesture that I'd like to talk to Dalton when she's finished. When I do, we exchange some banter about a dinner in Ottawa we'll both be addressing next week and then, reluctant to carry on my job-seeking next door to Gloria, I ask for an even more private chat later in the day. He gives me his home number.

2:40, the apartment: Dalton seems even more responsive than Barbara McDougall to my thoughts about literacy. He tells me of a recent meeting at which some Tory thinkers asked themselves what they'd do "if we had *tabula rasa*". Literacy was high on the agenda, he says, maybe even at the top. "It's obviously much cheaper than day care," he notes wryly.

Does he understand my ambitions?

"I'm enthusiastic," he says. "I'll mention it to the Prime Minister."

As in my conversation with Barbara McDougall, which I describe to Dalton, I find myself in the strange position of asking a political figure to keep mum about what I'm doing.

"Is it all right if I mention it to Barbara?" he asks.

"Of course. I didn't think there were any secrets in Ottawa anyway." I remind him of a passage in Michel Gratton's book in which he is quoted, at a meeting of party insiders, as having said, "Since it's impossible to speak privately around this table, I'm taking my comments directly to the PM."

"See what I mean?" he says.

Saturday, October 24, St. Lawrence Market, Toronto, 6:30 a.m.: No cottage this weekend. I have to go to Owen Sound tomorrow to flog books and, partly out of guilt, I agreed to let Gill drag me to a dinner party with some friends from the race-track last night, where I had, unexpectedly, a wonderful time.

Up at three this morning, though. Read, read, read. Bob White's autobiography, a new (and moving) novel by Jane Rule, Andy Russell's eloquent study of the Oldman River, the second volume of Peter Newman's history of the Hudson's Bay Company. Worked on White and Newman this morning (no possibility of confusion there, I hope), but grew hungry a while ago and decided to come over here for some cheese bread and Mennonite sausages.

The market next door may be the best thing about living where Gill and I do. (It still amuses me that after Jenny and I had slowly worked our way up town as we grew more prosperous, I have, like a lot of other aging Yuppies, tried even harder to get back to the foot of the city.) Though I haven't come here much since we rebuilt the cottage, I still enjoy a Saturday-morning prowl among the stalls of fresh vegetables and exotic meats–it is a myth that anything's cheaper here than in the supermarkets – and seeing who I'll run into. On Saturdays, this is the social centre of trendy Toronto.

Now, contemplating a booth of fresh herbs and garlic, I see Christina McCall and Stephen Clarkson, the political scientist and author she married after she and Peter Newman broke up. Stephen is resplendent in a beret.

We chat, mostly about the fall books. I give them some notes on what has impressed me so far–Sylvia Fraser's novel, the Starkells' canoe book, and a few others. Idle gossip. I am, however, careful not to mention what I've been reading this morning; who knows what feelings now exist between Christina and Peter?

Politely, Stephen and Christina ask me about my own book this fall. I say I'm just beginning the promotion, and repeat my usual lament about selling everyone else's work on *Morningside* but being unable–or unwilling–to push my own.

"Who's publishing it?" Stephen asks.

"McClelland and Stewart," I say, "–or, as we're calling it these days, Bennett and Clarkson. Adrienne's really having a wonderful time."

I am halfway back to the apartment, bread and sausages under my arm, before I remember Adrienne–Adrienne *Clarkson*, dodo –used to be married to Stephen.

The king of the social graces strikes again.

Sunday, October 25, Owen Sound, Ontario: This is more my element, I think. Maryann Hogbin, of the Ginger Press, one of the nation's most enterprising booksellers–I am not the first writer she has lured to this pretty, out-of-the-way corner of Georgian Bay to stimulate business – has sold tickets to a hundred and twenty-five of her fellow citizens to hear me talk over lunch about the wonders of *The New Morningside Papers*. After a brief turn on "sorry" (the *Reader's Digest* version), I flog mercilessly. Among other anecdotes, and to underline the sense of literary intercourse these volumes provide, I point out that the new edition includes a chapter of "memorable meals" written by some English-language students in China, whose teacher had brought the first

Papers from Canada as an aid in the classroom. Among the memorable meals in *that* edition, I remind Maryann's luncheon guests, most of whom seem familiar with both it and the program, was one of my own, on board the *Aleksandr Pushkin*. Jenny and had I been amazed to see the captain, at whose table we dined, cut a Ritz cracker with a knife and fork.

After the lunch, while I'm signing copies of the new book, I am summoned to a table by a young man whose name I fail to catch. As I watch in delighted fascination, he repeats the Soviet sea-dog's trick, neatly bisecting his own cracker, dispersing not a crumb.

"I mastered that after I'd read the first book," he says.

Ah, the literary life, drawing Canadians together in their common culture, from sea to sea to sea.

Monday, October 26, Morningside: Thanks to the trick with the cracker, or, perhaps, just the pleasure of meeting a lot of people in a new part of the country, I am energized again. Hal has said nothing further about the ACP. My own thoughts about becoming a figurehead for literacy are getting more complicated. I haven't heard from Crombie yet, of course. But as I've turned over in my mind the prospect of my fantasized new role (would I have a limo?), I have begun to wonder if a move to Ottawa would be perceived as – or, in fact, would be – an act of support for the Tories. If it were, I can't help thinking, I could kiss journalism goodbye.

We'll see. Right now, it's a pipe-dream. *Morningside* remains the reality.

Tuesday, October 27, the Northfield room of the CBC's Jarvis Street "Kremlin", 11:30 a.m.:   Eyes welling with emotion, Gloria addresses the meeting.

The unit comes here (or tries to, since time does not always permit) every Tuesday. We gather round an oaken conference table and, away from the phones and the distractions of the office, look at some of our long-range goals. We hear the latest ratings or budgetary announcements, get caught up on what Gloria puts on the agenda as "comings and goings" (notes on the steadily moving parade of personnel), and do some soul-searching. Without exception, I think, we find the process a nuisance

–no one, in fact, more than I, since I make a practice of not pre-taping on Tuesday afternoons and these meetings often stretch into my own time–but we have not yet found another way to maintain a perspective; even confining the daily story meetings to immediate ideas uses up all of their allotted half-hours.

Today, though, there's been a sense of anticipation. The producers have *asked* for this session. As Gloria says when she begins to speak, they want to clear up what they call "the poison in the air".

She's trying. It's difficult for everyone. There's a lot of paper-shuffling, and downcast eyes. Talin, to her credit–it's easy to forget, with her cheeky ebullience, that she is the producer with the longest record of service–has taken on the role of spokes-person. She's been frank about everyone's concerns–the over-work, the shortage of staff, Gloria's own apparent lack of dedication. And now Gloria is struggling to respond.

"Maybe I'm too isolated," she says. "Maybe my office is too far away from the centre of the action."

Talin looks impassive. One of the problems, I can't help think-ing, is that Gloria has become so caught up in such matters as office design that she has lost track of the program's soul.

Gloria keeps talking, trying to come to grips with the com-plaints. She talks of the people she's tried to hire, running through each of their reasons for turning us down. She apologizes, as if it's her fault, and says she'll keep looking. She asks for sug-gestions. When there are none, she smiles ruefully and carries on. She is so obviously upset by the atmosphere–so taken aback by the tone of the meeting–that sympathy is swinging to her. The paper-shuffling ceases. Eyes look up. There are a few smiles.

"I'll do better," Gloria says. You can almost feel the tensions easing.

From my seat at the other end of the long table–near a window, though I do not smoke in these meetings–I step in. I apologize for my own moodiness over the fall, and for my apparent lack of gratitude for everyone's support. I say I, too, will try to mend my ways.

"Oh, sure," says Talin, but she's grinning now. People begin talking of other things. Old jokes are recycled. A feeling of com-fort returns.

Gloria is visibly relieved.

As the meeting breaks up, I'm not sure we've put our problems behind us. But the session has helped. The pressures of the fall, which have taken their toll on all of us, may have strained the feeling of mutual affection at the heart of *Morningside*. But they haven't broken it. In the end, Gloria survived today's mini-insurrection–I wonder if it was the crash I thought I saw coming last week–not so much by what she's said as who she is. Even when we're mad at her, we *like* her. We'll carry on.

Czar of literacy, eh?

I wonder.

Adventures on the book tour. ABOVE: "Is that Anne with an 'e'?"
BELOW: with David Schatzky on Radio Noon in Toronto.

CHAPTER SIXTEEN

*Some wise advice on fame . . . Politics and
the Ottawa pen . . . Tempest in a cocktail-
shaker . . . Why, according to Fotheringham,
Bill Vander Zalm wears wooden shoes . . . A
book for Joanne's mother . . . Fathers and
father figures . . . Thanatos and Eros . . .
The luck of the draw with book
reviewers . . . Angels in the trees*

*Wednesday, October 28, the Château Laurier, Ottawa, 4:15
p.m.:* The last guest on the program we did from Toronto this
morning was the union leader Bob White, talking about his new
autobiography (well, the new autobiography the incomparable
June Callwood has written for him, as she earlier wrote the autobiographies of Otto Preminger and others). When we had finished, I asked White, whom I like and admire, if he thought the
attention the book was drawing to his personality would detract
from his ability to function as a union man, and, if that was the
case, whether it bothered him. My question wasn't all that different from the one I had asked Pierre Berton in September, and,
I'm sure, was based on the same introspective motives.

White's answer was more to the point. "If you go seeking
fame," he said, "you can't bitch when you get it."

Now, I'm not so sure. I'm getting the royal treatment here. I
have come to Ottawa to act as master of ceremonies at a dinner
to raise money for the Writers' Development Trust, a fund started
a couple of years ago by – who else? – Jack McClelland and some

others. There are variations of this event all over the country, evenings where the citizenry pays to break bread with the literati. (Last year, when some people in Windsor bought my presence for fifteen hundred dollars, Alison, who claims there are evenings when she'd pay *not* to dine with me, wondered what the essential difference was between my function and that of an employee of an escort service. The escort gets to keep the money, I said.) In Ottawa, for an evening called "Politics and the Pen", there's a whole anthology of us. I'll host, and Dalton Camp, Allan Fotheringham, Sondra Gotlieb, Ron Graham, Charles Lynch, Marjorie Nichols, and Jeffrey Simpson will each review a book by another member of the group. The organizers, a committee of very bright Ottawa women, have everything running with frightening smoothness, and when I checked in here a while ago I was whisked to this luxurious room on the Château's new Gold Key floor, where I found flowers, some wine (no thanks, I'm working), and a welcoming note.

I was tired. Even before I caught the plane this afternoon, I'd had a full day, which ranged from the American author Joan Didion in the first hour, who joined my list of most difficult interviews ever (Talin, sitting in for Hal, wanted to bail out after eight minutes, but, sensing that the audience would think me rude, I hung on for fifteen), through White in the third, and carried on to a pre-tape with Bruce Cockburn (my goodness, he's earnest) after the story meeting. With the prospect of a long evening ahead, I hung up my dinner jacket to let the wrinkles fall out and crawled onto the bed for a restorative nap. Just as I was dozing off, the phone rang. The manager.

"Anything you need, Mr. Gzowski?"

He meant well, I'm sure.

Ah, well. I pad down the hall to see Fotheringham, whose door, I have noticed, is open.

With a Scotch and soda from his mini-bar perched on the dresser beside him, the Foth is clicking the last few paragraphs of his newspaper column into a portable word processor. He looks, as always, like a sawed-off model for *Gentleman's Quarterly*, though his jacket is on the back of his chair, leaving his red suspenders on display, and he has loosened the white collar of his boldly striped shirt. My presence does not distract him. He gestures to the mini-bar (no thanks, again) and keeps typing. Click, click, click.

The prose, I know, will be as impeccable as his attire, carefully carved sentences that trip out with deceptive ease. I tried to hire him once, at *Maclean's*, but he was content in Vancouver then. Now, his column is the best thing in the magazine, even when he recycles old quips – I never want to read "the jaw that walks like a man" again – or makes up for his lack of reportage with polished insults. He's a verbal cartoonist, who takes himself as lightly as he takes his subjects. Behind the smart aleck, though, is a serious, perceptive writer; it's possible to miss that, laughing with and at him as we do.

He finishes the column (one of three he'll send this week to the Southam chain, as well as the weekly page in *Maclean's*), plugs his machine into the telephone, and, by technology incomprehensible to me, dispatches his *bon mots* to a waiting nation.

Gossip time.

I catch him up on some of the latest moves around the CBC, though I'm silent about the troubles at *Morningside*, and give him some notes I've picked up from travelling authors. I consider telling him about my tentative job application to Ottawa, but decide against it. He's a reporter, after all.

He's more frank than I am, too. "I'm in the glue with Southam," he says, and proceeds to tell me how he had come back from his base in Washington recently to address a meeting of the company's executives. "I thought it was the usual dog-and-pony show," he says. He trotted out some of his best one-liners, apparently, and spilled some of the beans he keeps out of his column. What he didn't know is that the Southam people had invited some guests to hear him, among them the U.S. ambassador, Thomas Niles, and his wife. The Nileses walked out. At the door, according to Fotheringham, Mrs. Niles said they were "not here to be put on a spit."

Now, evidently more amused than concerned by the trouble he has caused, he glances at his watch. A Piaget, probably. I can't tell.

Le Salon, the National Arts Centre, 6:30: At the urging of the organizers, I have prepared some introductory remarks for "Politics and the Pen", which I hope will set a tone for the evening of good-natured badinage. "The first thing a defeated politician does these days," I plan to say, "is write his memoirs, which means our history is being recorded by losers. . . . If Mackenzie King were alive today (and who knows that he isn't?), he'd probably be selling his diary to the *Globe and Mail*. . . ." And so on. Har har har. Well, maybe you'd have to be there.

Nothing I have constructed, however, could match the tempest in a cocktail-shaker that is raging about me now. The issue is whether the evening's speeches will be on or off the record. Most of the people who will speak tonight spend half their working lives trying to persuade politicians to say something for attribution. Now, when they're about to be in the limelight themselves, they're worried about reading their remarks in the morning paper.

Not all the evening's players, to be sure, are of this mind. Charles Lynch, the acknowledged dean of the Ottawa press corps, who has in the past fought nobly against such off-the-record events as the Press Gallery dinner, has no qualms at all. Neither does Marjorie Nichols, the gutsy, smoky-voiced westerner who is now writing for the Ottawa *Citizen*. Fotheringham, not unexpectedly, shrugs his dapper shoulders and says, "We have no choice." But, to my surprise, Jeffrey Simpson of the *Globe* – for my money the smartest journalist now writing in Ottawa (though so solemn that I plan to introduce him later on as his paper's humour columnist) – says he thinks we should be off the record. Sondra Gotlieb, the novelist and wife of our ambassador to the U.S., agrees. Ron Graham, author of the illuminating *One-Eyed Kings*, seems undecided, but Dalton Camp, whose wife is one of the organizers, says wryly that, on evenings such as this, "you need the right of deniability."

We huddle. Eventually we find a compromise. As compère, I will *announce* that the the speeches are off the record, but in a room full of politicians, reporters, and other denizens of the capital, I will say to anyone who thinks that makes him safe from hearing his remarks played back at some later date, "Good luck."

Le Restaurant, same building, 11:30: Nobody has said anything newsworthy anyway. There were some pointed shots – Marjorie

Nichols on Charles Lynch: he's "written more books about himself than Audubon has about birds"; Fotheringham on the MP Lucie Pépin (a non-participant, but what the heck?): "the only Member of Parliament who spends more on her hair than Tom McMillan", and on B.C. politics: "Why does Bill Vander Zalm wear wooden shoes? To keep the woodpeckers away from his head." At one point Mike Duffy, sitting at my table, passed a note over saying it was getting "more savage than a Press Gallery dinner". But, by and large, I thought, it was a clever evening, more fun than nasty, pleasantly Canadian. The highlight for me (though I can't think of a line that sums it up) was Dalton's hilarious appreciation of the gallant Marjorie Nichols's non-book on B.C. He is, surely, one of the best after-dinner speakers around, droll and urbane. I remember once when Roy McMurtry somehow got me invited to a black-tie dinner at the Albany Club in Toronto. That evening was ostensibly to show off, to a select group of influential men, the wit of Robert Stanfield, who had just been elected Tory leader. Dalton, along with Eddie Goodman, the Toronto lawyer who is also a champion of postprandial spieling, spoke first. After their turns, which had the audience daubing tears of laughter with their linen napkins and choking on their cigars, poor Stanfield had no chance.

That's true, by the way, even if Dalton denies it.

Thursday, October 29, Prospero Books, Ottawa, 12 noon: The healthy line-up that awaits me, *New Papers* clutched to chests, is an endorsement of Ottawa's reputation as both a good book town and a bastion of CBC radio. It is, I think, the only city where the local morning program habitually clobbers the commercial competition. Smart people, these Ottawans.

Because of the length of the line, I have less time than I would like to chat, even with the several of my fellow contributors to the *Papers* who've shown up. My head is down. Sign, sign, sign. "Is that Anne with an 'e'?" "And what's your mother's name?" "*You're* doing your Christmas shopping early, aren't you?"

I come to a stop, however, when a strikingly attractive young woman—I look up for *some* things—presents a copy of the book, opened to the middle of my introduction, her thumbs bracketing a particular phrase.

"I'm Joanne," she says.

It takes me a minute, but the phrase she has framed is the clue.

In December 1985, we had an unusually large response to a drama about adoption, and, in the weeks that followed, carried a number of personal letters and interviews based on it. After Susan Rogers and I–Susan produced the series–both thought we had rung every change on the theme, we learned of a moving incident. A woman in Northern Ontario who had heard the piece we did with an adopted child, explaining how deeply she would like to meet her birth mother, decided, twenty-two years after the fact, to search for her own daughter. With some difficulty she found her, and, because of *Morningside*'s involvement in the story, agreed to talk with her by studio link, Sudbury to Ottawa, with me, gulping back my emotions, in Toronto.

Joanne, as you will have guessed, is the daughter.

Now I'm gulping again. The intensity of the talk we had on the radio comes rushing back.

People who have listened to *Morningside* for a long time and, as they frequently say, feel they know me before they meet me in these line-ups are nevertheless sometimes stuck for words. ("But I'm cuter than you thought, aren't I?" I say to break the tension–I am, too.) Now I know how they feel. I have shared a moment of high emotion with the lovely young person who stands at my autographing table, asked her the most intimate questions, and now, face to face, I don't know what to say to her. Not at all. I long for the privacy of radio, with only a few hundred thousand people listening.

I blurt out that I would like her to have a copy of the book.

"But I've already bought this one," she smiles.

"I . . . uh . . . wouldn't you like another?"

"Sure. Okay."

"Maybe you can give it to your . . . er . . . mother."

I explain the story to the people in the line behind her, nearly all of whom are familiar with it. Sharing Joanne's pleasure, they are happy to wait.

I sign the book I have charged on my Visa. My handwriting is even shakier than usual. On the radio, I could have turned my mike off, and kept my sloppy emotions to myself.

Friday, October 30, Morningside, *Toronto*, *11 a.m.*: Here is a script I wrote this morning, after Patsy Pehlman, who told me the news, suggested I might want to say a word or two on the air:

This is an obituary of someone who never appeared on *Morningside*, and who didn't even listen to it much, but who in a not incidental way made everyone's life around here and around other radio programs more pleasant, and whom I would like to salute this morning before we get down to regular business.

Her name was Ruth. Yesterday, when I heard she had died, I learned her last name too, which was Burgess, but for me and for hundreds of other people who have come into this drafty old building over the years she was just Ruth. Ruth in the cafeteria.

She knew everyone's name.

This is a funny place to work. More or less like any other large institution, the CBC comprises not only those of us who own the voices you hear, but old guys with purple veins in their faces who have slugged away at the same jobs for years, and young kids with tank tops who wear Walkmans as they empty the garbage, and executives who wear suits and women who carry clip-boards wherever they go, and a whole lot of other people who see each other in the hall every day without learning each other's functions, let alone what they are called. But Ruth knew everyone, and you only had to work here a couple of weeks before she greeted you by name when you went down for your first cup of coffee in the morning. There are at least twenty other people in this building this morning whose names I know only because I heard Ruth address them.

She was always nice, too. Not cloying or artificially nice–I don't think she ever told me to have a good day –just pleasant and cheerful and good at her job, which she took pride in and did well; the cafeteria here isn't supposed to open until seven, but Ruth used to get here well before that, and, if she was ready, and had her galoshes off, she'd let you get a cup of coffee when you needed it most.

Ruth got sick a couple of years ago, with cancer, and

last year she went away to hospitals and her family. I talked to her on the phone a few times. She never complained. She was always grateful that you'd taken time to say hello.

I hope she knew how much everyone around here liked her, and how much the fact that she put a little humanity into this frequently anonymous place mattered to all the people she served coffee to over the years.

Evening of the same day, Ziggy's restaurant, Kingston, Ontario: Dinner with Glen Allen. A rare pleasure. We became friends, I would like to think, during the year Glen worked at *Morningside*, but, except for office functions, our social paths seldom crossed. I took him to the harness races one evening just after he'd signed on. He knew the ropes, and bet every race, sometimes with a zeal that reminded me of his father. But I don't think he had a good time. Any kind of social engagement—especially one where there are drinks around—is an ordeal for him. Compared to him, I'm Dale Carnegie. Much as I'd like to have, I didn't ask him again.

He'd been foreign editor of *Maclean's* before he joined us, but what he enjoyed most about the radio was the chance to celebrate the eccentric. He liked the mail as much as I do, and in preparing the current volume of *Papers* I leaned heavily on his editorial skills. He would come in early, and, without saying much, take a pile of letters to the smoking-area and read them quietly to himself. Through the day, you'd hear him murmuring on the phone to their authors, sometimes for hours on end, and at story meetings, when things got dry and all the earnest stories had run out, he'd always have a Ukrainian immigrant who played Hawaiian guitar to suggest, or a man who built model bridges out of spaghetti.

When Glen left the program last spring, the other people in the unit wanted to make a fuss over him. They do this for everyone who leaves, of course, usually preparing a special tape, or putting a lot of thought into a touchingly silly present. But, though Glen had been with us for a short time even by our standards, the effort that went into his presentation was extraordinarily warm. For days in advance, people sneaked down the hall to record tributes to him, satirical to be sure, and full of the kind of inside joke I'd never be able to capture here, but in the care and sheer hard work that went into them a measure of how much we'd all liked having him around.

When we were finished making the tape, the producers, led by the unquenchable Talin, insisted on playing it for him at the wrap-up party. I fought them, convinced Glen would be embarrassed by the the limelight. They won. They were right. He chuckled and grinned his shy, contagious grin all the way through the tape, and when it was finished made a gracious and funny speech. That evening, Glen and I came as close as we did all year to opening up with each other. Until then, we'd communicated mostly by note, each of us able to say things better at the typewriter than face to face, or in guarded, coded explorations of mutual interests, which are many, and vary from a woman we have each (at different times) had a crush on in Montreal, to the prose of A. J. Liebling, and from the politics of *Maclean's*, to, inevitably, alcohol, its use and abuse. On the abuse (he hasn't used it now for several years) he is an expert, a "recovering alcoholic", as he says, and that has deepened our curiously reticent friendship. I've told Glen about my father, things I glibly left out of these pages back in June—that Harold Gzowski, too, was an alcoholic, though unrecovered till his death. I haven't pussyfooted about my own occasionally scary history, either, and he, in his quiet way, has been of gentle support to me, even when that support has just been reassurance. Once, I casually mentioned that I'd had a couple of extra Scotches the night before, and said that I was sometimes not sure, between me and booze, that I knew "which was the horse and which was the rider." Next morning, stapled closed on my desk, I found a friendly and helpful note, PG from Glen.

Still, as I say, we never really talked. Men don't do that. Not men of my time or Glen's. Not with other men. I said that to Glen, in fact, when we were making our private goodbyes at his last *Morningside* party, and when, at last, we brought up the subject of our lack of real contact. "Well," he said, "sober men don't, anyway. One of the things I miss about drinking is those long evenings of just talking. You know, all the good bullshit."

"Except it really is bullshit," I said. "We both know that."

"Yeah. Well, you can't remember it in the morning anyway."

WHAT STANDS BETWEEN US, ironically, is precisely what–or who –most powerfully draws us together. Ralph. Glen's father, my mentor. Glen's relationship with Ralph is his own story. He has told some of it in a lyrical and gripping piece he agreed to put in the second *Papers* (the diary of his emergence from the mire of his addiction was in the first), and I am not willing to invade his privacy now more than to say the man he knew at home – the father–was a darkly different creature from the companionable exemplar I served under at *Maclean's*, and that the demons that have pursued the son stem in no small way from the tensions of his boyhood. "My . . . father and I," he wrote, "never spoke more than ten words to each other at a time. And these conversations were grim – they had all the flavour and fun of the Geneva arms talks."

And yet, I think as I look across the table in this crowded restaurant, watching him sip on soda water laced with lime while I–with his blessing but nonetheless self-consciously–work on a double Scotch, he is so much like Ralph. He is taller, dark where Ralph was a redhead, and the smile that ignites his face is more reminiscent of Birdeen than of his father. But he has the same hunch of the shoulders, the same impatient walk, the same intolerance of fraud and pretension, the same eye for a story, the same ear for language. "All the flavour and fun of the Geneva arms talks", eh? Only an Allen could have written that. And none could have written it better.

He understands, too, my hero-worship, and is reluctant to disturb it. When we first met, he told me he remembered my coming to the duplex when he was a child–he is about ten years younger than I–and, when I'd left, Ralph's making favourable predictions about my future. He knew how much that would mean to me, and reported it with pleasure. In other conversations, when I seek more details on the man I thought I knew, probing, the way a tongue searches for an open nerve, Glen's memories of Ralph's dark days at the typewriter staring at the wall and saying nothing, he brushes me aside, and changes the subject. His father, he knows, is my father *figure*, and, however uncomfortable his own relationship, he is too big a man to begrudge me that.

Saturday, October 31, the Hochelaga Inn, Kingston, 1 a.m.: Can't sleep. Too much on my mind.

The book tour has started in earnest now. As soon as the program finished in Toronto this morning, I jumped into my car and headed down the 401 towards Belleville, where, though I was late and left my aging BMW running outside W. and R. Greenley books, I was greeted by bagpipes and the town crier. I signed more in Kingston tonight, at A Printed Passage, where, as if as a reminder of that other current in my life, the subject of literacy arose. (A woman in the line-up asked me to donate something for an auction to support the local campaign; I bought a paperback of *Who Has Seen the Wind* and wrote something personal in it.) Tomorrow: Peterborough–another degree, I blush to say–and then the west. I won't be back on *Morningside* for a week.

What's keeping me awake, though, is an interview I did this morning. The guest was Clive Barker, an articulate young Englishman who has become a star in the world of horror fiction, but who was, on this trip, talking about a novel he has just published, called *Weaveworld*, a whimsical fantasy, full, as Barker said, "of all the magic in the world". The book had captivated me, and Barker responded warmly to my enthusiasm. We talked of magic, of how it's faded from our lives. He said a favourite story of his youth was of the young William Blake, whom he described as one of his great heroes. "He was taken for a walk on Peckham Rye when he was about nine," he said, "and, though his mum and dad couldn't see them, for Blake the trees were full of angels."

To Clive Barker, in the studio, I offered the observation that Hallowe'en (which, I see by the clock, has already begun) seems to be coming back into favour this year, that more people than I can remember since my childhood are planning to go to parties or somehow mark the occasion. The reason, I said, might spring from the same longings that lay behind my response to his novel: in a world of too many computers, too much television, too many bean-counters, we need more . . . angels in the trees.

Before we could explore the idea further, Barker was off for his next appointment. But the image he implanted has hung in my mind.

A COUPLE OF SUMMERS AGO, the writer and radio producer Max Allen, with the help of the researcher Brian Hickey, did an exten-

sive analysis of every story carried on CBC radio's hourly news
–a thousand broadcasts. Eighty-eight per cent of the stories were
about conflict of some sort, they reported; fifty-six per cent about
death. In only three per cent of the items on the news did "things
turn out well".

On one December 31, the year-end round-up of news reviewed
the year in obituary. Sixteen people were mentioned. Fifteen of
them had not been on the news in the past twelve months for
any other reason; all they did that we found worth reporting on
was die.

To Max Allen, a thoughtful man, those figures were a symbol
of the news department's fascination with Thanatos, the ancient
Greeks' personification of death – the death instinct, as a
dictionary I consulted later said, "especially as expressed in vio-
lent aggression" – and the antidote would be to have the news
pay more attention to Thanatos' opposite, Eros, the life force. I
agreed with his analysis when I heard it, and found it cast a light
on some of my own dissatisfactions with what I do for a living
–my own version, perhaps, of the feelings that led Ray Munro
to attempt his transformation of the *Chatham Daily News*. Now,
as I watch the glowing clock on the table count into Hallowe'en,
I realize that the Blakean symbol I have picked up from Clive
Barker has illuminated the same corner of my mind.

Eros, the life force. Angels in the trees.

Thanatos, the death force, the enemy, the scourge.

You don't suppose it would have occurred to me to talk about
Ruth in the cafeteria when she was alive, do you?

Saturday, October 31, the Hochelaga Inn, 6:30 a.m.: Up early to
write out my thoughts for the speech I will deliver this afternoon,
I make my way to the wickered sunroom of this comfortable, out-
of-the-way hostelry, and at the front desk, with a coffee and crois-
sant, pick up a Saturday *Globe*.

On the book page–hello!–is a review of the book I'm on the
the road to peddle. The headline (why do they have headlines
on book reviews anyway?) is non-committal, even mysterious,
The people who do talk back to radio, but the reviewer is–
oh-oh!–John Melady. The good news is that Melady is a writer
himself; the bad is that he's never been on *Morningside*. He had
a book out about the Korean war a couple of years ago and, for

one reason or another, we never got around to doing it. Wouldn't be surprised if he's still mad at me.

One of the problems with book reviews in this country – and there are a lot of them, which the Writers' Union is currently looking into – is the arbitrary nature of the decisions about who gets to make judgments on whom. I've had a lot of good breaks. The *Globe* gave my race-track book to Martin O'Malley, for example – before I started playing golf with him, admittedly, but still a guy I knew from around – and the *Star* gave *The Game of Our Lives* to Christie Blatchford, who, long before she became a newspaperwoman, worked in the ticket booth at North Toronto Arena (her father was the manager), where I took my sons to play hockey.

Other authors haven't been so lucky. Berton, for sure, gets beaten up regularly by academics who don't like the way he's brought his lively, journalist's prose into their bailiwick, or are jealous of his sales. But there are worse than that. Last summer, the *Globe* gave the book by the Kingston *Whig-Standard* reporters who had broken the story about Soviet defectors from Afghanistan to Victor Malarek, their own guy, who is a dogged and effective soft shoe himself but who, on that particular incident, had been cleanly beaten by the very people whose work he was asked to review.

There's no conspiracy here, just the breaks of the game, and they can go either way. This season, the same paper, the *Globe*, had a book by another of its own reporters, Linda McQuaig, reviewed by Arthur Drache, the Ottawa tax consultant (and an author himself), and I'm sure whoevever assigned the piece was unaware before he did it that Drache was one of the people Linda's book criticized – just as, I'm sure, they weren't aware that Peter Foster, whom they asked to review Gary Ross's *Stung*, is one of the people Gary thanks in his acknowledgments.

I don't know what to do about all this. There are few people in the community of writers in this country who don't know a lot of the other people. Paths cross. My own solution, reached after I was asked to review a collection of sports pieces by a friend, found it wanting and myself unable to say so in print, is simply not to accept for review any books by anyone I know. Whatever I say, I figure, I'm damned, and never more so than if I praise a work by someone I like. But if everyone were to take that course, who'd write the notices? As Jack McClelland says, it's not so much whether anyone likes your book, anyway. It's whether they mention it at all.

Melady? He loves me – and the *New Papers*. He's as flattering as Craig MacInnis has been calumnious. Whoopee! Says I'm cool, courteous, and curious, which the cutline, at least in the edition that has reached the Hochelaga before breakfast this morning, translates to cool, "couteous", etc.

That's me, boy. Couteous.

Smart guy, that Melady.

Trent University, Peterborough, Ontario, 2 p.m.: On a golden autumn afternoon in the heart of this lovely campus, amid the buildings that soared from the imagination of Ron Thom, who lived on Washington Avenue when Jenny and I came back from Montreal to live there, and with the memory of the university's former chancellor, Margaret Laurence, still lingering in the halls, I wish my fellow graduands a happy Hallowe'en.

"I hope you have learned some magic here," I say, "and how to see angels in the trees."

Krista Munroe's Longshot. This is the picture that adorned my bulletin board. Ben, 26 months old, is stirring cake batter – a substance of which, as Krista wrote, "a single tablespoon can cover a suburban split-level."

CHAPTER SEVENTEEN

The book tour in theory and practice . . .
Death of a democrat . . . Longshot comes to
breakfast . . . "Just let me make sure I have
all this" . . . Eros in Victoria . . . A Great
Canadian in Regina . . . Dizzy spells . . .
Why the news is the news . . . An
astrological clinker

Sunday, November 1, Richard Osler's house, Calgary, 7 p.m.: Over drinks – I have begged out of dinner, pleading a need to get to bed early before the whirlwind of the next few days – Richard says the stock-market crash has left him with more time than he thought he would have, and that he'd be interested in coming back to *Morningside* after Christmas.

Hurray. Our business column has continued to struggle without him.

This chance to talk with him is a pleasant side benefit of the book tour, and I can hardly wait to report to the office that he's willing to join us again.

9:45, the Delta Bow Valley Inn: Gordon Pinsent's *John and the Missus* is playing on the TV, its pace as slow as icebergs along the Avalon peninsula, and I am lulled to the cusp of sleep when a bulletin from the news department snaps me wide awake.

René Lévesque is dead. My first reaction – other than the chill of fear all heavy smokers must be feeling as they hear the news

–is one of sadness. He was a good man, the antithesis of a bean-counter. His vision for Quebec, his nation as he would have called it, was one I abhorred (even though, as I've said, if I'd been raised a francophone I'd probably have been among his supporters), but he fought for it with honour, and when the people he had tried to sell it to rejected it, he shrugged his shoulders and accepted their verdict. A democrat.

My personal response – and I am more moved than I can remember being by the death of a Canadian public figure –takes the form of an urge to talk about him on the radio tomorrow. Augusta LaPaix, a thorough professional, is sitting in for me while I travel, and the producers, even now, are probably hard at work. But, damn it, I want to be involved.

Thanatos? I don't think so. Lévesque's death is a real event, a landmark in our history. I'd just like to be part of the discussion, and contribute what I can.

Monday, November 2, still the Delta Bow Valley, over a wake-up coffee in my room, 7 a.m.: Not many years ago, when the book tour was a new phenomenon in Canada, a writer with any kind of national reputation could waltz into, say, Calgary, and be assured of his picture in the paper, appearances on all the chat shows, and, consequently, a pretty fair turn-out at his autographing sessions in the stores. Now, it's not so easy. Travelling authors, their peregrinations subsidized by the Canada Council, swarm like frantic water-spiders over the country every fall, running into each other at airports, swapping tales as they wait their turn in the line-ups for TV shows ("one guy in Winnipeg hadn't even read my *dust-jacket* . . ."), and usually, when they get home, writing one more account of their adventures. But people, especially the media, are more blasé all the time. ("Jeez, Sally, we talked to Peter Newman *last* year.") The reps – the publishers' representatives who chaperone us from engagement to engagement (and it's a good thing *they* don't write memoirs)–are having a harder and harder time filling our dance cards. The gimmicks get wilder and wilder all the time. My own thought is that, as valuable as the tour was when Jack McClelland and the other pioneers invented it, and as much as it has had to do with creating the Canlit scene (the days when Farley and Pierre sat around signing each other's books didn't last very long), it's outlived its usefulness. The money that goes into air fares and hotels could be spent a lot more usefully, on newspaper ads, maybe, or direct mail–or, heaven forfend, making Canadian books cheaper at the bookstore. But, since so much of it comes from the good old Council, the publishers don't seem to care, and here I go again, into the fray.

8 a.m., the Glencoe Club, southwest Calgary: On the way in to breakfast with two hundred people who have paid twenty-five dollars each to the enthusiastic proprietors of Sandpiper books for a copy of the *New Papers* and a chance to hear me talk, I am accosted by a man in a wheelchair. He has been waiting for nearly an hour, he says, and just wants to tell me about a story he thinks *Morningside* should do. I stop.

A mistake. The people coming in to breakfast, it turns out, also want their books *signed*, and before I finish hearing the case from the wheelchair, I feel like Bobby Hull at a hockey banquet, pinned to a counter in the lobby, surrounded by open books and flashing pencils.

Bob White, where are you now that I need you?

My petulance, however, is short-lived. At the periphery of the crowd I spot a slim young woman–she's thirty, I happen to know –with a handsome blond pre-schooler perched on her hip. Krista. Krista Munroe. The boy is her son, Ben Munroe-McFee, or, as I know him better, Longshot.

Krista first wrote to me in the fall of 1983. Ten months earlier she had learned she had Hodgkin's disease, and her letter, in response to a *Morningside* discussion of suicide, was a wise, sometimes funny, paean to life, which she had figured out better at twenty-six, I thought, than most people will have at a hundred. I put the letter in the first *Papers*, and, over the years, have kept in touch with her, and shared her joy in Ben's birth after the disease went temporarily into remission–he really is called Longshot–and some of her other ups and downs. Ben's picture, which she sent me, adorns my office wall.

Last spring, when I was speaking to some teachers in Medicine Hat, where she lives, I met her for the first time in person, and learned she'd been sick again, but was "eating chemicals" and fighting back. The letter that arose from that encounter is in the book I'm flogging now, another blithe, brave ode to Eros. So, and I don't know if she knows this yet, is the admission that her original letter was my favourite of all in the first volume.

In a sense, Krista is here at my invitation. The Calgary CBC morning radio program ran a phone-in contest last week to see which of its listeners could best imitate my stammering, prolix, circumlocutory style of questioning. The winners were to be given tickets to this morning's breakfast. The producers played the tapes for me on the phone and asked me to judge. Three of those I chose were devastatingly – and hilariously – accurate. (Actually, so was nearly everyone who called in.) For the fourth, which was funny too, I knew only that Krista was the first name and that the first three digits of the phone number matched those an operator told me meant Medicine Hat. I took a chance. She took the bus, and here they are, she and Ben.

In my after-the-coffee remarks, among other things, I talk briefly about Lévesque. Somewhat to my surprise–this is Alberta, let us not forget–the applause tells me my response to his death is a common one, even here. I wonder if the other politicians have noticed how people feel.

Before I close, I introduce the winners of the sound-alike contest. When I get to Krista–and Ben–my voice trembles, and I have to bite my lip to finish. When I go to her table to thank her for coming, I think I see her wink at me. Can't be sure, though. She's busy helping Ben finish up a blueberry pancake.

Friday, November 6, Air Canada 234, headed east, 10:30 a.m., B.C. time: I've almost made it, for now, anyway (there'll be an eastern excursion later on). I'm squeezed pretty dry. I was a little cranky in Vancouver–when was it, last night?–when I learned at the last minute that the Sav-On store where I was scheduled to sign in North Van was selling the book for $11.97. (It's supposed to be $16.95.) "I don't sign discounted books," I told the M and S rep. "It's not fair to the independent stores, who can't afford to discount, but can give the kind of special service the chains don't – like autographed books." But even that turned out all right. I knuckled under–the rep hadn't known about my quixotic principle when she'd made the arrangements–and I had quite a good time, standing in the book department, hard by detergents, watching people trundle by with their shopping-carts full of week-end groceries, wondering who the hell the bearded guy was, next to the All. For one surprised weekend shopper, I signed a grape-fruit. I'm a signing fool. By the time I finish all this, an un-autographed copy of *The New Morningside Papers* will be a col-lector's item.

The most unfortunate interview I've had was in Vancouver too. A woman from a suburban paper took me up to her apart-ment in False Creek–no, no, there was none of that; the rep was there as well–and, saying she'd been unable to get a press release from the CBC (no investigative reporter, she), pulled out a tape-recorder and asked me, I swear, "So, where did it all begin?" While the rep glanced nervously at her watch, I replayed some of the material from this journal, starting at Timmins. Twenty minutes or so later, when I was pulling out of *Maclean's* for the second time, she needed to change tapes. "Just let me make sure I've been getting all this," she said, switching her machine to "Play".

You can guess the rest.

Most of the interviews, though, have gone better than I expected. Nearly all the people who've talked to me have read the *Papers* at least as well as I've read the books by all the people I brag about. Calgary, Edmonton, Vancouver, Victoria, Vancou-ver again, and now, one more stop and I'm home.

Victoria was an almost unrelieved high. It started with a mem-orable dinner of oysters, scallops, and medallions of lamb at the Deep Cove Chalet, after which the owners – *Morningside* lis-teners, I hardly need point out–sent me back to the cavernous old Empress in their white Rolls-Royce. At a crowded breakfast at the University of Victoria the next morning (I talked about Lévesque again, by the way, as I have everywhere I've had the chance, and once again drew sympathetic applause), I shared the podium with the poet (and wife of the former diplomat and *Maclean's* editor Arthur Irwin) P. K. Page, who, now past seventy, stood hand on hip and read from her Brazilian journal about "swallows darning the threadbare air", and "a girl whose tight costume made her the ripest orange on the tree". Eros. After breakfast, I signed in a shopping-mall, where I was serenaded by the Raging Grannies, sprightly women in flowered hats who, when they are not singing in the plazas, patrol the coastline for nuclear ships, and whom I instantly added to the considerable file of potential guests I'm taking back to *Morningside*. After *that*, at a TV station, I met a woman named Kelly Rose, who introduced me to her daugher Kimberley, a Down's syndrome child. Kimberley was born, Kelly told me, after the parents, already aware through amniocentesis that she would be handicapped, heard David Suzuki talking on *Morningside* about the decision he and his wife had made to have their baby under the same circumstances. If the love I saw between mother and daughter is the measure, they did the right thing.

All in all, I'm feeling pretty jaunty.

7:30 p.m., same date, a drawing-room in Government House, Regina: The last event of this part of the tour—my travel schedule has been built around it, in fact—is my second dinner for the Writers' Development Trust, and now, decked out in the dinner jacket I've toted across the west for the occasion, I stand in a receiving-line for the two hundred people who've paid to eat buffalo steak and hear me speak. I'm surrounded by dignitaries: the Premier and his wife (Mr. Devine will leave later for a speaking engagement of his own), the Lieutenant-Governor and his wife, the chairman of the dinner committee and his wife. The guests promenade by, the businessmen in black ties (they have, I'm fairly sure, been dragooned by the energetic committee into coughing up two hundred bucks a ticket—"Hi, I'm Keith Hoover, as in vacuum cleaner," says one, "the best sucker in town"), the wives in ball gowns and silver lamé, often introducing themselves in the Zena Cherry style of "I'm Mrs. Keith Hoover", many of the writers (good old Saskatchewan) in sports jackets or suits. Ken Mitchell, poet, playwright, novelist, and Lenin look-alike (his friend and colleague Geoff Ursell could play Karl Marx in a duet with him if they chose), sports a red pin in his lapel.

"What's that?" I say.

"Tory pin," says Mitchell.

"Really?" I glance toward Grant Devine, whom Mitchell has already shaken hands with. He's talking with a later arrival. They're unlikely confrères, I think. Ken's play about Norman Bethune has just played to enthusiastic audiences in China. I peer more closely at the pin, and Mitchell raises the lapel so I can read the fine print.

"The only good Tory," it says, "is a supposi-Tory."

9:30, the dining-room: The dinner, prepared in the kitchen of this storied old building, has been spectacular. It began with small stuffed quail, moved on through a cold strawberry soup (Larry Kyle, a Regina lawyer and sometime *Morningside* columnist who is seated at my table, says, "There are some people here who'll say the chicken was small but the dessert was terrific"), the buffalo filet, a salad, and (good old Saskatchewan) one dessert – "chocolate soldiers"–for the women and one–I'm not sure, but "blueberry hockey puck" would be fitting–for the men.

The conversation too, at least at my table, has been engrossing. On my left is Mrs. Devine–Chantelle, as everyone at the table calls her (a custom I have easily adopted) – a prepossessing bilingue from Gravelbourg. On my right: the Lieutenant-Governor, a former Chief Justice of the province (I learn), who is splendidly suited for his current appointment. Over the buffalo and the blueberry pucks, His Honour has talked movingly of his love for the country, which he has explored fom Cape Spear to Long Beach, of his views on the constitution, and of–he looked slyly around the room before he said this, noting the presence of the owners of several private stations – his affection for the CBC.

The Queen's representative and I, in fact, are getting along like a house on fire. I tell him that once, on a winter vacation, I saw a highway in Jamaica, along which, at regular intervals, were impressively outfitted privies. I heard, I said, that the Jamaican government, in preparation for the royal visit that would open the road, plied one of its own citizens with as much water as she could drink and then drove her at a processional pace from Negrille to Montego Bay. Every time she held up her hand, they marked the site for a comfort station. But when the Queen herself arrived, she sailed right through, smiling graciously all the way. His Honour shook his head in admiration, and topped me by saying that when Her Majesty had been in Saskatchewan last month she had gone through seven straight hours of ceremony without once having to excuse herself. Then, eyes twinkling, he said, "and I didn't go either."

Charming man. I wonder how many dinners like this he has to attend every year, and keep the small talk moving along.

As Grant Devine rises to introduce me, the Lieutenant-Governor makes a flattering gesture to me. He picks up a copy of the *New Papers* which, along with some books by the Saskatchewan writers at the dinner, has been left at the table, and asks if I will sign it for him as a memento of the evening. Rather proudly, I reach for a pen.

And suddenly realize I have a problem. The question, class, is:

What is the name of the Lieutenant-Governor of Saskatchewan?

I can't believe I don't know it. Surely, when I was introduced to him before the receiving-line . . . no, that was "Your Honour, may I present . . ." and all through dinner I've just been saying "Your Honour, this," "Your Honour, that."

Chantelle? Too late to ask her now. At the podium, her husband has almost finished a surprisingly warm introduction and is preparing to leave for his later engagement.

I brandish the pen, as if trying to muster an appropriately sincere dedication – which, come to think of it, I am.

His place card! I peer past his coffee cup as he beams in anticipation. The card is lying on its face.

The Premier finishes, and begins to make his exit.

I write: "To His Honour–a great Canadian, Regina, Saskatchewan, November 6, 1987."

THE LIEUTENANT-GOVERNOR OF SASKATCHEWAN, by the way, is the Hon. Frederick William Johnson, BA, LLB, etc. That's Johnson. The Toronto politician is Anne Johns*ton*.

Wednesday, November 25, the apartment, Toronto, 3 p.m.:   I'm dry-docked. Tomorrow will be, as best I remember, the third time in my five-plus years that I've missed a program through incapacity. I succumbed to the flu for a couple of days in my first season, and last year missed half a week or so when my back, which has troubled me off and on most of my life, just gave out, and I hobbled off to a clinic and my bed. (I have one of those fancy back-rests now, which probably helps, but like a lot of other back victims, I'm sure, I use it–and remember to do my pelvic tilts–only when I start to feel pain.)

Don't know what the trouble is this time. I was crackling with energy when I returned from the western book tour, but gradually I started getting dizzy spells, feeling more disoriented than I wanted to let on – or, I hope, than came through on the air. In the studio, especially with line links, I've been covering my free ear – I wear a headphone on the other – with my hand. This is an old announcer's trick to hear your own voice (it works, too), but in my case, it's just been to stop my spinning head. Dave Amer has had some of the same symptoms, he says, and there are a lot of nasty viruses around this long, grey autumn. After the program today, I just told Gloria I needed to stop for a while. As always, she – and everyone else in the unit – understood. Whatever the tensions, they're all wonderfully supportive of me. Augusta will sit in tomorrow. I'll sleep and read and, if my head will stay still, write.

I haven't been as diligent about this journal as I meant to be. My notebook entries since I got back from Regina have been sporadic and unenlightening, a happy note one day (here's a rave about the artist and designer Heather Cooper, for example, and another for a man named Adolf Hungry Wolf, a European who has adopted the native culture and lives with his Blackfoot wife in the B.C. interior); a grumpy one the next – we're having trouble settling on a pair of columnists from Vancouver; so-and-so was too solemn, someone else (a first-time author) showed up stoned.

For every bad day – yesterday was a real stinker – there's an inspiring one. Even today, when I was fighting whatever it is I've got, there was a string of guests to carry me along: Kay Mac-Pherson, the peace activist who's getting one of this year's Person's Awards; Candace Savage, a naturalist from Yellowknife who talked about eagles (and who so enthralled me with her own soaring enthusiasms that Katz had to flag me down from the control room to get in the hour-two cutaway); Marion Quednau, another first-time novelist, who lives in a small town in B.C. and who turned out to be as brittlely clever in person as her book, called *The Butterfly Chair*, is compellingly sombre; and Trish Wood, a loquacious free-spirit who works as a producer at *Canada* AM and whom Carole Warren – who is really blossoming as a producer, by the way – is carefully nurturing to do the kind of pop-cultural reportage we never were able to get from Daniel Richler. Just writing their names down now lifts my spirits.

My thoughts on Eros and Thanatos have continued to nag me. On November 11, I copied the first sentence of the newscast into my notebook: "Remembrance Day, and the news is full of fighting, bombing, and bickering." The Sunday after I got back from Regina, the weekend news (according to my notes) consisted of a bombing in Ireland (twenty-eight dead), a car crash in Edmonton, when "both the north- and south-bound highways near the airport were hit by instant fog," and a train wreck in India. What does any of that have to do with *me*, I wonder, or, except perhaps for the people who were driving past Leduc, Alberta, some hours before the weather made the news, with anyone who could possibly be listening to the radio?

It's not only devoted to death and destruction–Thanatos–but it's remote, out of context, a score-card of disasters you can't do anything about. As Neil Postman says (in *Amusing Ourselves to Death*, the smartest book on the media I've read for a long while): "How often does it occur that information provided you on morning radio or television, or in the morning newspaper, causes you to alter your plans for the day, or to take some action you would not otherwise have taken, or provides insight into some problem you are required to solve?"

I have a theory about how this has come about.

A couple of years ago, I was invited to speak to a conference of the managing editors of Canadian newspapers. The conference was held in Winnipeg, as it happens, and Murray Burt, my old crony from the *Moose Jaw Times-Herald*, was, as m.e. of the *Free Press*, one of its organizers. At the first plenary session, I couldn't help noticing not only that all the delegates were men (which will change), but that nearly all of them were, like Murray, contemporaries or near contemporaries of mine. (I noticed they nearly all wore ties with diagonal stripes, too, but that didn't lead to anything.) They were, in other words, people who had started about the same time I did and built on many of the same foundations. They–we, for if Ralph Allen hadn't called me in Chatham, I'm sure, I could well have been among their number, wearing a diagonally striped tie of my own – began writing up speeches to the Beaver Club, or its local equivalent, and moved, as I did, through obituaries, police calls, traffic accidents, court cases, forest fires (or, again, their regional variations), and municipal politics. However idealistic we may have been–and I would wager that every man in that room in Winnipeg shared to one degree or another the romance that had infected me in Timmins – we were absorbing ideas of what was news and what wasn't, where you got it and where you didn't. Those ideas, I think, are with us still, and, as we have moved into positions of power or influence, they have continued to determine what gets into the press or onto the air.

What are those ideas? For one thing, an undue number of them spring from Thanatos: accident, pestilence, conflict, death. If it's awful, it must be interesting. Show the pictures of the raging flames; get the quotes from the survivors; film the body being wheeled to the ambulance. For another – even more fundamental, I think – they deal with received facts, facts that come from accepted sources. News is news not because it matters to anyone, but because it comes from the places you get news.

You cover the speaker at the Beaver Club not because what he says will affect the lives of your readers, but because you know that if you go there, someone with a title will say something you can quote. You phone the police, as I used to watch Austin Jelbert do in Timmins and then, on the night beat in Toronto, did myself, because you know they'll have a list of who's bumped into whom and who's been hurt. You cover court cases not because the events there are inherently interesting (even though they sometimes are), but because, in court, conflicts are paraded before your eyes; all you do is write things down.

And so on. And when you move up from Timmins or Moose Jaw or the Fredericton *Gleaner*, the habits are formed. The Beaver Club has become the Empire Club – or, for that matter, a conference of world-renowned scientists. Traffic accidents have become plane crashes; forest fires, wars. Sometimes the speeches and the catastrophes matter; sometimes they don't. Their importance to people's lives is all but irrelevant to those of us who cover them; the reader, the listener, the viewer, is left to sort it out for himself. *Our* motivation is simply that the events and the statements are there; we write about them or broadcast their "highlights" because we always have.

Two cornerstones of what we call news, I think, buttress my theory. One is our over-reliance on the press release and the "news conference" – in each case, I'd argue, a demonstration of picking up and disseminating information almost solely because of where it comes from: accepted sources. The other is the amount of ink and air-time devoted to the affairs of political institutions, whether or not what's going on in them has anything to do with the real world. Almost every day, for example, something from the parliamentary Question Period makes "news". The world hasn't changed. The only thing that's happened is that someone in a place where you get news has said something you can report. So you report it, just as you learned to report the city council meetings in Moose Jaw, many years ago.

Meanwhile, of course, the world does change. The two biggest stories of the time I've been in this business have not been the assassination of John Kennedy or the October crisis in Quebec (though each of them has left scars on a generation), or even, may the ghost of Foster Hewitt forgive me, the Canadian hockey victory of 1972. They've been the computer revolution and the change in the role of women. Yet in neither case can I remember them leading the 7 a.m. newscast, or making the major headline in the *Globe and Mail*. No one held a press conference, you see. There isn't any place that quantifies social change.

Too harsh a view? Sure. Too wide-ranging, too. Things *are* evolving – in many cases for the better. In spite of their earnestness, or, indeed, as a function of it, the young people coming into the business with Alison have a far broader understanding of what they're up to than we did at the same stage. They *do* seem to see some need for context. They *are* dissatisfied with the daily ration of Thanatos – even if they wouldn't agree with my use of the word. They *can* find the stories they'll be reporting by following their natural curiosity. But, thanks to us, they have a hell of a long way to go.

YESTERDAY'S PROGRAM, by the way, included the result of one of my own efforts to inject a little Eros into things, a little magic.

On the book tour, in the green room for the *Vancouver Show* on Channel 13, I had run into a man named John Rutherford, an astrologer with a long history of broadcast appearances. I rather liked him, and, though I think the whole thing is arrant mumbo-jumbo myself, tried hard when I returned to convince a story meeting that we should have an occasional *Morningside* astrology column–to put, as I of course phrased it, "a few angels in our trees".

A hard sell. As I wrote cantankerously in my notebook, "No one seems to get it." But Janet Enright, who at least confessed to consulting her own horoscope in the paper from time to time, agreed to give it a whirl. She tracked down John Rutherford and, as a partner for him, booked a woman named Eugenia Last, who lives in Toronto, and, among other pursuits, does a column in the Sunday *Sun*.

Boy, were they terrible. They were so serious they made our business column sound like *Monty Python*, and so convoluted that . . . well, they lost me somewhere between the cusp of Aquarius and the moon over Libra. They wouldn't even *predict* anything, for heaven's (oops) sake. They were, in fact, the main reason I called yesterday's program a stinker.

Sorry, Janet.

The CBC publicity department's idea of how Helen Hutchinson and I spent our time on This Country in the Morning, *1971. This may have been the last time my hair was combed for the next three years.*

CHAPTER EIGHTEEN

Katz, V.I.P. . . . In praise of Montreal . . .
The day the expert spoke with forked
tongue . . . Best wishes to room service . . .
Win-win with David Crombie . . . Crossing
paths with Tom Wolfe . . . Who was that
writer in the editor's office? . . . The facts vs.
the truth

Friday, November 27, 5:15 a.m., the Hotel Bonaventure, Montreal: Katz, meeting me in the lobby to share a cab to Maison Radio-Canada for this morning's program, says, "Friendly hotel, eh?"

"Huh?"

"Didn't you get the flowers in your room, or the matches with your name on the cover?"

"I had a hard enough time getting a key to my mini-bar."

"Jeez," Katz says. "I even had a note of welcome from the manager."

"But tomorrow," I say, "I'll be at the Prince George in Halifax, and *all* the matches there have my initials on them."

As we settle our accounts at the desk, the reason for Gary's special treatment becomes clear. Our reservations were made at the last minute, as we waited to see if a day in bed would cure my dizzy spells. (It did, of course, though the prospect of this trip may have helped as well.) Whoever made the arrangements presumably said only that one of us was to be given VIP treatment.

At the hotel, they chose "G. Katz". Why not? The staff here, I'm sure, is largely French. The small envelope of celebrity in which I glide through English Canada *ne traduit pas*. I remember touring with the *This Country* book, sitting in front of a bookstore in the heart of Place Ville Marie just when the office workers were breaking for lunch. Several thousand of them–*thousands* of thousands of them, it seemed–clattered by, stopping only, when they paused at all, to peer quizzically at the stranger grinning vacuously behind the table. By comparison, my session at the North Vancouver Sav-On this month was a royal wedding.

"Want a light?" says Katz.

5:35 a.m., a taxi: High snowbanks line Dorchester Boulevard, Boulevard René Lévesque as it will soon be known, but the sparse traffic moves steadily along. A blizzard dumped two feet of snow here just before we arrived, but, unlike a lot of Canadian cities, Montreal knows how to handle winter. In Toronto, still November-grey when we left, the first storm of the year will come, as always, as a surprise.

Even–perhaps especially–in the morning dark, Montreal looks lovely. This is how I remember it: wrapped in winter, lights twinkling, the rough grey stone of the old buildings outlined against the night. Just as I can't go to Vancouver without asking myself why I don't move there (the answer is simply that I have to live in Toronto to do the work I do), I can never come here without feeling the pull of nostalgia. For all its political and linguistic strife–or, maybe, because of it–people love this city, I think, as they love no other in Canada. It's more grown-up than other places, more alive. Even the people who've felt they had to leave miss it constantly, and talk about it all the time. I miss it, too, though my residence lasted only a year and I'm too unilingual to settle in now. The train trip from Toronto yesterday was more ordeal than luxury; towed backwards all the way, trying to balance an undercooked meal on a tray the size of a Kleenex box. But I'm pleased to be here this morning, snow and all. My dizzy spells are forgotten. Probably just a virus after all.

5:55, the security desk, Maison Radio-Canada: I fumble in my wallet for a CBC identity card. This is no formality. A couple of years ago, Mike Boone, the perceptive reporter who covers broadcasting for the *Gazette*, wrote an amusing column about my difficulties in getting in here. But I'm not surprised. For one thing, *everyone*'s anonymity is all but guaranteed in this hexagonal concrete tower–the J-cloth building, as someone has dubbed it. (I'm not among those who await with enthusiasm the move from our musty headquarters in Toronto to some equally anti-human monument.) More to the point, I work for the minority service: the English, and English radio at that. As at the hotel, I'm about as big a star in the eyes of the commissionaire here as I would be at customs in Thailand.

Still, the security is a nuisance. If I were going to blow this place up, I don't think I'd arrive in a cab at quarter to six in the morning.

11 a.m., Studio 42, deep in an underground corridor: In spite of the difficulties–riding the elevator fifteen floors from the English Current Affairs office and spelunking through the basement halls to find this site, trying to help Gary through the language barrier with a technician who has the right (though mercifully has not exercised it) to work in French, dealing with (as everywhere on the road) strange hardware in the studio (at least they let me smoke here, as in some places they do not) – the program has gone well. Gloria came down last night, cheered, obviously, by a chance to visit her old haunts. Through the morning she has been dispensing coffee and croissants, translating, handling the crisis when one of three panelists on life on the Main showed up twenty minutes late.

I stumbled a bit in the first hour when a rock singer named Michel Pagliaro compared, I think, singing in English to free trade, but musicians, with their nocturnal habits, are often difficult to comprehend in the morning, and we've had so much success generally with the artists of Quebec – even the biggest stars among them are far more accessible to us than their counterparts in English Canada–that it was hard to be upset.

Right after our musical interlude, I had a rare face-to-face chat with Daniel Latouche and Eric Maldoff, our regular Quebec columnists. Daniel has been growing weary of the amount of coverage we've been giving to the language controversy here, but he's a stimulating presence. He and Eric wrangle all the time on the air–they talked today about the racial tension in Montreal that has followed the shooting of a black teenager–but, as was obvious in the studio, there's affection between them. Their column, which we were so worried about in August, is working fine.

Later on, as well as our panel on the Main, we had an item on bagels and some other odds and ends.

In the third hour, my old crony Gérald Godin dropped by, he of the three-hour taping session for TV. He looked healthy, if pale; his recovery from the brain operation has continued. The occasion for his visit was his winning of the Prix de Montréal for his poetry–$10,000, as he said, for thirty years of work–but, inevitably, for he has stayed active in the PQ in opposition, our talk turned to politics. I asked him why, when he had come out earlier this autumn against Pierre-Marc Johnson, who had succeeded his old friend Lévesque as party leader, he had waited until Johnson was in France–it was, in fact, just a couple of days before Lévesque died–to do it. It had seemed ungallant, I said, an "un-Godin thing to do".

"I'll give you a poet's answer," he said. Then he paused and took a sip of water.

"I wanted to do it before Lévesque was dead," he said.

I was too shaken to ask more.

2 p.m., *Paragraph Books:*   The list of people I've encountered at these autographings grows longer all the time. I was at the Double Hook in Westmount this morning, an unexpected treasure-house of Canadian titles (it may be the only bookstore in Canada that still stocks *An Unbroken Line*, my book on the thoroughbreds, which I am sure is unrelated to the fact that one of its owners, Judy Mappin, is a daughter of E. P. Taylor, a hero of the racetrack). There, I met a violin-maker with a day-care button from Cape Breton Island on his chest, a poet who couldn't finish his sentences but who, having heard *Morningside* today, had figured out that we should have free trade in bagels, and Wayne McKell, a big, strong-handed farmer from St. Chrysostome, Quebec, who has a lyrical piece about fishing in the *New Papers.* Here, on Sherbrooke Street, I meet a cluster of McGill students from across the road (one of whom flatters me by speaking only French); a young man who brings bagels; and someone–I missed

the name—who astonishes me by recalling an occasion from *This Country in the Morning*.

"The day you got Helen Hutchinson," she says.

"Oh, dear. Do you really remember that?"

"I can't remember the name of the 'expert' you brought in," she says. "But almost everything else."

His real name was Schoichet, I tell her. Dr. Roy Schoichet, a psychiatrist in real life and a practical joker by avocation. He and a colleague had done some skits for us, send-ups of traditional radio fare, but I kept spoiling the jokes by breaking up on air. I think it was Frame's idea that Roy do something with an unsuspecting host, and, since Helen was doing occasional interviews for us, the conspiracy was born. We passed a pseudonymous Roy off as an experimental speech therapist from California, who had succeeded in making babies speak full sentences at the age of six months. When Helen, following a script prepared with unusual care, had asked how, he had said simply "hot forks".

HELEN: "Hot *forks?*"

ROY: "Yes. You heat the tines and then apply them to the baby's tongue until he–or she–speaks."

HELEN (outraged): "You can't be serious."

ROY: "Well, it does sound cruel, I know. . . ."

Helen struggled to retain her considerable cool, while Frame and I fought to keep straight faces in the control room. Now, in the bookstore, I recall that I was even then not sure everyone listening would know it was a joke.

"At first," she says, "I wasn't sure myself. But the last line gave it away."

"The last line," I say. "I don't even know if I remember it."

"Oh, I do. Poor Helen. You could hear her anger rising. But I guess you guys had made sure she'd get to the last question."

"Yes, I guess we had. I remember now. We had told her to make sure to ask what the babies' first words usually were."

"And he said . . ."

As the memory of almost thirteen years ago comes racing back to me, we say it together . . .

"No more fork."

Sunday, November 29, the apartment, Toronto, 9 a.m.: I'm autographed out. Once, a season or two after *An Unbroken Line* was published, and when (except for the stock at the Double Hook) it had disappeared from the stores, I went to Edmonton to speak at the Canadian Derby breakfast. The people who had brought me there suggested that I go to the track the night before and sign some copies of the book they'd managed to acquire. When I arrived, I was dumbfounded to see tables everywhere, piled high with my opus. "You'll *never* sell all those," I said, but rolled up my sleeves and set to work anyway. For the next couple of hours, solidly through the first four races, I didn't stop. I signed right through the wall of writer's cramp and up to the manual equivalent of lockjaw. (Next morning, when a waiter brought coffee to my room I signed the bill "Best wishes . . .") I think we moved eight hundred books in all – a record. It wasn't until the fifth race, when I finally had time to walk around, that I saw the sign that had been in front of all the tables: $2 a book. At the racetrack, as someone said later, they'll buy *anything* for two dollars, at least till their money runs out.

On the tour this season, I haven't come close to that dubious achievement. But, as I say, I feel I've done enough. In Halifax yesterday, after yet another breakfast (and yet another evocation of *This Country in the Morning*, when my speech was introduced by Janet Murray, who, as she reminded me, had given the name to Chinook Day, a holiday we invented in those carefree days but which, in the more sedate 1980s, we have let drop), I did two more stores. At one, the Pair of Trindles on the waterfront, I even signed a copy of *Following the Sea*, the diary of an old Nova Scotia whaler named Benjamin Doane, which was published this fall under the editorship of Doane's great-great-granddaughter, who unearthed the manuscript from the family's memorabilia. I was pleased to fulfil that request, as it happens. Hal spotted *Following the Sea* when it came from its publishers, with its gripping text set in an elegant design, and, as well as the usual interview with the editor, we carried readings all last week, by Chris Wiggins. So *Morningside* had some stake in its success. I even managed to conceal my jealousy over the fact that the person who wanted it signed hadn't bothered to pick up the *New Papers*, and was rewarded for my forbearance when a young woman three or four positions later in the line – who *had* bought the *New Papers* –turned out to be Heather (Doane) Atkinson, the editor of her progenitor's work.

With Halifax wrapped up, I've done something like forty sign-ings. *Morningside* interview or not, the *New Papers* surely have been flogged within an inch of their life. Now, I pick up the Sunday *Toronto Star*, which carries a list of the best-selling paper-backs in Canada. When I started on this grind, the *New Papers* were number two, right behind Gelsey Kirkland's *Dancing on My Grave*.

Today, we're fourth.

Thursday, December 3, the Morningside *studio, Toronto, 8:15 a.m.:* The first item on the program this morning is on tape. It's yet another Carole Warren production, a piece on comput-erized music we did yesterday afternoon with Adam Little, a ver-satile young producer at *As It Happens*. It's quite delightful, or sounds it now, since Carole has had to take out a few false starts and other moments of electronic confusion. But I'm hardly lis-tening. I'm talking instead with David Crombie, who, as soon as we finish the tape, will discuss his department's new bill on multiculturalism, but whom I'm questioning now to find out more of his ideas about literacy.

This is not the first time Crombie and I have talked. Late last month, while I roosted briefly in Toronto, he called me at home. He didn't say which of the lines I'd sent out to Ottawa–to Bar-bara McDougall, or to Dalton Camp–had snagged his interest, but he was, my notes say, "enthusiastic" about my possible par-ticipation. Without spelling out any specific plans, he said I could be involved either part-time or full-time. He was very flattering. He called me "my friend". Though I put our brief conversation on the back burner while I finished the book tour, it's been sim-mering away.

Today, his enthusiasm is unflagging, and, once again, I am impressed by both his knowledge of the literacy question and his commitment to dealing with it. He is an engaging man, as bright and (at least in private conversation) as irreverent as some of his cabinet colleagues seem pompous and overblown. He says, albeit vaguely, that the plans for a literacy secretariat are "falling into place", and repeats the idea that I could "have ten per cent or a hundred per cent". I say quickly that I don't think I'd like the ten; the last thing I want is another extra-curricular interest while I carry on with *Morningside*.

"So be it," says the Secretary of State. "It's still a win-win situation for us."

Imperceptibly (I hope), I gulp. A win-win situation? For whom? The Tories? Have I really taken a step towards a *political* involvement? Am I biting into something here I don't want to chew?

Before I can work up the nerve to pursue the subject, the computer-music tape has nearly run out. Katz gestures from behind the glass.

In the interview that follows, I am so intent on keeping my professional distance from the man who may hold my future in his hands that I do an unsatisfactory job. Crombie – and the listener – must wonder what the hell is going through my mind.

Sometimes, I'm not sure myself.

Friday, December 4, the office, 6:30 a.m.: Tom Wolfe, the American writer who is scheduled in hour two today for the first of two conversations based on his new novel, *The Bonfire of the Vanities*, has been a presence in my life ever since I first read him. We've never met, as it happens, but the writing he so exemplified in the early 1960s, the form he himself came to label New Journalism (there was a case to be made that it actually dated back to Daniel Defoe), shook the world as I knew it, and, as is true of virtually everyone who has been practising journalism since, has had a profound influence on the way I have tried to do my various jobs.

Superficially, the work Wolfe was publishing in the 1960s, which became a best-seller when some of his articles were anthologized as *The Kandy-Kolored Tangerine-Flake Streamline Baby*, was characterized by his unmistakable style: vivid, urgent, hip, exclamatory; run-on, baroque sentences full of brand names, modish argot, onomatopoeia, and . . . *original!* . . . punctuation. Some writers, in fact, picked up Wolfe-ish tricks of style without also picking up the structure that lay under them. (I remember one sentence, in the *Telegram*'s old "Showcase", describing the eyelids of Joel Aldred, who was doing car commercials at the time, as, going . . . *chunk!!!* when they closed, an image that would, I'm sure, have amazed even Wolfe.)

More fundamentally, and whether or not Wolfe invented it, the New Journalism departed from the tradition I had grown up with by bringing the techniques of the fiction writer to the craft of non-fiction. It employed realistic-sounding dialogue (even to the extent of internal discourse). It was made up of carefully constructed scenes, intercut with cinematic dexterity. It employed extensive descriptive passages of hitherto undescribed aspects of life – "the recording," as Wolfe wrote, "of everyday gestures, habits, manners, customs, styles. . . ." And it gave to the reporter – or assumed for him – the novelist's position of omniscience.

High-octane stuff, and, as I say, many of us got giddy on it. In Toronto, and not only at "Showcase", we talked about the new writing all the time. In *Esquire*, in *New York* (the supplement to the *Herald Tribune* that was such an inspiration when Michael de Pencier and I were looking for a way to do a magazine in Toronto), we read every word we could by Wolfe, Gay Talese, Jimmy Breslin, Hunter Thompson, Joan Didion, Gail Sheehy, and the other acolytes. We tried some of the new devices ourselves. Sometimes our efforts were successful; our magazine articles breathed with new life. Sometimes, as with the excesses of style that led to eyelids that closed audibly, or with pieces written by reporters who didn't realize that Wolfe and his colleagues did a lot of hanging out before they wrote a word – Wolfe, incidentally, has a PhD from Yale – they were disastrous. But we felt liberated. The magazine article, whose traditional form had been eclipsed by the television documentary, had a new respectability, and the New Journalism gave its practitioners a freedom to write in ways we had not tried before.

Almost from the beginning, though, there were doubts. In Toronto, I remember, Fulford, while fascinated by the new departures and a connoisseur of their evolution, kept his own clearheaded style steadfast against the winds of fashion, and raised alarms about their possible abuse. Others, too, had reservations. If the new writers were using the techniques of fiction, ran their arguments, what was to keep them from also using its licence to make things up? On the roof of the Park Plaza, and at other congresses of scribes, the arguments raged.

In New York, the debate was more furious. In April of 1965, Wolfe published, in *New York*, a two-part profile of *The New Yorker*, a bastion – *the* bastion – of the traditional way of doing things. The articles, called "Tiny Mummies", were both savage and scandalous, and they so raised the intensity of the debate that some of the staff of *The New Yorker* took the unprecedented step of firing back. In the *New York Review of Books*, Dwight MacDonald, a patriarch of *The New Yorker*, sprang to the defence of the magazine and its editor, the hitherto almost anonymous William Shawn. Listing a devastating number of factual errors, which ranged from the colour of the paper on which memos were written to the description of offices in which Wolfe had demonstrably never been, MacDonald labelled Wolfe's prose "para-journalism", and Fulford and the other skeptics chortled with I-told-you-so glee.

My own perspective on all this was a singular one. On the one hand, I had a vague connection with *The New Yorker*. When I was still at *Maclean's*, Edmund Wilson, on the visit to Montreal that led eventually to our memorable evening at the Park Plaza, had arranged to put me in touch with Shawn. I had taken some time off in Toronto and written what I hoped would be the first of a regular "Letter from Canada" for his magazine. Though Shawn hadn't accepted it, he had been mildly encouraging–had sent me, in fact, a cheque for a thousand American dollars along with his rejection slip. (Which led me, since I had never received as much for a *published* article, to volunteer not to write for him every couple of weeks.) Later, as a free-lance, I had visited him at his office on West 43rd Street, and, though I hadn't written anything further, I had stayed in touch.

On the other hand, I was splashing around the periphery of the newer wave. I had made friends, for instance, with Barbara Long, a loquacious denizen of the East Village whom I'd looked up–and written about, for *Saturday Night*–because of some striking sports-writing she was doing in the *Village Voice*. When Wolfe's attack on *The New Yorker* appeared, I was caught squarely in the middle. In the lead paragraph of his first part, he had described in lavish detail a scene in Shawn's office. A prospective contributor was visiting. While Shawn huddled behind the stack of manuscripts on his desk, the visitor, nervously and unthinkingly, lit a cigarette. After a couple of drags, he noticed to his dismay (though Shawn said nothing) that there were no ashtrays in the room. Desperately he reached for an empty Coca-Cola bottle and deposited the offending cigarette, point down, into its base. The barely smoked weed–all smokers will recognize this picture–continued to burn, and, as the visitor watched in mounting anguish, and Shawn smiled enigmatically from behind the barricade of his manuscripts, the brown smoke curled acridly into the unventilated room.

For me, the scene had the ring of perfection. It was *exactly* what had happened to me on my visit to Shawn's office–closed window, Coke bottle, brown smoke, and all.

And yet, as we learned from Dwight MacDonald, Wolfe had never been there. He had, unforgivably, made the incident up.

I DWELL ON THIS MINOR INCIDENT NOW, more than two decades (and, in my case, several careers) after the fact, because it has always seemed to me to sum up the debate between the daredevils of the New Journalism and the defenders of the original faith, and to put nicely a question that is at the heart of what I do for a living. The debate is between "facts" on one side, attributable, witnessed data, and "truth" on the other. A story is true, the priests of New Journalism would argue, if it *could* have happened, if it fits with what is known about character and situation. If telling it casts light on the subject, then telling it is legitimate. To the traditionalists, that's heresy. The writer of non-fiction, they say, has an unspoken contract with his reader to report only what he has witnessed. To do otherwise is to assume for himself the totally different licence of the novelist, and it is this redefinition of the contract that has led to, for instance, the description in a Pulitzer-prize-winning story (the prize was later rescinded) of an eight-year-old heroin addict in Washington, D.C. There was, it turned out, no such person, although, of course, there *could* have been. Like the visitor in Tom Wolfe's imagined office scene, the situation was "true", but not factual.

In the end, disciple of Ralph Allen that I am, I have sided with the conservatives. If you can't check it, I have decided, or if you didn't see it, you can't write it. Still, as I prepare at last to meet Wolfe this morning, I want to know how he got something he made up so precisely and exquisitely right.

10:25 a.m., the studio: Wearing his trademark white suit, Wolfe is as insouciantly charming in our interview as his writing is energetic in print. After much palaver–Hal has gone along with my plan to talk about journalism today and get to the novel on a return visit Monday–I pop the question. Does he remember the scene? Of course. Where did he get it? He has, he confesses disarmingly, no idea now. He'd have to look at his notes. Concerned lest I take an already self-indulgent interview further down the lane of autobiography, I turn to other matters.

10:30:   As Wolfe – Tom, now, since we've talked – gathers his angular frame to depart, I make a bit of small talk.

"Do you ever hear from Barbara Long?" I ask.

"No, not for a long time," he says. "Why? Do you know her?"

"Used to, in the days we were talking about."

"You know," he says, "she was one of the people I talked to about *The New Yorker*. She'd been in Shawn's office, I think. Maybe I got that story from her."

And she, I think, may have got it from . . . No, it's too much of a coincidence.

The apartment, 2:30 p.m.:   I call Barbara Long in New York. She is astonished to hear from me after so many years, she says, but launches immediately into one of the long and name-drenched anecdotes that so bedazzled me in the 1960s, this one involving, so far as I can make out, William Buckley and his sister.

At last, I turn her attention to the *New Yorker* anecdote in Wolfe's piece. She has, she says, no memory at all either of my having told her the story or of retelling it to Wolfe.

"Why would I tell him that, anyway," she says, "even if I did hear it from you? I smoked a cigar in Shawn's office myself."

"Well," I say, crestfallen. "Just wondering. Thought I might add it to this journal I'm . . ."

"Listen, Peter," says Barbara Long. "If it makes a better story, just *say* it came from me."

So, okay, Fulford, you win. But I still say the story took place.

Stephanie Anne Gzowski Zufelt, in her first year.

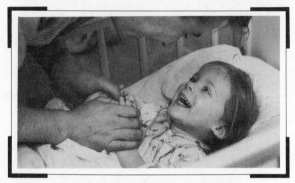

Her mother, not much older, in the early 1960s.

The Colonel, her great-great-grandfather.

CHAPTER NINETEEN

Winter reflections . . . Gorbachev's
birthmark . . . Throwing the hoolihan . . .
Comings and goings of the staff . . . The
hawk in the cedar . . . "Welcome back and
Merry Christmas again" . . .
"Basically" . . . The family together . . .
Grandfather/grandson

Sunday, December 20, the cottage, 6:30 a.m.: The day ahead promises grey, and even now a cold rain drips off the eaves, stippling the seamless snow on the deck. Wet slabs of snow adorn the golf-course evergreens, too, dollops of whipped cream topping the dark branches. Here, inside, tiny cracks have appeared in the plaster where Jack and his Finnish cohorts taped last spring, and on the Hedge Road, the line of adolescent cedars we planted in the fall is tipped with brown. I'm unperturbed. I slept last night like an angel, stirring only when the moon broke through and filled the room with silver light. Now, a fire glows in the fireplace. Coffee burbles. While Gill sleeps, I spread my notes on the butternut table to see where I have been.

Elmer Iseler, Eric Peterson, Clare Coulter, Lorna Crozier, Jacques Parizeau, Jack Webster, Roch Carrier, Roch Demers, Gordon Pinsent, Monique Mercure, Veronica Tennant, Joe Clark, Timothy Findley, Morley Callaghan. Lefolii *is* right: people I'd want to talk to anyway. (Lefolii was in town last week. *Claims* is doing splendidly, no thanks to me, though he doesn't need the royalties. He's making so much money from his investments that he's thinking of setting up a foundation for non-fiction writers. Over dinner, he said he'd like me and Fulford to be on its board. I said the hell with that; I want to apply for a grant. He paid for dinner anyway, and announced, to my surprise and admiration, that he is well into the writing of a novel, which he's basing on the life of Norman Bethune.)

One day, after an interview with Greg Curnoe, the artist from London who was in Toronto promoting one of his shows – he's doing splendidly too, I should add; his paintings are selling for twelve thousand dollars apiece – I learned that it was he who'd said "paint the whole – – – – ing thing blue" in the *This Country in the Morning* incident I now dine out on, and another day I learned that Lucille Starr, a singer Carole Warren presented as part of a series on the stars of Canadian country music, had been weeping for real over her own lousy marriage when she recorded her huge hit, *"Quand le soleil dit bonjour aux montagnes"* – or, as the American producers called it for convenience, "The French Song".

Not all has gone smoothly. I had a contretemps with the producers when Robbie Robertson, the former member of the Band who has been touring with a solo album, wouldn't come into the studio and insisted on doing a complicated "double-ender" (a tape recorder at his end of a telephone, with the answers to be edited in with the questions later on) from his hotel room at the corner of Yorkville and Avenue Road. ("If Joe Clark will come in . . ." I said, but lost.)

On another day, there was a technical foul-up that almost spoiled one of Stuart McLean's best pieces. Stuart had been at Mutual Street arena in Toronto to do one of his stylish oral essays. He'd been talking to an especially gorgeous roller-skater there, he was saying, about how much that old landmark has changed, and just as he was about to roll his tape-clip, the control room accidentally plugged into my ear the hook-up for our next item, the attorneys general. As a result, when Stuart played his punchline, instead of hearing it and responding to it (the gorgeous skater said, "You think *this* is different? *I* used to be a man") I was listening to Brian Smith, the attorney general of B.C., coughing and spluttering in Victoria.

On still another, a panel of teenagers we tried to do from

Edmonton on their views of sex and the AIDS crisis turned into an incomprehensible shambles. And on a fourth, when we were taping the panel we'll run next month as my New Year's levee, I stupidly blurted out a question about Mikhail Gorbachev's birthmark ("What's that on his head, anyway – a map of Viet Nam?") that I'm sure will draw some mail.

On that same panel, by the way, Nathalie Petrowski, the perceptive young cultural columnist of *Le Devoir*, responded to a long segment eulogizing Margaret Laurence by saying, "I'm sorry, I don't know who Margaret Laurence was." Nathalie, of course, was just being honest. For all our provincialism, English Canadians have reached out to try to understand the artists of French Canada harder than the Québécois have reached out to ours. For their English culture, they turn to New York, and they have no more idea who our luminaries are than, say, the clerk at the Bonaventure knows whether to send flowers to G. Katz or P. Gzowski. But we'll get mail about Nathalie's comment all the same, as if she'd insulted Margaret Laurence's memory. Two solitudes.

(Which reminds me: We haven't talked to Hugh MacLennan for a while.)

On the days when it's not bitchy, which is nearly every day, the mail continues to turn up the most extraordinary stories. I went this month, as I rarely have time to do, to a meeting of the Book Person's Club in Toronto, and there, Harry Campbell, a Sinophile as well as the former chief librarian of the Toronto Public Library system, told me about a Canadian doctor I'd never heard of who was about to have a statue erected to his memory in Beijing – a kind of unsung Norman Bethune. The doctor's name was Tillson Lever Harrison. Excitedly, I suggested that Harry come in to talk about him on the radio. Two days after he did that, we had a letter from – not surprisingly – Tillsonburg, Ontario, in which a relative of Dr. Harrison, whom we also booked, told us what a black sheep his great-uncle had been. Wired his wife once from China to say he was coming home; after she'd travelled all the way from New York to San Francisco to meet his boat, he waved to her from the passenger deck and then sailed away again into the distance.

From a more compatible family, a woman wrote from Cloyne, Ontario, after she'd heard me talking to the Saskatchewan folklorist Bob Cosbey about cowboys, to say I ought not to have been ashamed of my ignorance of what a hoolihan was–as in throwing the . . . She had spent three years, she said, travelling the rodeo circuit doing rope tricks – including hoolihans – and even the most learned fans didn't know what it was. She had, she went on to say demurely, also just come second in the world championship of rope-spinning, a contest in which contestants do as many consecutive tricks as they can until they flub one, and the person who does the most wins. Our correspondent had done ten. The winner, she said, had done an incredible thirty-eight. But the winner was, ahem, her daughter, and wouldn't we like to book her? Of course.

The champ came in a couple of days later. Her name is Kim Gowan. She is Korean-born, adopted as a baby, and her picture hangs now on my office wall, her almond eyes beaming under her Stetson, a twirling loop in each hand, right beside Longshot and Evelyn Hart and, of course, Stephanie Anne Gzowski Zufelt. With the rope in her right hand, Kim, I think, is throwing a hoolihan.

We've had our share of Thanatos, to be sure: panels or experts (or both) on pain, insomnia, rural poverty, the crisis over P.E.I. mussels, AIDS. But death and pestilence haven't been dominant, the way they sometimes are, and those reports, I think, have been balanced by, for instance, three tuba players (Carole Warren again!) who came into studios in Montreal, Toronto, and Vancouver and oompah-pahed their way over the wires through, among other pieces, "The Flight of the Bumble Bee", or two cooks Talin hooked up between Vancouver and Toronto to have a latke-off, a confrontation over the best way to cook potato pancakes.

I've had–or maybe made–the occasional lucky break. On Friday, I was still in the preliminaries with Bill Kelly, the federal labour mediator who's just been through the Air Canada strike, when I heard, from the studio in Ottawa where he was sitting, the click of a lighter. I had an instant flash from the research that morning. He'd been a pack-and-a-half-a-day smoker, I'd read, but he'd quit for four years. He had fallen off the wagon only once in that time, during a particularly tense set of negotiations in Thunder Bay. On the click of the lighter, I asked if it had happened again with Air Canada. Bingo! He chuckled with recognition and the piece took off. It might have been good anyway – he's a remarkably frank and appealing man – but when the little tricks you've built up over the years, studying the research for the unexpected fact, fencing around till you see your opening, and, most of all, listening, you can feel pretty good, like a cagey old pitcher striking out the last batter with his knuckler.

If things have been going well since I came back from the book tour, far more of the credit belongs to the producers than to me. This often happens. When I'm away – sorry about this, Augusta – they save the good stuff up, and when I come back, with notes on Dutch poets and Raging Grannies and (oops) astrologers (I've lost the name, dammit, of a woman I met in Regina who raises llamas with her husband), and sometimes just a little better sense of what's on people's minds – we seem to settle in for the kind of strong run we've just had.

But they're also reaching into their own feelings more now, trying new things. The panel on AIDS I mentioned so casually, for instance, was in fact three eloquent gay men talking movingly about what the presence of the disease in their community has meant to their daily lives. Janet Enright put that together, and, I confess, she had first to overcome my objections; I felt there wasn't much left to say. The series on pain, which (and probably in spite of my eye-rolling at the story meeting) took us to some fascinating frontiers of research as well as opening up the lives of people who live with chronic agony, came from Gail Kotchie, a quiet young mother Gloria hired last month to take over the spot David Langille has vacated. (Gail, who has a background in theology, is so young that when I suggested she book Jack Webster for a *Morningside Drive* on smoking, she had to ask me who Webster was, but in spite of that – oh, okay, maybe because of it – she seems so far at least to be the best addition to the staff since Susan Rogers.)

Insomnia was another Puff and Pain production – Nancy Watson and Susan – and, again, coupled research with real experience. The truth is, for all my years and wisdom, I don't know how they put these things together. The subject comes up at a story meeting. I roll my eyes (or don't) and – presto – a few days later we have an assembly of people willing to share their secrets. Or, when we have to scramble, as we did this month when the mussel story broke from the east coast, they just come roaring into the office early in the morning – Nancy and Ken Wolff in this case – and find people who know the scene.

On the producer front, however, things are not all rosy. Patsy Pehlman, curses, is leaving. She's going back to Thunder Bay, where she'll run the CBC's local morning show, and live with a man she's fallen in love with. She's even decided to have a shower for herself before she goes – "Why not?" as she says, "I've given enough presents to people who are getting married." But I suspect, as well, the desk has wrung her out. She's been putting in about twelve hours a day, reworking the new producers' greens, huddling with Dave Amer to make sure the music fits, writing promos and links, assuaging egos, kicking butts, and just generally making sure everything's in shape before she leaves.

Wisely, I think, Gloria has decided to move Susan into the breach. She'll do swimmingly, I'm sure. She's a bear for work, with a solid story sense and the kind of discipline the desk needs. Furthermore, everyone likes her, and, as I've thought from the beginning, she'll probably run the joint some day. But right now, we – I – will miss her steady, reliable output of stories. As I told Gloria, it's as if the Edmonton Oilers had decided to make Mark Messier a coach. (Hal, I guess, is Wayne Gretzky.)

Sue Kilburn is leaving too. I think she's just tired of being everyone's office mother, and wants to go back to something that would better match her qualifications. But I wonder, as well, if Gloria has worked hard enough at maintaining the friendship that brought Sue here in the first place. It would be difficult: the executive producer and the receptionist – "Get some more paper clips, will you, and I'll see you tonight at dinner" – but . . . well, I probably haven't been very good either. We all take too much for *granted* around here. In any case, I'll miss Sue. Her work may not have had a direct effect on what's been going on the air, but things go better when there are nice people around.

And, of course, Lynda. The week that starts tomorrow is her last. I've written her a letter of recommendation for Australia – that'll go over big, eh? – and told her to frame what I wrote about her in the *New Papers*, but I hate to see her go. The good news is that, with Gloria's enthusiastic agreement (she, after all, pays half the salary), I've hired Shelley Ambrose, the young woman who approached me in Windsor. There were other applicants, as word got around—including, in fact, two more who approached me at other signings—but Shelley was a clear winner. She's been working with Lynda for the past few days, and the more I see of her the more I like her. It's possible (touch wood) that the pleasant eagerness she showed at South Shore Books will lead her to heights of assistantship even Lynda couldn't scale. But even if that happens, I'll miss my cheerful little friend.

Comings and goings, comings and goings. There are forty-six people listed in what I've called the credits for the *New Papers* —the producers, directors, production assistants, and technicians who worked on the program in my first five years. Only twelve of them are still with us. Only two, Carol Wells and Janet Russell, were at *Morningside* when I arrived, and neither of them, it's hard not to note, is a producer.

Gloria? She is—for certain now, though it's not yet public—on her way up and out. I can't tell exactly from my notes how I know this, but I do. Frame has continued to dangle a bigger job in front of her, most recently a national project to revitalize the 4-to-6 spot (heaven knows we need it), and she's talked openly about her need for a break. She'll last the season, though, or be here until, somehow, we figure out who should succeed her. It's a mark of who she is—this *is* in my notes—that when we had a closed-door heart-to-heart last week and talked, each of us, as the friends we have become, about our dissatisfactions and restlessness, she said, just as we were finishing, "You know, I'd still kill for *Morningside*." On days like this, cozy in this house, with Christmas coming and the rigours of the fall behind, and looking back over the people *Morningside* has introduced to me and the issues it's allowed me to join, I feel the same.

9:30: Drive to Sutton to pick up a *Star*.

On the last best-seller list before Christmas, the *New Papers* are number three.

1:30 p.m., Peter Sibbald-Brown's: While we sip a sherry around the fire, discussing the Ridley book and plans for the holidays, a sharp-shinned hawk (confirmed by Gill) poses nobly on a branch of cedar at the window. There was a kestrel on a wire when we drove up yesterday, and, before the ice began to form a crust on the lake, we stood one day and watched loons diving.

They can go farther under water than I can hit a nine-iron in the air. Straighter, too.

It's still raining. The hawk is wet. It's a long time till golf.

Monday, December 21, the Morningside *studio, 3 p.m.:* Everyone's cranky. Katzie is twisting a lock of his beard as if he's trying to tear it out. Even the unflappable Janet Russell is biting her lip. We've been here since 12:30, right after the story meeting, trying to tape a couple of hours for Christmas morning – one is already in the can – and nothing will go right. The LP that carries the cut Dave Amer has chosen as a theme for the day – the Canadian Brass's "Wassailing" – is scratched. The CD player keeps jamming. Nothing fits. This seems to happen every year. We pre-tape a program so we can spend Christmas Day with our families – on *This Country*, when the kids were little, I used to say hello to them on tape and watch their faces when we turned on the radio at home – but the trouble of doing it sometimes outweighs the pleasures of having got it done. Meanwhile, a piece we'd planned for tomorrow's program has fallen through, and the producers working to replace it keep running down the hall for suggestions. Bah, humb –

Oh, sorry. . . . Take five. . . .

"Hello, welcome back, and Merry Christmas again. This is *Morningside*, hour . . ."

Better than magazines, I guess, where you have to do this in August.

Tuesday, December 22, the office, 11:15: Out of the blue, the Toronto Symphony calls. After their tour of the Arctic this fall, they've commissioned a musical setting for some northern poetry, and they'd like me to read the words when they present the new work at a concert in – my goodness they work a long time in advance! – February of 1989. Will I? Are you kidding? I'm ready to start rehearsals now, I say.

Maybe I can cover it for the Timmins *Daily Press*.

I AM, when I sober up, under no illusion as to why I have received this flattering offer. They have not, let us say, made it to the author of *The Game of Our Lives*.

Wednesday, December 23, the studio: 8:11 a.m.: For a couple of weeks now, in response to a pet peeve of mine (though Patsy Pehlman claims she started hearing it first), every time a guest or a contributor has said the word "basically" on the air the control-room crew has made a note. Last Friday alone we caught nine: two from Deborah McGregor on our Ottawa column (what a pleasant addition she's been, "basically" or not), two from Jasper McKee, the physicist who does occasional science pieces from Winnipeg, and a world-record five from Robin Pascoe, who does our Ontario notes from Ottawa. By yesterday, we had a formidable collection of tape clips, and the estimable Tom Mac-Donnell—even though he thought the idea was snobbish, and an attempt to impose the standards of print onto spoken language –has assembled them into a hilarious and graphic montage. At the top of the program this morning, after a brief introductory essay from me–it's empty language, I say, a word that does nothing but vamp for time till the speaker thinks of the next one – we play it.

Point made.

Except that Richard Osler, who has returned to our business column even sooner than we'd been counting on, hears himself cited from some old appearances. When I bring him on after Tom's tape, at first he is tongue-tied, so conscious of trying to avoid saying "basically" (one slips out anyway, which makes it even worse) that he can hardly finish a sentence. Still, he's wonderful. The column lives again. Maybe, from now on, I should leave well enough alone.

Sure glad *I* don't have any patterns of speech people could make fun of. (Glad I'm likely to be elected Miss Grey Cup next year, too.)

Thursday, December 24, the apartment 4 p.m.: Shopping done at last–just one last teddy bear for Stephanie before I called it a season–I am napping before the evening's festivities when the phone rings.

David Crombie.

As I shake the sleep from my head, I realize how little I've been thinking about the plans for my next career. Still . . .

We make a date for a breakfast over the holidays.

98 Lytton Boulevard, North Toronto, 7 p.m.: The family's last Christmas Eve in the house the kids know best – Jenny's house now, according to our agreement, but an empty nest for her and on the market. We bought this place in 1971, when Mickey, who's wearing leather pants this evening; and told raunchy jokes at dinner, was six, and it's full of memories for them all, I'm sure.

Alison has brought moose meat and caribou from Newfoundland, but we'll eat that another day in other places. Tonight: Chinese food, as we've had delivered every Christmas Eve since we discovered how much it took the pressure off. The kids–kids? Peter will be thirty in the year that starts next week–are all blasé now, or pretend to be, but the talk is good at dinner, with much laughter. With Jenny shopping for a smaller house, I wonder if this is the last time we'll all be together like this. The marvel is, surely, that we've held on this long, and I'm grateful again to Jenny for that.

Over the beef and snow peas, Stephanie, nearly a year old now – she'll spend tomorrow at her other grandparents' – reaches up from her high chair, as Maria used to do, and pokes a sticky finger into the beard I didn't have when her mother was a child. Clear as a bell, she says:

"Doggie."

December 25, the apartment, 9 p.m.: It was a lovely Christmas, rich with food, gifts, laughter, memories, games. Stephanie, before she left for her other date, appeared to like her teddy bear, which plays "The Teddy Bears' Picnic" if you pull a string in its back. She played with it almost as long as she played with the wok John and Mickey chipped in to buy for me.

Next week, for Stephanie's birthday, I'll bundle up as much of this manuscript as I'm happy with and add it to the other treasures we're all putting into a box Scott and Maria have planned for her. She's not to open the box till she's twenty-one. Peter and Heather have bought a bottle of Glenlivet and written an offer to help her drink it, and the others . . . well, let's wait for her to open it, shall we?

Wonder what she'll be like then, and what she'll make of her grandfather, and what was going through his mind. She is, I realize as I pour a nightcap, almost precisely the same number of years younger than I am that I was younger than the Colonel.

Even Aislin, I take it (he drew this cartoon in 1986),
knows about my three Js. Note the reminder
pinned to my shirt.

CHAPTER TWENTY

*Frontiersman at the cottage . . . New Year's
Eve . . . My breakfast with the Secretary . . .
"The people I would like to
talk to anyway" . . . Who did they think
Wayne would marry? . . . The interlocutor
of P.E.I. . . . A message from Ottawa . . .
A decision, at last*

Sunday, December 27, the cottage, 10 a.m.: Two days after the Christmas rush has ended, and with the bookstores facing a month of remainders, returns, and empty aisles, *The New Morningside Papers*, which I haven't flogged since I did a quick last-minute trip to Winnipeg in the middle of the month, hits number one.

Tuesday, December 29, the cottage, 2:30: Crombie calls from his home in Toronto to postpone our date till next week. That's fine with me, as it happens. I'm not due back at *Morningside* until January 11. I've burrowed in up here, with the wind howling round the clerestory, to wrap up – at last – the Ridley book. The writing's going slowly, but this morning I split a log into kindling, one blow per stick. Last night: caribou stew. What a frontiersman! I'll watch *"Crocodile" Dundee* on the VCR tonight, and feel superior.

New Year's Eve, the cottage, 11 p.m.: A happy gaggle of good friends for dinner: O'Malley and Karen, Peter S-B and Marion, Katzie and his Sarah, Tina Srebotnjak, who left *Morningside* a couple of years ago to work at *Midday* but who I hope will come back some day, and her man Brian Stewart, who's settling in at home after long service as a foreign correspondent for the CBC. Honey-cured ham (Gill knows a place), baked beans, turnips in honey and black pepper, sliced potatoes and onions, steeped in cream and cheddar and broiled in tin-foil on the barbecue, broccoli and hollandaise sauce, fruit, cheese, and a too-sweet sparkling wine from the Sutton liquor store. This house, with its open spaces, is perfect for parties, but we'll all weigh three hundred pounds in the morning, and now, playing Scruples, are having a hard time staying awake till midnight.

Gloria was supposed to come too, but, at the last minute, called in sick. What a rotten year she's had. May the new one, as it will, bring her the fresh start she deserves.

Monday, January 4, 1988, the Victoria Room, the King Edward Hotel, Toronto, 8:30 a.m.: David Crombie, half an hour late for our breakfast date, quickly mollifies my impatience with the charm and self-deprecating candour that made him the unbeatable mayor of this city for so many years. I ask him, to make small talk, if he sees anyone who might follow in his tradition –step in now, as he stepped in after a period of boom and development, and slow things down. "I don't think people realize how hard you have to work," he says, "how many meetings you have to speak to where there are nineteen people. God, it took me ten years." I ask him if, with hindsight, he has any thoughts on how to control what's happening now, with the overloading of downtown and the soaring prices it's brought with it. "Not now," he says. "In my day you could get all the developers together in one room. They all knew each other–hell, they were all in the same grade ten at Harbord Collegiate–and you could lay down the law to them; they heard you. Now, the money comes from all over the world, Germany, Hong Kong, Japan, half of it in numbered companies. The people who put up the buildings don't have to live with the consequences."

If only, I think, *we could get politicians to talk that insightfully on the radio. Or–who knows?–maybe he would.*

As a waiter brings more coffee, we turn to literacy. The

Secretary of State's enthusiasm is unalloyed. He quotes Peter Calamai again, and talks of what might be done. He's had a couple of people in his department working on some stuff he'd like me to go over with . . .

. . . a panel on municipal affairs . . .

. . . could set up a meeting, either here or in Ottawa to . . .

. . . maybe Elsie Wayne in Saint John, New Brunswick, and . . . no, Mike Harcourt's not mayor of Vancouver any more . . . but . . .

. . . John O'Leary of Frontier College?

"Yes, sorry." I'm back at the table. "Sure I know John. He's the person who first got me hooked on the cause."

I tell the minister about how it all started, the *Morningside* series, O'Leary's letter (he knows John, it turns out, and shares my sense of wonder at his powers of persuasion), the golf tournament, my subsequent conversion.

"What you should do," he says, glancing at his watch–he has another meeting at ten – "is sit down with O'Leary, and rather than us telling you what we should do, you and he write me a letter and tell us what *you*'d like us to do, and what part you'd like to play in it. Then I'll get a couple of my people and we'll proceed from there."

O'Leary, I know, will be excited. It's the breakthrough to government he's been looking for. He has, I happen to know, some bold ideas.

I'm excited, too. Something will come of all this, I'm sure. I'm glad I placed those calls in November.

Crombie, shrugging himself into his dark-blue politician's overcoat as he goes, walks me to the door, and grasps me warmly by the arm as we shake hands. He walks off down King Street. I stand on the sidewalk for a moment, before going back to the apartment to get my car.

The people I would like to talk to anyway, I think.

Friday, January 15, the Charlottetown Sheraton, Charlottetown, Prince Edward Island, 12:45 p.m.: It occurs to me, as I wait to make phone connections with Dalton Camp in Ottawa, that the program we did this morning, with our regular P.E.I. columnists, and a panel of lobster, oyster, mussel, quahog, and snow-crab fishermen, and Joe Ghiz, the premier, among other guests, kind of filled in the map for us. We haven't covered every corner of the country yet, of course, and never could. This spring we're off to Yellowknife, where I'm supposed to fire a shot-gun to start the dog derby, and there's a chance for Labrador in the fall. I'd still like to do Quebec City some day, and Moose Jaw, Timmins, Sept-Iles, the interior of B.C., Corner Brook, and . . . well, the list is endless, but, as of today, we've done at least one program from every province, and that's – what the hell – not bad, eh?

We had some trouble getting here. Barely made the last connection. I'm supposed to do a piece on Wayne Gretzky for *Maclean's* this weekend – he's just announced that he's going to marry Miss Janet Jones of St. Louis, Missouri, and Hollywood, California – and, to brush up, was thumbing through *The Game of Our Lives* on the plane from Toronto, when the steward sidled up and said, "Always read your own books so people will recognize you?" Then, when we were late getting into Halifax, he spent a lot of time running back and forth to the cockpit, so he just may have arranged for the plane to Charlottetown to be held for me and Katz. Or, maybe he knows the clerk at the Bonaventure and held it for Gary. Anyway, we made it. (Don't know what I'll write about Wayne, by the way. Who did they think he'd marry? Margaret Atwood?)

The occasion for this trip – where's Dalton? – was a debate last night at Confederation Centre, the last in a series they've been having here on whether to build a fixed link to the mainland (they vote on Monday in a referendum), and, as I wait for the phone to ring, I turn that over in my mind, too.

An extraordinary evening. Something like eleven hundred people (no one seems to know the exact count) gathered in a public forum to hear, and then question, the same arguments they've been having here since approximately 1873. I was the moderator, imported from away on the grounds, perhaps, that no one on this island is impartial. Not sure I'm impartial myself, though I tried to behave as if I were.

To a remarkable degree, I couldn't help thinking, the debate on the fixed link – the flink, as they call it here – is a scale model of the national discussion on free trade. On the one hand: progress, facilitated commerce, perhaps increased prosperity. On the other: a particular and very special way of life, which could – just *could* – be threatened by making the crossing of fourteen miles of strait physically easier. As with free trade, my instincts are conservative. (Funny, eh? A "conservative" position that leads you to oppose a program being put forward by a "Conservative" government.) But, also as with free trade, I think the arguments should be weighed. In P.E.I., at least, they're weighing. No minds may have been changed at the meeting last night–it was pretty easy to tell which side of the argument each questioner was coming from, and, indeed, the microphones in the audience were labelled "yes" and "no" to make my job easier–and the debate may have once or twice bogged down in a welter of unfathomable detail. But at least they were talking about what's at stake, trying to grapple with what they mean by "the island way of life" and whether easier access to and from the mainland threatens it. Even from the platform, the people who presented the cases for and against were not politicians, but people whose lives would be directly affected by the outcome: In favour, a distinguished businessman from Stanhope (which the organizers carefully coached me to pronounce "Stan-up"), and a lawyer; opposed, an historian from UPEI and an eighteen-year-old high-school student from Summerside. Invigorating stuff, the same grassroots politics I saw in Saskatchewan in the 1950s or, later, at the Créditiste rallies in Quebec.

The other thing that occurred to me as I sat at my interlocutor's table–"You're on the island, now, Peter, give them time," someone shouted from the audience when I tried to move the debate along–was how much last night's meeting was a scale model of *Morningside*. Not as it is, perhaps, for we have not yet figured out how to line people up in front of microphones across the country and let them ask the questions, or to allow, as last night's format allowed, everyone who wants to to have his say. But as it aspires to be–or could aspire to be. If our mail, as I once said, is a "kind of village bulletin board for the nation", then maybe the program is, or could be, a kind of village meeting, a place where people who are interested enough can gather to consider the things they hold in common.

Pompous? Sure. We're a *radio* program, for goodness' sake, a little background talk and music people turn on when they're doing their ironing or driving to their next appointment, or riding their tractors over the fields. The edition we just finished this morning, as well as a chat with the Premier and a panel of fishermen, had a piece about two dead fleas in a museum in

Fredericton, dressed in tiny little wedding costumes. A man who lives in Ontario now had seen them when he was a child, and this morning, in the third hour, just before the Premier came in, we . . .

1:12: Dalton's call comes through. He tried to reach me in Toronto this morning, and with Shelley quarterbacking from the home base – she is turning out to be every bit as efficient as I'd hoped – has chased me down here, while Gary and Talin polish off the scallops downstairs.

He apologizes for taking so long in responding to my initial inquiry about literacy.

"Is this on or off the record?" I ask, partly, I think, to postpone a question I'm not sure now I want to deal with.

Chuckling, he ignores me.

"I've been thinking about it," he says. He goes on, in his casual insider's way, to talk about the importance of the cause, how they – the Tories – *are* interested, how something will be done. He knows, I infer (though there's no reference to the programs we've discussed), that I've been talking to Crombie, and appears to approve.

Maybe *this* is how things are done.

Then, somewhat to my surprise – and without, I feel, having come to the point on literacy – he switches to the CBC. He says nothing earth-shattering, of course ("It's impossible to speak privately at this table"), but I sense his concern for it, his understanding of its importance, and am grateful, even as I do, that he is where he is.

"And you're important to it, too, you know," he says. "You're doing something that matters now."

It takes a moment for the message to sink in. But I realize, as I thank him, that what he has told me is, whether I have been consciously aware of it or not, what I have been feeling all along. Faced with a truly difficult decision, my mother used to say, toss a coin; you will know by your visceral reaction to its result where your true emotions lie. Now, as Dalton's well-meant advice closes the door on my aspirations to the bureaucracy, I know where my heart lies.

Ah, well. The bureaucratic czar of literacy probably couldn't have a golf tournament anyway.

1:25, the dining-room: In *The New Morningside Papers*, the famous number-one best-seller of post-Christmas 1987, I introduce a chapter called "Why I Live Where I Live" by describing a place on Prince Edward Island introduced to me by "an old friend from my Moose Jaw days". Now, as I join Talin and Gary and a couple of the P.E.I. producers who are lingering over coffee, I spot him across the way. He is Bill Hancox, a pleasant man, who was the publisher of the *Times-Herald* in 1957. After I left, Thomson sent him down here to run the *Charlottetown Guardian and Patriot*. Later, he resigned to manage the Confederation Centre, where he was working when he gave me directions to the beach I have described – and where, as I say, I might live if I could – but he's retired from that now, too, and, as I learn when he comes over to say hello, is dabbling in real estate.

After introductions and a quick obeisance to old times (or times and heralds), I ask, like every other tourist, if he happens to know of any properties a guy from away might be able to . . . you know.

"Well," he says, "as a matter of fact . . ." and proceeds to describe – in an islander's low-key way, mind you – a certain piece of land that juts out into the sea. *Thirty-five thousand dollars*, he says, *for fifty acres.*

Hmmm.

I *could* live there, I think, and write novels like Lefolii, or, like Dave Amer and Travis McGee, take my retirement in instalments. I could start a magazine, perhaps, or have another try at television, or do the book about my mother and father, or, maybe, just dig for mussels on the beach. There is a golf course not far from the property Hancox has described. Stephanie could visit me, and here in the gentle air, Gill could plant honeysuckle and the hummingbirds would come.

But not for a while, Bill, not for a while.

EPILOGUE

As is true of all the events and circumstances in these pages, the decision I made in Charlottetown in January 1988 was real. Indeed, I not only finished my sixth season as host of *Morningside*, but, as I write this now, at the end of the summer that followed it, I am preparing to begin my seventh.

At the same time, the point at which I have chosen to end my story is an arbitrary one. Any point would have been. The temptations of literacy that arose in the winter of 1987–88 were new ones, but they were not the first I had experienced in the years after I returned from the wilderness of Rockwood. Nor, I'm sure, will they be the last. For six years, the satisfactions of the job I have been lucky enough to hold have outweighed the weariness it engenders. But some day, inevitably, the balance will swing; I'll move on.

Morningside, I realize after working on this book, is a river more than a lake. It was flowing before I jumped into it and, I trust, will carry on long after I climb out. So the several months I have tried to capture in these pages are typical only in that they are unlike all the others.

In the months that followed our visit to Charlottetown, in fact, change continued at so fast a pace that before the seventh season began I wondered if the exodus of 1987, when four producers departed at once, still stood as what I had so blithely called a record.

Gloria Bishop, as we had all known she would, left to take up newer challenges within the CBC. Susan Rogers, of whom I had written "she'll probably run the joint some day," decided instead to run another one, and took over the weekly *Media File* as executive producer. Talin Vartanian, the only producer who had been at *Morningside* when I started, left for CBC radio's public relations. Janet Enright returned to other forms of journalism. Jim Summerfield, our loyal technician, moved up the ladder to management.

Hal Wake, "the Wayne Gretzky of producers," moved behind the bench into Gloria's job. But by the time we held our 1988 summer meeting at the cottage, there were more new faces than I could ever remember, and some of the people who appear in these pages as rookies had become, at least by comparison, grizzled veterans.

There were changes in the other parts of my world as well. David Crombie, whose own enthusiasm had had so much to do with my flirtation with the idea of becoming a bureaucrat, left politics. A couple of the relationships I have described in these pages (not my own this time, I am happy to report) flew apart. Others solidified. Carol Wells and Carol Ito each had babies. Carole Warren got married. The baby Hal and Jennifer Wake had been expecting when I bailed out of the CBC's television coverage of the winter Olympics arrived fat and healthy. And so on and so on. Life went on.

Although I abandoned the idea of moving into the literacy movement full time, I have continued to serve it in my self-indulgent way. In June 1988, the third edition of my golf tournament raised even more money than the first two. (Sandra Post, playing in my foursome, described my swing as the perfect example of "fire and fall back".) Later in the summer we began to make plans to hold a tournament in Ottawa in the fall. By the end of August 1988, literacy, it seemed to me, had become fashionable. I celebrated that development, and toasted its success with John O'Leary. But there was still work to be done.

Joey Slinger behaved himself at the 1988 tournament; by the way. But at the party the night before I heard someone else telling two of my more sedate neighbours on the Hedge Road that marijuana increased the joy of sex. Shortly after, my neighbours went home.

Also in June, the Ridley book Peter Sibbald-Brown and I had been working on was published.

In April, I won two ACTRA awards, one for the Trudeau interview I had just completed when this book begins, the other as host. When I was aw-shucksing my acceptance my old *Varsity* colleague Liz Gray could be heard shouting from the audience the suggestion that I could now stop complaining about the number of times I'd lost.

I will.

Writing this book has taught me many things. Perhaps the most important is how lucky I have been to be where I am. As I begin my seventh season at *Morningside*, I am as full of trepidations as I was when I began my sixth, or, I now realize, as when I began my fifth or fourth or first. When I finish typing these words, in fact, and leave the cottage to begin the season of 1988–89, my heart is full of . . .

But that's where I brought you in, isn't it? And that's what my life has been.

ACKNOWLEDGEMENTS

The author and publisher gratefully acknowledge the use of the photographs and cartoons that appear throughout this book. They are the work of the following.

DEDICATION PAGE:	Vera Gzowski
CHAPTER ONE:	Peter golfing as a boy: Vera Gzowski
	Peter golfing, some time later: Terry Hancey
	Gill: Toronto *Star*
CHAPTER TWO:	Maria and Alison: Courtesy of the Gzowski family
	The family at Ward's Island: John Reeves
	Peter and his sons: Courtesy of the Gzowski family
CHAPTER THREE:	*Maclean's*
CHAPTER FOUR:	Timmins *Daily Press*
CHAPTER FIVE:	Louise Keenan
CHAPTER SIX:	*Maclean's*
CHAPTER SEVEN:	Bruce Macaulay/CBC
CHAPTER EIGHT:	Toronto *Star*
CHAPTER NINE:	*Morningside* at dawn: CBC
	Gloria editing: Don Pennington
CHAPTER TEN:	'Before' photo: CBC
	'After' cartoon by Aislin. Reprinted with permission of The Toronto *Star* Syndicate.
CHAPTER ELEVEN:	Akos Arnold
CHAPTER TWELVE:	Jack McClelland: Terry Hancey
	Peter and Wayne Gretzky: Edmonton Oilers
CHAPTER THIRTEEN:	Ted Blades
CHAPTER FOURTEEN:	Both photos by Hilary Armstrong
CHAPTER FIFTEEN:	Konrad Ejbich
CHAPTER SEVENTEEN:	Krista Munroe-McFee
CHAPTER EIGHTEEN:	CBC
CHAPTER NINETEEN:	Stephanie: Scott Zufelt
	Peter with Maria: Lutz Dilla
	The Colonel: The Milne Studio (Courtesy of the Gzowski family)
CHAPTER TWENTY:	Cartoon by Aislin. Reprinted with permission of the Toronto *Star* Syndicate.

The excerpt from *Sarah Binks* by Paul Hiebert, copyright Oxford University Press Canada, 1947, is reprinted with the kind permission of the publisher.